TO LIVE AND DINE IN DIXIE

SOUTHERN FOODWAYS ALLIANCE
STUDIES IN CULTURE, PEOPLE, AND PLACE

The series explores key themes and tensions in food studies—including race, class, gender, power, and the environment—on a macroscale and also through the microstories of men and women who grow, prepare, and serve food. It presents a variety of voices, from scholars to journalists to writers of creative nonfiction.

SERIES EDITOR

John T. Edge

SERIES ADVISORY BOARD

Brett Anderson | New Orleans *Times-Picayune*

Elizabeth Engelhardt | University of Texas at Austin

Psyche Williams-Forson | University of Maryland at College Park

To Live and Dine in Dixie

The Evolution of Urban Food Culture
in the Jim Crow South

ANGELA JILL COOLEY

The University of Georgia Press   *Athens & London*

© 2015 by the University of Georgia Press
Athens, Georgia 30602
www.ugapress.org
Designed by Erin Kirk New
Set in Minion Pro by Graphic Composition, Inc.
Printed and bound by Thomson-Shore
The paper in this book meets the guidelines for
permanence and durability of the Committee on
Production Guidelines for Book Longevity of the
Council on Library Resources.

Most University of Georgia Press titles are
available from popular e-book vendors.

Printed in the United States of America
19   18   17   16   15   P   5   4   3   2   1

Library of Congress Control Number: 2015931434

ISBN 978-0-8203-4758-5 (hardcover)
ISBN 978-0-8203-4759-2 (paperback)

British Library Cataloging-in-Publication Data available

Contents

Acknowledgments

Over the years, I have heard stories from various food studies scholars that at some point in their education or academic career they encountered a professor, colleague, friend, family member, or total stranger who informed them that the study of food was not a serious or important scholarly topic. I have been lucky to have avoided such experiences. On the contrary, I have always received a significant amount of support, especially from my friends, colleagues, and professors, for my desire to study how foodways inform southern culture and society. I would like to thank the following people, who have supported me with their funding, their time, and their expertise. I hope I have not left anyone out.

I am grateful for the financial support I received to research this book from the University of Alabama History Department, the University of Alabama Graduate School, the Bankhead family, the Teaching American History Program (and its Tuscaloosa coordinator, ZuZu Freyer), and the William L. Clements Library at the University of Michigan. Thanks also to the staffs at the many libraries and archives in which I conducted this research, including the interlibrary loan librarians at the University of Alabama's Amelia Gayle Gorgas Library, the University of Mississippi's J. D. Williams Library, and Minnesota State University, Mankato's Memorial Library; Lee E. Pike at the University of Alabama's Angelo Bruno Business Library; the reference librarians at the University of Alabama's Bounds Law Library; Jim Baggett and the staff at the Birmingham Public Library's Department of Archives and Manuscripts; Jan Longone and the staff at the Clements Library; Maria David at the *Charlotte Observer*; and the staffs at the Annie Crawford Milner Archives and Special Collections at the University of Montevallo's Carmichael Library; the Special Collections of Georgia College and State University's Ina Dillard Russell Library; and the Atlanta History Center's Kenan Research Center.

Thanks to friends, colleagues, staff, and professors at the University of Alabama for making graduate school a positive experience in my life. I received much support and encouragement from my friends Megan Bever, Becky Bruce, Stephanie Chalifoux, Colin Chapell, Matthew Downs, Ryan Floyd, Jonathon Hooks, Christian McWhirter, John Mitcham, and R. Volney Riser. Thanks to History Department staff members Kay Branyon, Fay Wheat, and Ellen Pledger for helping me to negotiate the bureaucratic side of academia. Many thanks to professors John F. Beeler, Tony A. Freyer, Michael J. Mendle, Joshua D. Rothman, and Maarten Ultee. Particular appreciation goes to my dissertation committee—Lisa Lindquist Dorr, George C. Rable, and John M. Giggie of the University of Alabama and Grace Elizabeth Hale of the University of Virginia—for encouraging me to revise and publish this book. My dissertation advisor, Kari Frederickson, deserves special acknowledgment because she encouraged this project when it was just the germ of an idea for a seminar paper and because she helped me to successfully navigate the vagaries of the academic job market.

Much of the work of revising my dissertation to turn it into a book manuscript took place while I served as a postdoctoral fellow at the University of Mississippi's Center for the Study of Southern Culture. I owe a great deal of gratitude to Ole Miss faculty, staff, and students and especially to the Southern Foodways Alliance (SFA) and its board, staff, and members. The center's director, Ted Ownby, and SFA's director, John T. Edge, gave me the invaluable gift of a two-year postdoctoral fellowship. Not only did I have the time to revise my dissertation, I had the opportunity to teach the center's southern studies students, who are among the most enthusiastic and creative individuals in academia. They, along with faculty members Michele Grigsby Coffey, Deirdre Cooper Owens, Barbara Combs, Darren Grem, Adam Gussow, Andy Harper, Katie McKee, Zandria F. Robinson, Jodi Skipper, David Wharton, and Charles Reagan Wilson; center staff members Ann Abadie, Mary Hartwell Howorth, Sarah Dixon Pegues, Jimmy Thomas, and Becca Walton; SFA staff members Sara Camp Arnold, Amy C. Evans, Melissa Booth Hall, Emilie Dayan Hill, Mary Beth Lasseter, Julie Pickett, Sara Wood, and Joe York; and former Nathalie Dupree Graduate Fellows Roy Button, Susie Penman, and Anna Hamilton, gave me a safe and inviting space in which to develop my interpretation of southern food culture. The center and the SFA do important work by educating students and the general public about the constantly evolving and ever-diverse culture of the American South, and I am honored to be part of the SFA family. I offer special thanks to Anna Hamilton, who helped to secure permissions for the images that appear in this volume, and to SFA's managing editor, Sara Camp Arnold, for helping to edit this manuscript, to secure image permissions, and to educate me on the publishing process.

I would like to acknowledge my colleagues in the History Department: Kim Greer, the former dean of the College of Social and Behaviorial Sciences and Maria Bevacqua, the acting dean of the College of Social and Behavioral Sciences at Minnesota State University, Mankato, for giving me time to revise this manuscript for publication with much-needed course releases and for their support and encouragement throughout this process. Thanks also to the University of Georgia Press, especially Patrick Allen, for seeing value in this project. I appreciate the close attention of the anonymous readers and their help in making this manuscript as strong as possible. I am also grateful to the editors of the Southern Foodways Alliance Studies in Culture, People, and Place series—Brett Anderson, John T. Edge, Elizabeth Engelhardt, and Psyche Williams-Forson—for including this book among the exciting scholarship coming out in the area of southern foodways. Special thanks goes to SFA board member and University of Texas professor Elizabeth Engelhardt for the vital role she played in helping me to revise this manuscript for publication.

Finally, I appreciate my family—especially my mother, Frances; my father, Gene; my sisters, Susan and Jesslyn; my brother, Shane; and their families—for their constant love and support through the uncertainties of an academic career.

TO LIVE AND DINE IN DIXIE

The Ollie's Barbecue Case and the Foodscape of the Urban South

In 1926 Ollie's Barbecue was little more than a shack with a screen door. James Ollie McClung had founded the barbecue stand after years of selling bread to the growing number of quick-service eateries in Birmingham, Alabama. Barbecue quickly became the McClung family business. James's brother Leonard owned a joint named American Barbecue. James's son Ollie McClung Sr. and grandson Ollie McClung Jr. would inherit the family business, including Ollie's sauce recipe. When the restaurant finally closed in 2001, the name lived on through the bottled sauce, which was sold in grocery stores in the McClungs' hometown.[1]

For James McClung, the restaurant business offered an independence that even the middle-class income of a salesman could not match. He joined other entrepreneurs—black and white, native-born and immigrant, rural-migrant and city-dweller—who cultivated spaces in which the many appetites of an industrial New South city could be satisfied. James likely served the lunch crowd from nearby companies. Like other proprietors, he sought to cultivate a regular base of customers who, in the busy, clock-centered environment of the city, had no time for the leisurely midday dinner of southern lore.

By 1941, when James died and his son Ollie Sr. inherited the business, Ollie's Barbecue was located in a light industrial area on Birmingham's Southside. Barbecue and homemade pie were its best sellers. Ollie Sr. and his son Ollie Jr., who entered the family business as a partner, professed to run their restaurant on Christian principles. They were closed on Sundays and did not serve alcoholic beverages. A sign on each table read, "No profanity please. Ladies and children are usually present. We appreciate your cooperation." They wrote religious verses on the walls. Their politics were conservative. In 1964 the McClungs proudly displayed a picture of the Republican presidential candidate, Barry Goldwater.

The McClungs referred to most of the customers who stopped by for lunch or dinner as "regulars." They knew them by name or by face. Ollie's, however, reserved the status of "regular" customer for whites. Although Ollie's Barbecue was located near many African American homes and a couple of black schools, prior to December 1964 the McClungs had never knowingly served a black customer in their dining room. Since 1914 the city of Birmingham had prohibited cafés from serving blacks and whites in the same dining room. Like other white café owners, the McClungs accepted this governmental restriction and infused white supremacy into the day-to-day operations of Ollie's. White customers could sit in the dining room or purchase takeout at the register. Black customers were relegated to a takeout station at the far end of the counter. Although the McClungs employed many African American workers to cook, serve, and clean up after their white customers, black employees ate in the kitchen.[2]

In 1963, the Birmingham city council repealed the ordinance that required racial segregation in public eating places, but Ollie's continued to deny seating to black customers. A year later, the U.S. Congress passed civil rights legislation requiring the desegregation of the nation's restaurants, based on its power to regulate interstate commerce. Ollie's, however, continued to be segregated. The McClungs challenged the notion that their business operations crossed state lines and filed a suit claiming that the federal law did not apply to their restaurant because it was purely local. They had a strong factual case. Ollie's engaged in no off-site advertising. The McClungs purchased their ingredients from local suppliers. Ollie's was located many blocks away from highways, airports, and train and bus stations. The restaurant never actively solicited travelers.[3]

Despite these facts, in December 1964 the Supreme Court, led by Chief Justice Earl Warren, determined that Ollie's Barbecue was involved in interstate commerce because most of its meat originated outside Alabama. The McClungs' supplier, the Hormel Company, delivered meat to Ollie's

FIGURE 1. Rare photograph of Ollie's Barbecue, ca. 1964. Courtesy of Birmingham, Alabama, Public Library Archives.

from its Birmingham warehouse. But the meat came from sources outside the state—which the McClungs likely did not know until they brought suit.[4] This fact satisfied the legislative standard requiring desegregation if a "substantial portion" of the food a restaurant served crossed state lines. Moreover, the Warren Court determined that Congress's reliance on the commerce clause to pass civil rights legislation passed constitutional muster because, even if Ollie's Barbecue did not order enough meat to substantially affect interstate commerce, the aggregated meat purchases of Ollie's Barbecue and all similarly situated restaurants certainly did.[5]

In short, *Katzenbach v. McClung* demonstrated that by the second half of the twentieth century, no restaurant could operate in the United States without engaging in interstate commerce—whether it wanted to or not. The Ollie's Barbecue decision expanded our constitutional understanding of interstate commerce and thereby increased congressional authority. It expanded civil rights law by allowing Congress to prohibit discrimination in an activity that had previously been considered "private action" and therefore beyond the power of federal regulation.[6] For these reasons, virtually all law students read and analyze *Katzenbach v. McClung*.

Although I grew up in the Birmingham area, I first encountered this case in a constitutional law class during my first year of law school in the mid-1990s at the George Washington University Law School in Washington, D.C. Most of my classmates had grown up in the Midwest or the Northeast, and they had moved down south for school. I had gone up north. I was the only one in the class who had eaten at Ollie's—at that time still located on Birmingham's Southside. I was the only one in the class who appreciated the special irony that Ollie's Barbecue—which moved a few years after this case to make way for the new interstate highway—at that very moment sat nearly underneath I-65. Even then, I wondered about the social and historical context of this decision. Why, I asked myself, had white Alabamians considered it acceptable to eat food that had been prepared and served by black hands, but inappropriate to eat that same food sitting beside black diners? In part, this book stems from my continuing attempt to answer that question.

In graduate school I gravitated toward the very issues of race and access that the Ollie's Barbecue case implicated. In particular, Grace Elizabeth Hale's *Making Whiteness: The Culture of Segregation in the South, 1890–1940* inspired me to think more closely about questions of racial construction and how segregation represents not racial separation, as is so commonly thought, but rather the privileging of whiteness in the consumer sphere. Hale reminds us that the actual separation of the races never really occurred in the Jim Crow era. Blacks and whites came into contact with each other and interacted in a variety of ways—on the sidewalks, in neighborhood stores, and in white homes.[7] In restaurants designated as "white," like Ollie's Barbecue, African Americans often cooked the barbecue and homemade pies that whites consumed in the whites-only dining rooms. Black hands transferred the food from barbecue pit to plate and carried that plate from kitchen to table. African Americans bused the dirty dishes and utensils that whites left behind after a meal. In other words, a typical white restaurant during the Jim Crow era involved constant interactions among blacks and whites.

Hale reconciles this paradox by explaining racial segregation as a cultural system that privileges whites as consumers in an increasingly consumer-based society. Segregation marks African Americans as "inferior" because they occupy inferior spaces. This is not a "natural" distinction, as white supremacists often claim. In fact, the emerging black middle class of educators, business owners, and other professionals, who enjoyed significant buying power, belied this idea even as white authorities implemented the system.

Hale offers up the notion of the black professional as the primary impetus for white supremacists to impose segregation.[8] Indeed, if it were not for the "whites-only" signs, then a black male lawyer could have stepped into the café across the street from the local courthouse and had a white working-class woman serve him lunch. This situation would have called into question many of the racial, class, and gender assumptions that formed the basis for white supremacy in the New South.

Hale addresses segregation as a cultural system that involves all public spaces, including railroads, theaters, and mass media, in the modernizing and urbanizing South. She suggests, however, that there may be something about the "intimate" action of the "touching of the product to lips" that made eating in transracial spaces different from other types of interactions.[9] Indeed, a vast body of white southern memoirs marks the act of "eating with Negroes" as unthinkable. Georgia native Katharine Du Pre Lumpkin, for example, calls it "a grievous Southern sin for which were allowed no mitigating circumstances."[10] In her memoir, *Killers of the Dream*, Lillian Smith identifies a horrendous incongruity in the fact that lynching was more acceptable to whites than was sharing a meal in public with African Americans. "A 'nice white girl'" could share a soda with a member of a lynch mob, Smith writes, "but she would have been run out of town or perhaps killed had she drunk a Coke with the young Negro doctor who was devoting his life in service to his people."[11] Hale's *Making Whiteness* provides a theoretical framework to explore this paradox as well as the legal and cultural questions that emerge from the Ollie's Barbecue case.

The Changing Southern Foodscape

As the American South became more connected to a national industrial and consumer culture, the region's food norms necessarily changed. *Katzenbach v. McClung* frames two parallel issues that arose from these transformations. The first concerns civil rights in southern public eating places. How and why did southern eateries become subject to formal and informal codes of segregation, and what efforts did activists pursue to achieve equality in those spaces? Second, what were the legal and cultural manifestations of the expanding regional and national food systems? And how did white southerners react to the changes wrought by increasing standardization in food practices? This book explores these issues of consumer equality and expanding national markets. It tells the story of food culture in the modern and urbanizing South.

In studying foodways, I join a cadre of interdisciplinary scholars exploring how culinary practices reflect, among other things, politics, society, culture, history, economics, and social justice. A dynamic group of academics use food practices to look at these issues from global, national, and regional perspectives.[12] In the American South, such scholarship is critical to overcoming common misconceptions of the region's food practices as static and monolithic. In popular literature, southern cuisine is venerated above all other aspects of the culture and is used to validate the broader fallacy of an unchanging South. Southern foodways are often described as "traditional"—a term loaded with racial stereotype and privilege. Far from being static, however, southern food practices are constantly evolving, a dynamic facet of a diverse regional culture. The emerging scholarly literature on southern foodways seeks to make connections between cuisine and other aspects of southern society and culture.

The twentieth century was a period of significant change in the ways in which southerners obtained, cooked, served, consumed, and thought about food. Changing food patterns in this period intersected with shifting power relationships in an increasingly consumer-oriented society. In *Building Houses Out of Chicken Legs: Black Women, Food, and Power*, Psyche Williams-Forson explains how black women have used their cooking skills and knowledge to support their families and build better lives for themselves. Along the way, they frequently confronted stereotypical, condescending images in white media that associated African Americans with fried chicken. In truth, men and women of both races prepare and consume fried chicken. Williams-Forson's work demonstrates the role of food in racial identity formation, and its capacity to simultaneously denigrate and empower.[13]

In addition, foodways reveal changing constructions of gender in the region in the twentieth century. In *A Mess of Greens: Southern Gender and Southern Food*, Elizabeth Engelhardt describes how food offered a path for southern women to claim a more modern consumer sphere. Tomato clubs gave adolescent girls in rural areas the opportunity to earn their own money, which they could spend on education or consumer goods. Baking biscuits instead of cornbread introduced previously self-sufficient Appalachian women to consumer markets. In these and other ways, food practices helped shepherd many southern women into the twentieth century.[14] This book builds on the work of Engelhardt, Williams-Forson, and other scholars to reveal how foodways served as a source of empowerment, disempowerment, and modernity in the twentieth-century South. It focuses on the social and legal effects of changing regional foodways and how those changes reflected a new urban culture and power hierarchy.[15]

White southerners generally approached the changing southern foodscape with a sort of cognitive dissonance. They eagerly accepted the new products, methods, and institutions that made life more convenient and that situated the region as a modern example of technological progress. But they bitterly denounced any changes that seemed to interfere with what they considered to be long-standing regional traditions. In 1955 Mary R. Wheeler of Waynesboro, Virginia, wrote an angry letter to the editor of *Life* magazine, complaining that the so-called southern fried chicken recipe included in an earlier issue was not "authentic." The recipe in question instructed readers to simmer the chicken in water for thirty minutes. Wheeler described the recipe as "steamed chicken" and considered it a "sacrilege" to use such a dish to represent the South. The editor responded to Wheeler's complaint by assuring his readers, "*Life's* fried chicken, the specialty of a real southern cook, is both authentic and crisp."[16] Wheeler's willingness to consult a national periodical for recipes and her dismay when the magazine botched this regional specialty reflects a propensity among the broader southern populace, especially whites, to embrace nationalized modes of food consumption while rejecting new consumer practices they deemed antithetical to "traditional" southern ways.

These contradictory tendencies emerged in the American South from roughly 1900 to 1970, as regional food practices became increasingly public and standardized. As national standards permeated southern foodways by way of consumer products, advertising, scientific cookery, public eating places, and chain restaurants, southerners responded with a mixture of eager acceptance, wary application, and determined intransigence. Some southerners recognized that more modern foodways offered convenience, luxury, and participation in the national culture. White urban southerners living on professional salaries who adopted these new foodways identified with a growing national, white middle class.

At the same time, some white southerners saw that modern food practices had the potential to undermine white supremacy. In urban areas African Americans had the opportunity to dine out, operate eateries, and purchase, prepare, and serve commercialized food in a manner that depended more on socioeconomic status and less on race. The emerging white middle class perceived such practices as threats to the region's racial hierarchy. They responded by increasing public regulation and scrutinizing black participation in the region's foodways.

All southerners did not experience this changing food culture at the same time nor in the same way. The historical question of who was included in, and who was excluded from, modern foodways is an important theme of this book. Cultural changes take place gradually and unevenly. Certainly, the lower classes, black and white, had less access to new food practices. Modern approaches to preparing and consuming food required a certain amount of financial means. But in the urban South, even affluent African Americans were increasingly excluded from the spaces in which southerners enacted their modern food practices. Instead, blacks tended to be relegated to spaces where their most visible role was as servers. This book explores the culture of de jure segregation as a modern, urban phenomenon in the South. While white supremacy had long been a reality in the American South, Jim Crow represented a particular way in which white southerners reformulated this trope to conform to post-Reconstruction society.[17]

Intersections of Food, Race, Class, and Gender

In public eating places, racial segregation implicated socioeconomic class and gender as well as race. During the twentieth century, the concept of eating outside the home changed. At one time, dining out was limited to elites, but the new quick-service cafés and lunchrooms expanded access to the middle and lower classes.[18] A southerner did not have to be wealthy to eat at a local café, pick up lunch at a sidewalk stand, or grab a cup of coffee at a lunch counter. The proliferation of quick-order eateries in the early twentieth-century urban South enabled a greater number of African Americans to consume food in a manner equal to whites, thereby undermining white supremacy. One goal of Jim Crow segregation at all socioeconomic levels was to reestablish the antebellum racial hierarchy in southern cities.

Whites often applied the language of impurity (such as "dirty") to African Americans as a rhetorical justification for Jim Crow. Anthropologist Mary Douglas writes that cultures often establish social order through constructions of purity. Although there are no universal definitions of what is and is not considered to be impure—such understandings change across space and time—in her research on "primitive" religion, Douglas finds that certain purifying rituals represent attempts at "positively re-ordering [the] environment, making it conform to an idea."[19] In the early-twentieth-century South, white supremacy was the "idea" around which middle-class Progressives established order in nascent cities. Other Progressive-era initiatives, including pure food, scientific cooking, and moral crusades, offered tools for establishing social order around race.

Middle-class notions of cleanliness played key roles in changing twentieth-century foodways. White Progressive-era southerners advocated for pure food regulation, scientific cooking education, restaurant health codes, and racial segregation. Class-based understandings of sanitation underlay the campaigns to ensure that industrial food satisfied notions of purity; that housewives learned how to maintain a clean kitchen; that public dining areas satisfied certain sanitation standards; and that a community identified by the white power structure as unclean did not share in the public ritual of dining out. To be fair, food purity was a genuine concern for the emerging industrial food system. But in the South, the white middle class conflated food purity with racial purity and used notions of cleanliness to reassert the antebellum racial order that urbanization and consumerism undermined.

Racial segregation in eating places also implicated issues of gender, especially the white middle-class belief that white women needed protection in public spaces. The body has long been significant to legal developments. Legislators focus on its color and gender, among other aspects, as a basis for regulation.[20] The development of segregation law in twentieth-century southern cities, especially concerning restaurants, privileged both white bodies and the white women responsible for reproducing them. Lillian Smith recalls that southern mothers used a combination of verbal and non-verbal cues to teach their children to "be careful about what enters [the] body." This warning applied to sexuality and to the consumption of food and drink.[21]

Two southern taboos connect the physical issues of race, class, social order, cleanliness, and gender. The first prohibited blacks and whites from engaging in sexual activity with one another, and the second barred blacks and whites from eating together. Laws against interracial marriage and in favor of restaurant segregation regulated these taboos in southern society, but white families perpetuated them by instilling these two prohibitions in their children, usually in nonverbal ways. Smith describes the eating taboo as "woven into the mesh of things that are 'wrong.' . . . it pulled anxieties from stronger prohibitions and attached them to itself." She recalls that members of a biracial group for the prevention of lynching transgressed the eating taboo when they took communion together. The white women expressed feelings of righteousness for overcoming their childhood training to take the Lord's Supper at a transracial altar. The black members, Smith notes, resented the fact that "white women felt so virtuous when eating with them."[22] Emotions ran high for many white women who crossed boundaries at the dinner table because they felt a familial commitment to maintain the racial status quo. In 1922, during Virginia Foster Durr's sophomore year at Wellesley, administrators forced the Alabama native to eat with a black student. Durr's white roommate pointed out that Durr hugged and kissed the family's black cook. "Why, I just love the cook," Virginia replied, "but I don't eat with her." Although the taboo made little intellectual sense—even to Durr—the notion had been ingrained in her since childhood. She reconciled the transgression by refusing to tell her father.[23]

Both of these taboos—interracial sex and interracial eating—stemmed from their connection to racial purity.[24] (They were regularly transgressed, often at great peril.) Sexuality and sustenance play similar roles in forming the human body. Both activities involve a foreign substance entering the human body and potentially contributing to the development of flesh. For white southerners, sexuality represented the foundation of racial purity and the means by which a parent transmitted whiteness or blackness to a child. In cities, sex and food shared other attributes too because both represented a product that could be bought and sold, sometimes in restaurants that fronted for brothels. For white southerners, the body that emerged from intercourse and depended on food for growth and survival related directly to constructions of whiteness.[25]

As purveyors of both sex and food, women played important roles in perpetuating race. Segregation arose, in part, as another link in a historical chain that limited women's access to the public places where food consumption took place. If twentieth-century laws did not prohibit white women from patronizing modern cafés and lunchrooms, as they did saloons, white male legislators would attempt to eliminate the potential harms such women might face in these establishments.

Food in the Southern City

This book is a study of the development of cities in the twentieth-century South. Changing food norms, in domestic and public spaces, entered the region through its nascent urban centers. The historian Don H. Doyle describes New South cities as "nerve centers" that birthed a new economy and culture.[26] Doyle's work is an example of how the story of the New South generally emphasizes the "masculine" activities of city building, commercial development, and railroad construction. I reconsider the gendered assumptions that underlie our assessment of the region during this period. Food plays an important role in urban economies and social mores. Whereas Doyle focuses on the men who brought railroads and commerce to the region, this book emphasizes the significant role of their wives and daughters, who brought change in the form of evolving foodways. Such transformations were not subsidiary. They were integral to urbanization. The modern city required new modes of eating, from the length and timing of meals to where and with whom to consume fare. Modern culinary practices began in cities and reached rural areas and Sunbelt suburbia through government initiatives and the efforts of private capitalism.

I conducted much of the research for this book in Birmingham and Atlanta. Both cities represent the New South—Birmingham with its emerging industrial economy and Atlanta as the center of southern commerce in the twentieth century. Moreover, Birmingham and Atlanta have played important roles in the history of food and race, as the homes of the McClungs and of cafeteria owner Lester Maddox, respectively, all of whom stood firm against restaurant desegregation. When it comes to segregation in public eating places, the civil rights histories of the "most thoroughly segregated city" in the nation and the "city too busy to hate" are more closely connected than former Atlanta mayor William B. Hartsfield would want to admit.[27] While no two cities fully represent the whole South (especially in the case of cities like New Orleans or states like Texas, where ethnicity perhaps plays a larger role in race construction and food culture), examining the histories of Birmingham and Atlanta can inform our understanding of how southern food practices have intersected with race, class, ethnicity, and gender. These two cities provide a starting point for a broader regional story of food culture that needs to be told.

This story, of course, cannot be told without discussing the women who toiled in southern kitchens and dining rooms. Black domestic servants played a significant role in southern history—one that has been popularly mythologized, idealized, and diminished into the "mammy" image.[28] The leading scholar on black domestic service in the South, Rebecca Sharpless, breaks through the common stereotypes to examine the lived experiences of black cooks. She views cooking jobs as a bridge that provided African American women with compensated employment between slavery and civil rights, a period during which they had few other opportunities. Because of the intimate spaces in which domestic servants labored, and the fact that cooking in white kitchens was often less than desirable work, Sharpless describes a constant power struggle between white employers and African American cooks. White women jealously guarded their authority in their homes and over their servants. Black women, on the other hand, attempted to exercise their rights as free laborers—however circumscribed—over their working conditions.[29]

In the South, the power struggle that Sharpless describes set the stage for the "servant problem" that some white clubwomen (who participated in Progressive-era organizations committed to social reform) in New South cities bemoaned in the first few decades of the twentieth century. A few white middle-class women reacted to the autonomy claimed by black servants in ways that contradict our assumption that black domestic service was a foregone conclusion in the South. In particular, there was a short-lived and controversial suggestion among clubwomen in Birmingham and Atlanta to replace their black domestic servants with white working-class women because they considered black servants to be degenerate in a number of ways.[30] This book is not a history of domestic service. Many other scholars have ably analyzed this topic.[31] But the controversial and unsuccessful effort to remold domestic service in these two cities is important for what it reveals about the white middle class. It shows the anxiety of some white middle-class women about a changing racial environment and provides greater insight into the inner workings of white society in the formative years of Jim Crow. No institution—not even the family kitchen—was too sacred to consider upending in the broader interest of reestablishing white supremacy in the urban foodscape.

By the 1930s segregation law and culture were well established in southern urban areas. Meanwhile, federal influence and education expanded access to modern modes of food preparation and consumption. In the decades that followed World War II, the expansion of consumerism and the development of the Sunbelt economy gave most southern whites access to the American consumer culture.[32] A broader acceptance of national markets and government regulation, however, also prompted white southerners to re-create "southern" cuisine by imagining "traditional" rural foodways as particularly distinct and superior to other means of sustenance.

Eating out became a key feature of American food consumption after World War II. The industrial food system, national chains, and fast food spread to or emerged in the South in the postwar years. In theory, fast-food establishments, primarily a product of the Sunbelt, epitomized democracy in food consumption. They offered quick, cheap, standardized fare at walk-up windows, with no dining rooms to segregate. In reality, however, the early fast-food chains envisioned their customer base as predominately white, middle class, and Protestant. They cultivated this image through advertising, and they also targeted white customers by placing their restaurants near white neighborhoods and churches and by favoring the new automobile culture. In this way, fast-food chains maintained the status quo of reserving southern eating places primarily for white customers. Nevertheless, fast-food chains completed the transformation of dining in the South into a national, public, democratic activity. In so doing, they helped set the stage for successful civil rights legislation based on Congress's power to regulate interstate commerce.

The sit-in movement in the 1960s brought national attention to the civil rights struggle in the South. The perpetuation of racial exclusivity at lunch counters—ubiquitous downtown spaces with affordably priced food—represented an increasingly untenable hardship for black customers, especially women and young people. These two constituencies led the fight for desegregation. Black college students served as shock troops, planning and executing demonstrations. Older black women boycotted the downtown stores that featured segregated lunch counters and provided behind-the-lines support by making sandwiches, mobilizing volunteers, and guiding activists' efforts. By the 1960s, sit-ins already had a long reputation in the history of peaceful protest. This extensive history, as well as the commitment of whole black communities, made the sit-in one of the most successful tactics of the civil rights era for forcing change in the legal and cultural environment. The Ollie's Barbecue decision reveals the impact of these changes.

Food Culture and the Law

Other scholars have used *Katzenbach v. McClung* as a point of entry into the larger legal and social processes of the twentieth-century struggle for civil rights. Legal scholars have examined the significant impact of the Ollie's Barbecue decision on twentieth-century constitutional development. Historians have identified the *McClung* case as important to understanding the history of white southern reactions to the changes brought by desegregation.[33] *To Live and Dine in Dixie* combines these approaches by considering the historical progression of food culture in the urban South and how the law evolved to regulate practices previously considered to be private.

This book covers a broad period—from the end of Reconstruction in the 1870s to the aftermath of civil rights legislation in the 1970s—and is divided into three chronological parts. Each part includes two chapters: the first describes how the food culture changed during the period and the second explores the corresponding evolution of law and society concerning public eating spaces.

Over the years 1876–1935, southern food practices transitioned from local patterns of consumption to more national and standardized practices. In the home, many white middle-class women purchased new products, adopted scientific methods, and relied on cookbooks with modern recipes. They used such practices to distinguish their white cooking from the lesser standards they imagined to be at work in African American kitchens. A disregard for black abilities in the kitchen enabled the white middle class to imagine whiteness as superior and to develop legal and social practices that privileged whites in public eating establishments. Although the cultural groundwork for white supremacy began at home, the laws regulating public eating practices revolved around this concept. In more accessible quick-service cafés and lunchrooms, the exclusive consumption practices that once relied on class became race-based.

From 1936 to 1959, the national consumer culture became even more accessible to white southerners. New Deal policies and public education encouraged modern kitchens, and rising socioeconomic standards following the Depression enabled many white southerners to adopt more modern consumption patterns. Firmly established Jim Crow policies allowed whites to view African Americans as quaint for their supposed old-fashioned cooking methods. Well-established racial segregation policies allowed white southerners to encourage more democratic spaces for food service and consumption by those of their own race. As quick, accessible, and inexpensive spaces, fast food epitomized this new democracy in public dining—at least for the white customers targeted by such chains.

From 1960 through 1975, the civil rights movement encouraged an even more inclusive food culture. The struggles of sit-in activists and other civil rights demonstrators encouraged many moderate whites and city officials to expand downtown eating spaces to include black customers.[34] Eventually, the civil rights struggles forced the U.S. Congress to pass legislation that prohibited segregation in public spaces across the country. College students who grew up in the region generated much of the momentum for civil rights progress in public eating places.[35] Moreover, as the Ollie's case demonstrates, the success of civil rights legislation lay in the more national and democratic processes that brought food to tables across the South. Greater standardization in food consumption enabled the success of proprietors like the McClungs. The existence of quick-service eateries like Ollie's, the financial ability of white southerners to eat out, and the ready supply of reasonably priced meats to slow cook in barbecue pits all contributed to greater standardization in southern food culture. Yet the McClungs and other white proprietors saw the end result of these nationalizing tendencies—civil rights legislation—as a burdensome intrusion on their businesses. Although they had established their business models around Jim Crow laws, they argued that they could not accommodate laws that necessitated inclusion. By tracing the changes in twentieth-century food culture and the corresponding alterations to the laws and society trying to protect white supremacy, this book illuminates how whiteness emerged for some white proprietors as a necessary ingredient in southern eating places.

PART 1
Southern Food Culture in Transition, 1876–1935

THE TWENTIETH CENTURY was a period of great change in southern eating practices, especially in the more public ways that southerners experienced food. The number and variety of public eating places increased significantly in southern cities around the turn of the century. In Atlanta, for example, the city directory listed around 40 eateries in each of the years 1900, 1901, and 1902—mostly high-end restaurants. Starting in 1903, however, the number of public eating establishments rose to 144 and continued to grow in the years that followed.[1] This boom took place primarily in the quick-service segment of the industry—cafés and lunchrooms offering low-priced fare and fast service. Many of these places may have existed prior to 1903, but only appeared for the first time that year in the city directory. Even so, this sharp increase reveals a significant shift in the way southerners identified, recognized, and thought about the public table. Unlisted eateries attracted neighborhood crowds or close associates of the proprietor, but they would not have been easily available to strangers looking for a quick lunch in the city. So even if these public places were not entirely new, they were at least newly public.

This dramatic proliferation of public eating establishments in Atlanta reflected a broader evolving food culture in the region designed around more national practices. Although the changes were most evident in the public sphere, they were cultivated in southern middle-class homes. Urban-dwellers faced new challenges with regard to food. They often did not have the space or time to cultivate crops, so they purchased food at city markets. Middle-class white women gained power over the food culture in the city by implementing domestic science principles in all aspects of their home life, especially cooking. Home economics education encouraged middle-class white women to help modernize the region and to incorporate national norms into regional food practices.

When middle-class people took control of the regional food culture at home and in public, they began to define food practices according to race. In the cities, white middle-class women especially worried over the degeneration of the white race because lower-class whites often worked and lived in degrading conditions. They also desired to reassert white supremacy in an era when middle-class African Americans were succeeding compared to working-class whites. Food culture provided a tool by which the white urban middle class could distinguish race. Many Progressive-era whites interpreted white practices as superior because they were based on science, knowledge, and education. At the same time, many whites assumed black practices to be inferior. This process was most obvious in the public sphere. City officials successfully implemented racial segregation in public eating places, transforming a culture that had once been governed primarily by class into one regulated by race.

CHAPTER ONE

Scientific Cooking and Southern Whiteness

Eugene Walter's childhood memories start in his grandmother's kitchen. Growing up in an urban middle-class household in Mobile, Alabama, in the early twentieth century, Walter recalls food preparation as a combination of tried-and-true methods and the eager application of modern technologies. His grandmother signified this intermingling of old and new by keeping two stoves side by side in her large kitchen. The modern gas range made cooking quicker and more convenient. But she used an old-fashioned iron stove for baking biscuits, cakes, and breads. Walter's grandmother handled the iron stove with a practiced hand. Even though the older technology did not have a precise thermostat, she had learned as a child how to gauge the oven's temperature by watching her family's black cook. In her old age, Walter's grandmother continued to rely on African American labor in the kitchen. The family's cook, Rebecca, arrived early each morning to prepare breakfast and stayed to help with the afternoon meal.[1]

Walter's culinary memories reveal a southern food culture in transition. Cooking methods based in an agrarian past and passed down through oral instruction and experience were giving way to new practices propelled by modernity and consumerism and dependent on scientific knowledge and technological advancement. Although, like Walter's grandmother, some women continued to hang on to the former model, by the turn of the century the latter vision had captured the southern imagination. Modern technology and a new consumption-based culture conspired to alter culinary practices too often considered to be static. For this reason, the term "New South" means more than the conventional images of new industries and new cities. The "New South" also implies an emerging modern food culture whereby women learned to cook from experts in the field, administered their kitchens with scientific precision and businesslike efficiency, used written recipes, embraced new foods, and purchased technologically advanced products and appliances.

White middle-class women were the first to adopt these changes in the South. The new food routines soon took on racial and gendered meanings that helped to establish white supremacy in the new century. Despite the deep African American roots of southern foodways, many white advocates of modern eating practices attempted to redefine southern food as "white" by standardizing recipes and mandating the preparation instructions for even the simplest foods. These practices contrasted with a white perception of African American cooking as slapdash and unsophisticated. Many white, middle-class, urban and small-town women, who had greater access to consumer markets than did their African American, lower-class, or rural counterparts, considered these advancements to be "white" knowledge. Black domestic workers could practice these techniques under white supervision, but could never really own them.

Gender, like race, was a significant component of white middle-class southern domesticity and the New South's food culture. The women who embraced this new food culture believed that knowledge, thrift, and cleanliness reflected feminine ideals when directed toward the domestic sphere. They also believed that only white women possessed these virtues. Many interpreted homemaking as empowering in that it enabled women to manipulate and control society. An educated woman read cookbooks and other household manuals. She recognized a quality cut of meat and understood its market value. She attended pure food lectures and cooking demonstrations offered by home economists. Her feminine attributes played an important role in identifying her class status and also in the construction of whiteness. White women determined which foods would be consumed by, and thereby become a part of, the white body as well as how such foods would be prepared. They embraced modern theories of nutrition and pure food as tools for building a stronger white race and maintaining racial purity.

Although this new culture was not universal, it had significant influence among clubwomen in certain New South cities, such as Birmingham and

Atlanta. Those women were in the best position to spread their influence by offering classes, sponsoring speakers, funding schools, supporting legislation, and participating in consumer markets. They served as "new food" boosters, committed to using culinary knowledge to improve southern society, starting in the kitchen. They were the wives and daughters of the rising urban business class in New South cities—the "new men" described by Don H. Doyle in *New Men, New Cities, New South*. For Doyle, white southern business leaders became a cohesive social class as they built new cities and recognized their common worldview.[2] Their wives and daughters experienced the same cohesiveness as they developed new food habits for the urban, business-focused society that their husbands and fathers were creating. Moreover, as Doyle's "new men" implemented race-based segregation laws in the urban public spaces they controlled, their wives and daughters sought to uphold white supremacy in the domestic sphere that was their domain.

This new food culture was limited at first to a salaried elite. Even then, some women may have rejected many of the strict rules of scientific cooking. Nonetheless, a significant cultural change spread through education, individual acceptance, and government initiative. World War I soon served to extend access to this new food culture to the lower classes because conservation efforts expanded the spread of food knowledge.[3]

Technology and Food

Modern food culture owes its existence to technological advances and increased consumerism. The antebellum South lagged behind the nation in updated cooking technology. Although iron stoves were commercially available by the 1830s, most southern households did not adopt them until after the Civil War. An engraved picture of the nineteenth-century kitchen at the Virginia governor's mansion shows a large cooking fireplace that took up most of the wall and rose well above the head of the enslaved cook, who had to stand nearly in the fire to tend the food. Older cooking technology—namely, fireplaces and early stoves—led to unsystematic processes and imprecise results, and there was little concern for sanitation. Cooking fireplaces needed to be large enough to accommodate sizable pots and skillets. Kitchens were filled with messy wood, ash, heat, and smoke. Unpredictable temperature controls made cooking imprecise and required flexible recipes and creative, experienced cooks. Because cultural change can be slow and uneven, nineteenth-century southern cookbooks often gave recipes for both stove and fireplace cooking.[4]

By the late nineteenth century most southern homes relied on iron stoves fueled by wood or coal. Stoves eliminated much of the mess and danger of cooking because the fire was contained. But the necessity of controlling the fire still contributed to unpredictable results in unpracticed hands. Oil-fueled and, later, gas and electric models allowed more ease of use and less mess and heat, and modern stoves enabled the use of lightweight aluminum pots and pans. Although technology simplified matters in the kitchen by making cooking more convenient and comfortable, it also required cooks to purchase new equipment and utensils. Middle-class homemakers accumulated measuring spoons, paring knives, doughnut cutters, bread knives, ice cream freezers, and meat grinders. The convenience and availability of twentieth-century train travel allowed these finished commercial products, often made in the North, to be transported for sale in southern markets.[5]

In addition to the new pans, utensils, and appliances, southern grocers stocked new food products that housekeepers previously had produced at home. An 1806 recipe reveals the time and effort necessary to make yeast for baking bread. Nineteenth-century women soaked hops in hot water. They poured the resulting tea over mashed potatoes and combined this mixture with flour and brown sugar. After this dough cooled, they left it to ferment.[6] By the end of the nineteenth century, however, southern cookbooks assumed that women purchased yeast. Among the earliest to take this approach, *The Dixie Cook-Book* suggests several name-brand yeasts that the homemaker could trust, including Twin Brothers, Stratton's, Eagle, and National.[7] Later, southern cookbooks called for baking powder.[8] In 1906 an Atlanta baking company announced its new sanitary bread factory. Now, Atlantans did not even have to bake their own bread. They could purchase the patriotically named Uncle Sam Bread at their local grocery store.[9] By the early twentieth century the salaried class in southern cities and small towns could purchase a wide variety of ready-made food products, from canned chicken to bottled salad dressings.[10]

New technology and products brought southern women of means into the national consumer culture. They also changed how women thought about the physical space of the kitchen and the activity of cooking. Antebellum southern kitchens were usually detached from the house because of the danger of fire. This architectural practice reflected a cultural understanding of the kitchen as a space separated from the white family—at least in the white twentieth-century imagination. Although only an elite few would have had enslaved help in the kitchen, many turn-of-the-century white, middle-class women interpreted antebellum kitchens as "mammy's" space—an area of black authority.

Pre-twentieth-century kitchens differed from their successors in many ways. Black and white women learned to cook based on oral tradition, observation, and trial and error. Girls served as apprentices and learned by doing—at first helping an older woman to perform her kitchen duties and later taking on these responsibilities in her own home. In short, the processes of cooking in the South before the twentieth century tended to be private and unsystematic.

The Servant Problem

Social change contributed to evolving notions about southern kitchens and the art of cooking. Only a small percentage of white antebellum women had the benefit of enslaved labor in the kitchen; nevertheless, the emergent postwar middle class imagined that emancipation had created a "servant problem" in the South. By the turn of the twentieth century, many among the southern white middle class believed that dependable, competent servants, especially cooks, no longer existed among the region's African American population.[11] This perception most likely stemmed from the new ability of free African American women to make employment choices that benefited themselves and their families. Most black women building new lives in the South's urban areas had two job options—they could either take in laundry or cook for white families. In 1918 researchers surveying conditions in Athens, Georgia, found that the majority of black women chose the former. Most black women preferred to work as laundresses because they could work at home, which allowed them to take care of their own families. In addition, they could take in laundry from more than one white household to increase their earning potential. One of the many downsides to cooking in white homes, not addressed by the Athens study, was the increased risk of sexual abuse by white men. For these and other reasons, many black women, when given a choice, preferred not to work in white kitchens.[12] This inclination contributed to a perception by some southern white women that black cooks were inexperienced and undependable.

Although the truth behind the South's so-called servant problem lay in the ability of African American women to leave unsatisfactory jobs, the white clubwomen of Atlanta and Birmingham tended to interpret such choices as personal slights that left them suddenly responsible for their own kitchens. One Georgia clubwoman described her experiences with a black cook who refused to show up for work even after the employer went to look for her. Other white women complained that northern recruiters came to southern cities promising black cooks better situations in the North.[13] The white women who complained about servant inadequacies saw themselves as part of a national, or even international, problem. On February 21, 1899, the author and lecturer Charlotte Perkins Gilman, who at that time used her first husband's name, Stetson, announced to a full house at the Atlanta Woman's Club: "the whole civilized world is now finding difficulty in the servant question."[14] Gilman no doubt intended the "civilized world" to mean western nations. White Atlantans, however, saw the southern problem as more acute because they considered early twentieth-century black help to be less skilled and less reliable than either their nineteenth-century enslaved forebears or their foreign-born white contemporaries in the North.

Certainly, social and economic changes particular to the American South affected both racial and class dimensions of the so-called servant problem. The twentieth-century South offered few job opportunities for African Americans, and whites still considered black southerners to be the region's laboring class. Lack of opportunity devalued black labor so much that African Americans did indeed constitute an inexpensive servant class. As a result, even relatively poor white families could often afford a servant, at least part time, to cook and clean.[15] Katie Geneva Cannon, who worked as a domestic servant during her childhood, recalls cleaning and cooking for a family of white textile workers whose house was smaller and simpler than her own. Because she was black, however, she could not get a textile job at that time. Her race forced her to follow her mother and other female relatives into domestic service.[16]

White southerners remembered longtime family cooks as "loyal" servants. "Sally used to cook wonderful breakfasts, with grits and gravy and broiled chicken and sweet potatoes," Birmingham native Virginia Foster Durr recalls in her autobiography. "She never came to prayer service, because she was cooking breakfast. . . We always thought breakfast was God's reward to us for the prayer effort."[17] Durr's white family considered Sally's hard work and her neglect of her own spiritual needs to be a providential gift. Durr internalized the need for black domestic labor as necessary to maintaining her own class and race status.[18] When she moved to Washington, D.C., as the wife of a liberal New Deal administrator, she continued to employ a black cook from Alabama.[19] Certainly, American culture in general encouraged the image of blacks as servants, but such representations found their fullest realization in the South, where most African Americans lived.[20]

The relationship of some white southern clubwomen to black domestic service was complicated. Although they generally relied on black labor and bought into the servile stereotypes represented by the Aunt Jemima image, a short-lived campaign emerged in Birmingham and Atlanta to replace black domestic servants with white working-class women. This controversial suggestion resembled similar discussions taking place on a nationwide basis as white middle-class women attempted to find a reliable and submissive source of domestic labor. In northeastern and West Coast cities, this debate often centered on replacing Irish women with Chinese men—an effort thwarted by the Chinese exclusion legislation in 1882. As the historian Andrew Urban explains, many native-born, white, middle-class housewives preferred Chinese men as domestic servants because they were considered to be more subservient than Irish women. In growing cities across the nation, white middle-class women sought dependable domestic help to maintain their class and race privilege, and the discourse they used to discuss these objectives revolved around racialized and gendered standards of respectability.[21]

In Birmingham and Atlanta, this debate implicated the relationship between the workers who were laboring in white homes and the welfare of the white race as a whole. Contrary to the servile images of black women circulating in the popular imagination, Mrs. James A. Kirk, the president of the Fenelon Club in Birmingham, thought African American women were inherently unfit for domestic service. She contrasted their supposed faults as a race—"dishonesty and utter disregard to morality and cleanliness"—to the alleged assets of lower-class white women, who were "intelligent" and "self-respecting."[22] Kirk expected good service from white women because she thought they had the capacity to learn to keep a modern household. She questioned this ability in black women. The Atlanta clubwoman Mrs. Lewis Beck agreed with this assessment. Beck emphasized the "dignity" that white girls would bring to domestic work and argued that white women "had been discriminated against" because they did not get household jobs.[23] Both women expressed concerns about the welfare of the white middle-class home and the white race in general, but neither was concerned about the desires or needs of working women.

To the extent that clubwomen did consider the situations of the working women whose lives this discussion most affected, their concern revolved around the plight of lower-class white women—or, more precisely, the effect of factory work on the welfare of the white race. Many southern white club-women considered factory work to be morally and physically degenerating to white women—and thereby to whites in general. Clubwomen generally agreed that providing domestic education to lower-class white women was a positive step in improving white society. In the years after emancipation, northern philanthropists had funded African American schools, and many of these schools offered some sort of domestic instruction for girls. In Georgia, Rebecca Latimer Felton encouraged the funding of domestic education for poor white girls. Echoing Kirk's and Beck's calls to hire white servants, Felton stressed that such schooling would prepare poor white women for a career in domestic service and would improve their own homes and families.[24]

A general recognition that white supremacy necessitated a strict status differentiation between black and white, however, complicated the call for white domestic service. The Atlanta clubwoman Mrs. Edward Brown cautioned against the practice. Although she agreed in domestic education for lower-class whites, Brown did not want to disturb the racial status quo. "I do not believe it would do justice to either race," Brown argued, "to develop in Georgia a class of white woman who would be recognized as identified exclusively with domestic service."[25] Birmingham and Atlanta clubwomen never pursued the initiative as a consistent, coherent effort, and in the end, Brown's position prevailed, and white domestic service failed to emerge in the South. The historical connection between domestic service and racial inferiority had doomed the suggestion from the beginning, and white lower-class women refused to take the jobs.

The call for white domestic labor was controversial and unsuccessful. But the debate, short-lived as it was, reveals the racial and gender anxieties of white, southern, urban, middle-class women at this time. The tendency of some white women to question the competence of black servants reflects a broader turn-of-the-century cultural belief among many whites that emancipation had resulted in a degeneration of the black race—that without the supposed civilizing effect of slavery, African Americans made poor servants.[26] And in this context the suggestion reveals the complicated and anxiety-ridden relationship that some white women had with black domestic service and its relationship to race construction. For a generation of newly urban and consumer-oriented southern women, the notion that "unclean" black women cooked meals in "clean" white kitchens seemed inconsistent with the idea of racial purity, especially since lower-class white women labored in dirty factories. Black cooking might somehow "pollute" the bodies of white families while, at the same time, factories seemingly polluted the bodies of laboring white women. This discourse in the halls of privileged white women's clubs allowed some middle-class women to question the state of affairs. Yet those who opposed white domestic labor revealed similar anxieties about the welfare of the white race if white working-class girls became associated with servitude.

The so-called servant problem gave impetus to new industrial products as manufacturers, publishers, and advertisers promoted goods for the home in southern markets. Early commercial imagery encouraged the perception that white women could not take care of their kitchens without assistance. In 1883 *The Dixie Cook-Book*, a national publication originally published as

"LOVE IN A COTTAGE." — "NEVER MIND; DON'T CRY, PET, I'LL DO ALL THE COOKING." AFTER DRAWING BY SOL. EYTINGE, JR., (BY PERMISSION OF HARPER BROS.) ENGRAVED BY WILLARD.

FIGURE 2. Engraving from *The Dixie Cook-Book* (1883) illustrates the "servant problem."

Practical Housekeeping and repackaged to appeal to southern housekeepers, promoted this perception with an engraving that features a distraught white housewife standing in the middle of her kitchen in tears. The kitchen is in complete disarray. Pots and pans, broken dishes, and food litter the floor. A cat eats out of a pan on the kitchen table. A fire rages on the stove. Outside the window, a cook loaded with her possessions walks away from the house. Inside, a white man holding his burned dinner tries to comfort his wife. "Don't cry, Pet," he says. "I'll do all the cooking."[27] After setting the stage in this way, *The Dixie Cook-Book* then offered solutions for the distraught housewife dealing with the "servant problem." Other manufacturers followed suit. An 1899 Campbell's soup advertisement in an Atlanta newspaper identified condensed soups as a solution, saying, "The cook can't spoil the soup . . . Her part is just [to add] 'hot water.'"[28] Such images encouraged the view that white middle-class women could not perform kitchen work without help, in this case in the form of consumer goods. The image of the hapless white housewife in need of an alternative to inadequate labor helped to sell a wide range of newly available food products.

Home Economics in the South

While national manufacturers offered solutions to the servant problem on grocery store shelves, many white middle-class women believed that they could, and should, take control of their own kitchens. In so doing, they emphasized a scientific approach to cooking and housekeeping and changed the way women gained knowledge about their principal household duties. This new field, commonly referred to as domestic science or home economics, could not be learned at home through an informal apprenticeship and could not be based on trial and error. It required the discipline of a classroom and the precision of a laboratory.

Professional scientists and educators, mostly women, who were concerned about the effects of an industrializing nation on the home and family started the American domestic science movement in the Northeast. Domestic scientists imagined that industry threatened the American family by moving productive work to factories and bringing costly manufactured products into the home. At the same time, however, they believed that modern thought and technology provided tools for women to organize their households more efficiently and to rebuild the foundations of the home. This new professional discipline combined chemistry, nutrition, economics, and aesthetics to teach women how to run their households like businesses. Although home economics had antebellum precursors, such as Catharine Beecher's household manuals, its twentieth-century incarnation first took form at an upstate New York conference in 1899, hosted by the American Home Economics Association. Within a decade, it achieved many of the hallmarks of a scholarly discipline—organizing a professional association, publishing a journal, and developing a curriculum.[29]

Food formed an early core component of the broader field of domestic science. Scientific cooking required precision. Proponents of this new discipline compared the home to a factory and advocated scientific management in the kitchen—including the use of modern equipment, strict schedules, store-bought products, precise recipes, and standardized measurements. Students were also expected to understand the chemical processes of nutrition and digestion.[30] In the South, the urban middle class was the first constituency to adopt this new culture. Clubwomen embraced the movement because it helped them to negotiate the South's emerging consumer markets.

In addition to suiting their twentieth-century urban lifestyle, home economics also met the needs of the South's white supremacist and class-conscious society. At a basic level, white southern women championed domestic science because they saw that its methods could help to sustain white supremacy, establish class lines, and promote racial purity. They did not have to read too much into its principles to draw out these ideas. The architect of the national domestic science movement, Ellen H. Richards, explicitly envisioned a profession that would help to improve the white race. During an initial naming controversy for the new discipline, Richards suggested the term "euthenics." She explicitly saw it as a companion to, and an improvement on, eugenics. "Eugenics deals with race improvement through heredity," Richards wrote. "Euthenics deals with race improvement through environment." Through euthenics, Richards hoped to improve the white race by imposing certain household standards that would better the health, well-being, and overall circumstances of whites.[31]

The connection Richards made between eugenics and domestic science is significant for understanding the domestic science movement in the South. Eugenics was a turn-of-the-century pseudoscience intended to improve the human race by preventing those who were not considered fit to reproduce from doing so. In the American South, eugenics focused primarily on improving the white race by confining the vaguely defined "feeble-minded" in mental institutions and through forced sterilization. Southern white clubwomen understood and actively supported this effort. In Louisiana and Georgia, among other southern states, white middle-class women took leading roles in lobbying for institutionalization and sterilization laws. Although such laws primarily affected poor whites, they were nevertheless race-based. They aimed to build a stronger white race by preventing those who were thought to bring down the race from breeding.[32] For the southern white women who supported eugenics, domestic science represented a more affirmative approach to achieving the same ends by ensuring that white children received proper nutrition and healthy food, thereby becoming physically and mentally stronger. Unlike eugenics, domestic science had the added benefit that it was an approach that white women could implement in their own homes and communities.

Scientific cooking supported the South's racial and class hierarchy in a variety of ways. White middle-class women were in the best residential and financial position to implement its principles. Home economics started with a properly arranged kitchen. The kitchen needed to be located near the pantry and dining room in order to save the time and energy of the server and to make sure that foods were presented at the appropriate temperature. A proper housekeeper stocked her kitchen with the "necessary kitchen equipment," including a variety of utensils, pans, dishes, towels, and cookbooks, and with modern conveniences, such as running water, an ice cream freezer, a refrigerator or icebox, and an electric toaster. She purchased foods as an informed consumer, selecting, for example, only a fresh, choice cut of meat and obtaining it at a reasonable price.[33] All of these decisions and improvements had to be made before the homemaker performed or supervised any actual cooking or food preparation.

In addition to keeping up the kitchen and managing the shopping, a middle-class housewife was responsible for meal planning, which required her to understand food chemistry, nutrition, and digestion. The knowledgeable housekeeper planned her family's meals according to scientific standards by considering the chemical composition of each ingredient and the nutritional needs of each family member based on their age, gender, and occupation. A young person generally needed more tissue-building proteins than an older person, while a family member who worked outside needed more calories than an office worker. In this way, food itself became gendered. Energy-generating and muscle-building foods, such as red meat, potatoes, and other heavy starches, became associated with men and their particular roles in society. Lighter foods, such as salads, sandwiches, and so-called dainties, became associated with women and their assumed lighter duties and responsibilities.[34]

To prepare food for home consumption, domestic science advocated cooking foods to improve their appearance, flavor, and digestibility, as well as to destroy harmful bacteria. Complicated home economics recipes served several purposes. First, they prescribed cooking methods based on chemical principles. For example, some foods might be made more digestible through the process of boiling, whereas boiling other foods would make them lose vital nutrients.[35] Second, domestic science recipes standardized measurements and clarified recipes to avoid confusion. Older cookbooks often used antiquated or vague measurement standards. Mary Randolph's early nineteenth-century recipe for rice waffles, for example, calls for "two gills of rice . . . [and] three gills of flour," and her cornmeal bread recipe requires "a piece of butter the size of an egg."[36] By contrast, the new domestic science cookbooks used teaspoons, tablespoons, and cups, requiring the associated measuring spoons and other utensils, which women could purchase and rely on to be exact.[37]

In addition to making recipes easier to follow, scientific cooking encouraged variety in the southern diet to ensure that people received sufficient nutrition and to make cooking and eating more interesting. Most devotees insisted that drudgery and monotony at mealtimes prevented people from receiving proper nutrition. Finally, a major purpose of domestic science recipes was to make food look and taste better. Domestic science advocated taste and presentation as scientifically proven digestion aids. "The tempting appearance or flavor of a food increases the flow of saliva and digestive juices," wrote one expert, "thereby adding to the ease of digestion."[38] In this way, domestic scientists took what had previously been considered an art and turned it into a science. Although the new consumer products had simplified a housewife's responsibilities to some extent, scientific cooking imposed a strict regime that ensured that its adherents could be identified and distinguished from those who did not belong.

Even for dishes that required little or no actual cooking, such as salads, home economists still suggested intricate recipes that served many of the same purposes. Older southern cookbooks had paid little attention to salads and offered few recipes. *The Young Housewife's Counsellor and Friend*, published in 1875 by Mary Ann Bryan Mason, provides a recipe for chicken salad and for a dressing (essentially mayonnaise) that could be used on "lettuce, slaw, tomatoes, lobster, cucumbers, celery, etc." But Mason offered no exact directions or precise ingredients and invited the cook to assemble the salad in any configuration she saw fit.[39] A generation later, domestic scientists eschewed such ambiguity. They considered salads necessary for supposedly daintier feminine appetites. Salads soon became a staple of club luncheons as well as an appetizer for formal dinners.

Scientific cookbooks usually included a large number of salad recipes and emphasized their preparation and presentation. The *Athens Woman's Club Cook Book* includes over forty different recipes for salad or salad dressing— all of which involve precise combinations of fruits, vegetables, meats, cheeses, mayonnaise, and, in some cases, gelatin.[40] The *Atlanta Woman's Club Cook Book* includes a recipe for the ironically named "As You Like It" salad, consisting of tomatoes, lettuce, mayonnaise, and boiled eggs that had to be combined in a very specific manner. The cook peeled the tomatoes, hollowed out the centers, and stored them on ice. Before serving, the cook was to fill the center of the tomato with mayonnaise and one-half of a boiled egg so that "the rounded top [of the egg] r[o]se a little above the tomato." The hostess was then instructed to serve the finished dish on a lettuce leaf.[41] The specification of the exact combination of ingredients and the detailed instructions for serving the finished product made this relatively simple dish quite complicated. In this way, its proper preparation and presentation helped to distinguish those who belonged from those who did not.[42] Although all domestic science devotees may not have strictly followed the curriculum and instructions of this demanding discipline, its principles still reflected a new way of thinking about cooking.[43]

White southerners contrasted this new scientific approach to cooking with the inferior standards they imagined to be at work among the world's black populations. Despite their reliance on black labor in the kitchen and their commitment to certain individual black cooks, some white middle-class adherents to domestic science belittled African Americans in general for not using written recipes or exact measurements. Whites often mocked the perceived illiteracy among black cooks, which of course had resulted from a lack of access and opportunity. The *Atlanta Constitution*, for example, described one cookbook as a "very useful book . . . if only cooks knew how to read."[44] In nearby Milledgeville, the local paper described black cooking as "slip shod . . . as if a man had the stomach of a hog or ostrich."[45]

Unlike white cooking habits, which they considered to be changeable and learned, white southerners considered black food practices to be immutable and innate. They imagined that primitive food cultures existed among all black populations. A February 1908 *Atlanta Constitution* article erroneously described African food as plain, raw, and unprocessed: "It is eaten as it is found, with but little preparation."[46] These two opposing perceptions—white food practices as methodical and scientific compared to African food culture as primitive and simple—established "white" food as normative and "black" food as the other. These contrasting images emphasized the importance of having an educated white housekeeper oversee the black cook—at least in the minds of the turn-of-the-century white middle class.

Such a distinction in the kitchen mattered a great deal for white southerners during the Progressive era. They connected diet to morality, brain function, and mental capacity. So a population that did not eat properly was considered to be inherently deficient in those areas as well. Citing the importance of cooking education at Georgia's white female state college, the *Milledgeville Union Recorder* wrote, "Let me know what a people eat, how they eat it, and I will tell you their character, their habits and their mental power."[47] By undermining the ability of Africans in general and African Americans in particular to cook properly, white southerners offered a justification for reestablishing white supremacy on terms that elevated the race and class status of white professionals and their families.

Many white middle-class women thought that scientific cooking could prevent the degeneration of the white race. In the middle-class home, proper food and nutrition maintained the productivity and purity—and thereby the supposed superiority—of white bodies. The presumed ability to regenerate the race with proper food, or alternatively to degenerate the race with improper sustenance, reveals the exaggerated importance attached to the white body. One white southern liberal, Lillian Smith, described this importance in terms of religion, health, and morality. The body was a gift from God and, therefore, maintaining physical health was a religious imperative. According to Smith, southerners tended to the health of the white body through a series of important rituals, including "taking baths, eating food, exercising, and having daily elimination." Consumption and the white body were related to morality.[48]

Smith's explanation of this understanding of the white body sheds light on the cultural importance of food. "Eating food" was one of several activities, according to Smith, in which southerners engaged in order to regulate the body's health.[49] And for those middle-class mothers focused on building healthy white bodies to contribute to the race, consuming the "right" types of food was important to maintaining racial purity. These women believed that feeding their children nutritious, pure food would contribute to a stronger white race.

The 1928 cookbook published by the Georgia Branch of the National Congress of Parents and Teachers, *P.T.A. Interpretations of Food*, instructs mothers to build strong children and families through the appropriate use of food, starting in the womb. The Georgia P.T.A. interpreted the responsibility for building strong white families as a new and important duty for white mothers. One nostalgic recipe for "Mammy's Mush Bread" explains, "This recipe is dedicated to the old colored mammies, whose pleasure and duty it was to administer to the wants and needs of the mistress of the household, in the 'fore de war days.'"[50] In other words, the plantation kitchen had put the care of the white family in black hands, but modern food practices placed this responsibility on the white mother. The P.T.A. cookbook, like other southern cookbooks of its day, relied on home economics experts to advise the white mother on how best to build the white bodies under her care.

Pure Food in the South

In an age of increased consumerism, pure food became a significant political and social issue. With a large number of families no longer raising food, the fear of adulterated products grew. At the same time, industry created new products and additives that may or may not have been healthy. In 1894 the *Atlanta Constitution* charged the relatively new industrial food system with "wholesale adulteration," describing grains mixed with "sweepings from the mill floor" and seasonings composed of "bakers' refuse."[51] In unregulated consumer markets, middle-class southerners had good reason to worry about contaminated food. But white southern women interpreted pure food to mean more than simply unadulterated products. Pure food meant food fit for white consumption. In this way, pure food contributed to racial purity.

As Lillian Smith describes, white middle-class southerners believed that food consumption affected health as well as racial identity. This point is best illustrated by the clay eating practiced by a small number of lower-class southerners. In various isolated parts of Maryland, North Carolina, Tennessee, Georgia, Alabama, and Mississippi, a few black and white southerners made a habit of eating dirt for both sustenance and pleasure. Clay or dirt eaters, as they were commonly called, fed on a white or yellow oily clay, called kaolin, that had a subtle but sweet taste. Some clay eaters rolled the clay into a small ball that dissolved on the tongue. Others chewed and swallowed the substance raw. Still others preferred to cook the clay until it became hard and crumbled in their mouths.[52]

Journalists and writers who observed the practice revealed a simultaneous fascination and revulsion with the custom. Fascination stemmed from the exotic nature of clay eating among global cultures considered to be "primitive" and "tropical"—namely, Asians, Africans, and Native Americans. The *Montgomery Advertiser* informed readers that the women and children of Siam considered a certain type of clay to be a "delicious dainty" and that "no means of persuasion" would convince the "negroes of Guinea" to halt the practice.[53] Such discourse marked those who ate dirt as part of an exotic other—a group within which whites easily placed African American clay eaters.[54]

White clay eaters, on the other hand, received a great deal of public criticism. Contemporary media labeled them "indolent," "worthless," "barbarian," "miserable specimens of humanity," and "the lowest type of the white race." The practice called their racial status into question. White middle-class observers styled white clay eaters' complexions as "bluish-yellow," "yellow," or "ashy"—descriptions often applied to persons with African ancestry. By contrast, journalists described non-clay-eating white complexions as "fresh pink and white," "milky white," or "red-faced."[55] Such terms identified one important marker of race: skin tone. Lillian Smith recalls white skin as being "the source of . . . strength and pride . . . a symbol of purity and excellence . . . [that] proves that you are better than all other people on earth."[56] Consumption practices that threatened such an important symbol also endangered what it symbolized. In this way, the consumption of the wrong type of sustenance brought racial identity into question.

Journalists also questioned the morality of white clay eaters in ways that mirrored turn-of-the-century white perceptions of African American behavior. They consistently described white clay-eating families as degenerate. "Their morals are lax," the *Atlanta Constitution* wrote of white clay eaters in eastern Maryland. "A man and woman will live together and rear a family without troubling themselves about a marriage ceremony."[57] Contemporary white southerners similarly attributed supposed moral failings, such as sexual wantonness, to African Americans.[58] Again, white clay eaters shared this racialized trait.[59]

One journalist writing about white clay eaters in North Carolina blatantly suggested that dirt eating affected racial identity by saying that clay eaters "may without exaggeration be spoken of as a race, so widely are they separated in the matters of social customs, education, and manner of living from all other classes of people in America."[60] In other words, whatever else they may have been, clay eaters were not purely white. In truth, clay eaters of both races were an extremely small percentage of the southern population. Yet their cultural significance belied their numbers, especially for white middle-class southerners who consumed stories about these odd rural folk and their lifestyle. Clay eating served as a cultural reminder of the tenuous nature of race at the turn of the twentieth century—and of the significant relationship between food consumption and race. For a white middle class newly dependent on uncertain consumer markets for its sustenance, the peculiar complexion and behavior of white clay eaters confirmed that the consumption of food related directly to racial standing and cultural identity.

The racial significance of food gave the pure food movement a special resonance among the southern white middle class. Like domestic science in general, southern women's clubs embraced the national movement to ensure the purity of the commercial food supply. One observer, writing in the *Atlanta Constitution*, suggested that impure additives, such as the practice of adding clay to sugar and flour, might lead all Georgians to become clay eaters.[61] Although such additives may have been limited to the journalist's imagination, white urban women did attend pure food expositions where national manufacturers assured them of the safety of their products. In March 1900 the Atlanta Retail Grocers Association sponsored a pure food show at the local armory, where national food manufacturers exhibited their products. This exhibition, designed after similar events in the North, was one of many such events that occurred in cities across the South.[62]

Food Education in the South

White middle-class women encouraged domestic science education in order to elevate the race and perpetuate white supremacy. Women's clubs offered cooking classes at public forums, such as the 1908 housekeepers' exhibition in Atlanta, sponsored by national food manufacturers.[63] Girls also learned how to cook at school.[64] In 1891 Georgia became the first southern state to implement public scientific cooking education for white girls with the founding of the Georgia Normal and Industrial College.[65] The founding president, J. Harris Chappell, required all students to take domestic classes in order to prepare them for their future roles as wives and mothers. The school also offered several vocational departments, such as stenography, sewing, bookkeeping, and teaching.[66] Other southern states followed suit. In 1898 the new Alabama Girls Industrial School in Montevallo offered a domestic science degree.[67] Cooking programs at these postsecondary schools followed national standards for scientific cooking education. They modeled their programs after northeastern institutions and hired northern-educated teachers.[68]

Considering the debates of Birmingham and Atlanta clubwomen over the suitability of white women for service jobs, such schools walked a fine line between presenting the act of cooking as an appropriate white occupation while at the same time separating their students from black domestic servants. They highlighted the enhanced standing a white woman held in the home if she knew how to cook—and if she knew how to instruct her servants. Despite the opinion of some white middle-class women that state schools should produce white domestic servants, the schools denied any such objective. Even though scientific cooking represented Chappell's pet project at Georgia College, he nevertheless ranked cooking at the bottom of the school's various industrial departments based on "what [cooks] are worth in the market . . . as a means of making a livelihood." Rather, Chappell insisted, cooking skills for white women benefited the white home.[69]

Industrial education expanded scientific cooking into more rural areas and exposed a larger number of women to this new food culture. The young women who studied scientific cooking at Montevallo tended to be the daughters of small-town professionals or landowning farmers. A typical student grew up in a nearby county and came from a family that had lived in Alabama for at least two generations. Most graduates married, presumably bringing a scientific understanding of cooking into their own homes.[70] Mary Louise "Mamie" Meroney was one such student. Born in 1891 to a Montevallo merchant and his homemaking wife, Meroney graduated from the Alabama Girls Industrial School in 1911 with a domestic science degree. After graduation, she taught at Montevallo until shortly after her marriage in 1917. She wed Dr. William Earl Wofford and moved to Cartersville, Georgia, where they raised a family.[71]

Another student was Vera Law, who was born in March 1895 in Elba, Alabama. Her father was a traveling salesman; there is no information about her mother. In 1915 she graduated from Montevallo with a domestic science degree. There is no indication that Law ever married, but she taught in rural schools around the state. This alternative path, traveled by Law and other cooking-school graduates, enabled some southern white women to become financially independent in a gender-appropriate manner and facilitated the spread of domestic science knowledge to the rural areas where these educated women taught.[72]

In addition to industrial schools, home demonstration work helped domestic science knowledge to spread from the urban middle class to other southern populations. In 1914 federal monies provided by the Smith-Lever Act funded female home demonstration agents to travel the countryside and teach homemaking to rural women. Home demonstration agents organized rural women into home demonstration clubs, which were modeled after urban women's clubs. Yet, despite the intent of the Smith-Lever Act to improve rural life for all farming families, home demonstration primarily benefited wealthy, white, landowning families.[73]

Cooking education and home demonstration reveal the tendency of domestic science to make previously private spaces a matter of public debate. Rural kitchens became the subject of public concern when federal monies sent educated women into the countryside to change and monitor food

preparation. But this facet of home economics extended beyond the legislature. In southern cities and towns, displaying a mastery of domestic science
skills, including the management of black domestic servants, was a mark of
racial and class status. Women displayed their achievements at luncheons,
teas, and parties during which they opened their kitchens and dining rooms
to their peers for inspection and approval. In this way, private spaces became forums for public performances of white middle-class respectability
as hostesses certified their allegiance to modern food practices. The society
pages in southern newspapers were filled with lavish descriptions of these
occasions.

As important as the kitchen had become to southern society, in the early
part of the twentieth century modern food culture remained limited primarily to the educated or salaried elite. Home-front mobilization during
World War I helped to disseminate this knowledge to a broader population. In August 1917, Congress passed the Lever Food Act, authorizing President Woodrow Wilson to take control of the nation's food supply. Later
that month, Wilson created the U.S. Food Administration and asked Herbert Hoover to head the wartime agency. Its primary goal was to conserve
American food supplies through a combination of compulsory and volun-
tary measures. Among other initiatives, the Food Administration mobilized
home demonstration agents to implement food conservation efforts.[74] In so
doing, they expanded access to domestic science knowledge.[75]

Black Domestic Servants

Despite the assumption among many white women that home economics
was a "white" occupation, some African American women took advantage
of the opportunity to gain formal domestic education. In Alabama, domestic science education began at the black Tuskegee Institute three years before
Montevallo opened its doors. According to the 1895 catalog, Tuskegee's program educated students in every aspect of homemaking, from proper table
settings to the preparation of meals to the chemical processes of food and
digestion, and included other curricula that Montevallo would later adopt.
Like white schools, Tuskegee saw its domestic program as crucial to training

homemakers, not necessarily laborers, even though many of its graduates would likely work in domestic service.[76]

In 1908, a Philadelphia Quaker, Anna Thomas Jeanes, donated $1 million to provide industrial education to African Americans. Across the South, Jeanes teachers instructed black women and girls in home economics. The main role of Jeanes teachers was to supervise rural southern teachers in black schools, but in some areas they spent a good deal of their time promoting better living conditions and organizing black women. These teachers empowered black communities to build better homes in the same ways that white women's clubs encouraged domestic social reform among whites. The work of Jeanes teachers actively contradicted the contemporary white southern belief that African Americans did not possess the capabilities to care for their own homes.[77]

For their part, white women encouraged their black servants to take cooking lessons for the purpose of improving white homes and families. Despite evidence to the contrary, white employers did not think black women had the ability to apply domestic science principles on their own account. While white households attempted to safeguard racial purity through the implementation of food knowledge and scientific methods, out of perceived necessity they also continued to rely on African American labor in the kitchen. In 1906 Booker T. Washington pointed out that "everything depended upon to make blood and muscle and bone and health and prosperity is at the mercy of the [black] cook."[78] White women agreed with this assumption, yet they worried that this reliance threatened the well-being of the white family.

Again, domestic science offered a solution. New technology, new food products, and new kitchen appliances helped to ensure that no hands, black or white, ever had to touch the food. The use of baking powder to make biscuits rise did away with the necessity to knead the dough for extended periods of time. Electric mixers and the wide variety of spoons and other utensils that stocked the modern kitchen had a similar effect. Packaged foods promised sanitary production facilities where clean machines, not humans, prepared the food. One cracker company boasted that its product was "cleaner than bread because the material is mixed by machinery and barely touched with the hands."[79] Once again, modern consumer products promised a solution to domestic problems that southern housewives had not even known they had.

Food culture was in transition in the turn-of-the-century South. The way that the white salaried class, in particular, thought about food and cooking was changing from a system based on tradition to one based on scientific knowledge. The new food culture also served to disparage other southern constituencies, especially African Americans and lower-class whites. Lack of access and financial resources prevented these two groups from participating at first. Nevertheless, the white lower class found itself in a better position to join the new culture when its situation improved. And despite the implementation of this new culture in many white southern middle-class households, the truth was that African American servants supplied most of the food-related labor in those homes.

Finally, although the domestic sphere was important to the development of new foodways, southerners at the turn of the twentieth century did not limit themselves to eating at home. The South at this time saw an explosion of public eating spaces. There, the white middle class identified another opportunity to mold society in its own image. It is in these public spaces that the race-based food culture found its most effective, popular, and oppressive outlet.

CHAPTER TWO

Southern Cafés as Contested Urban Space

In William Faulkner's novel *Light in August*, the character Joe Christmas visits a restaurant for the first time in the fictional town of Jefferson, Mississippi. Faulkner describes the entrance to the café as "a narrow dingy doorway between two dingy windows" with no sign outside or any other indication the establishment serves food. Inside, the "restaurant" consists of a long counter with backless stools and a cigar case up front. Joe, a socially awkward and racially ambiguous teenager, and his foster father sit at the counter, which is populated entirely by men and smells heavily of cigarette smoke. Ordinarily, the two pack a lunch to visit town, located five miles away from their farm, but on this occasion they have not because they had expected to be home by the lunch hour. Joe's foster father takes him to the restaurant reluctantly. Faulkner describes the fare as "simple" and "quickly prepared." A young waitress named Bobbie serves them. They eat quickly, pay at the cigar case, and leave.

Outside, Joe's foster father warns Joe against returning. "There are places in this world where a man may go but a boy, a youth of your age, may not," he informs Joe. Indicating the restaurant, he concludes, "This is one of them." "What is the matter with it?" Joe asks, but his foster father refuses to elaborate. Eventually Joe does return to the back-alley restaurant. He establishes a sexual relationship with Bobbie, a Memphis woman who turns tricks on the side. The restaurant's owner, Max, brought Bobbie to Jefferson to work as a prostitute. As he spends time with Max and Bobbie, Joe encounters various women from Jefferson and Memphis—"waitresses" who also seem to turn tricks for Max.[1]

In this tale, Faulkner identifies several significant themes surrounding early twentieth-century public eating places in the American South. Like Faulkner's unnamed restaurant, many of these spaces were small, simple affairs that focused on serving food quickly. They also were predominately male spaces where a woman's presence often raised suspicions—either over her respectability or over whether the public sphere was appropriate for women at all. Joe's foster father's warning that the restaurant was a man's place coincides with Joe's own foreboding. "I know that there is something about it beside food, eating," Joe reflects after his first visit. "But I dont know what."[2] Both teenager and grown man recognize that activities other than eating take place in such public spaces.

In the early twentieth century, cafés such as the one Joe visits were relatively new spaces. Although some public eating establishments no doubt continued to be reserved for the upper echelon, a variety of public eating places developed, including sidewalk stands, cafés, and lunchrooms. Such places multiplied in urban areas at the turn of the twentieth century and provided opportunities for people of various classes, ethnicities, races, and genders to gather for working, socializing, eating, drinking, and intermingling of all sorts.

Because of this diversity, urban eateries were contested spaces where proprietors, employees, customers, civil authorities, and the general public all attempted to express their own priorities, which were often at odds with each other. Conflict sometimes escalated into criminal activities, but more often clashes in public eating places involved more subtle cultural conflicts as proprietors, employees, and customers vied with each other and with civil authorities to promote and defend their vision of appropriate public discourses and activities. This was particularly true in the case of the newer quick-service establishments, where cultural attitudes toward class, race, ethnicity, and gender often differed from those of more established high-end restaurants.

Public eating establishments met many needs in the urban environment. Proprietors and employees found opportunities for financial reward and social advancement. The legal, and sometimes illegal, activities that took place inside urban eating places offered opportunities for profit and to consolidate local networks and power that may not have been available to the average workman elsewhere. Many proprietors improved their own circumstances and those of their extended families through partnerships, financial assistance, and employment. Employees, many of whom in the early twentieth century were immigrants, African Americans, or working-class whites, saw opportunities for upward social mobility by opening their own eating places.

For the mostly male customers, such establishments provided public spaces for grabbing a quick lunch, eating an evening meal, drinking an alcoholic beverage, smoking cigarettes or cigars, socializing with other men, discussing matters of public interest, and in some cases engaging in illegal gambling and illicit sexual interactions. Men also sometimes brought women to restaurants on dates. Women might eat together in such spaces if work schedules or shopping trips necessitated it. But unaccompanied women were a small proportion of customers, and their presence often aroused suspicion. Race complicated these issues further. Blacks and whites could intermingle in southern eating places, even if their status was unequal. This constant interracial interaction led urban authorities to greater vigilance in regulating these public spaces.

Some other activities that took place in public eating establishments violated the public trust. Civil authorities often sought to regulate, obstruct, or even shut down these operations. In the twentieth century, urban and town governments imposed specific licensing requirements for eating places. Such regulations reflected the importance that white authorities attributed to food, the Progressive concern for health and approval of government regulation, and white southern anxiety over the purity of the white body.

Whether or not they frequented eating establishments, the general public took great interest in these facilities. They believed that illicit activities in such establishments threatened the general order or public health. To many in authority, cafés were spaces where vice could take place, which threatened to disrupt public order, and where citizens could get around ordinances intended to protect public morality—especially those related to alcohol and prostitution. In particular, authorities feared that these spaces acted as fronts for illegal drinking, gambling, and illicit sexual activity.

Restaurants in the Southern City

In the late nineteenth century, patronage at public eating establishments in the South was regulated primarily by class. This is not to say that race played no role. Certainly few African Americans possessed sufficient socioeconomic resources to dine among the region's white elite, but no formal legislation regulated public eating places. The mores that determined proper etiquette in these spaces were class-based or derived from the individual discretion of the proprietor.

The Gilded Age's restaurants in nascent southern cities were high-end establishments where the New South elite of industrialists, financiers, and other businessmen dined in the manner to which the antebellum planter class had been accustomed. The Vienna Restaurant in Louisville, Kentucky, for example, exuded Old World elegance in its name, fare, and design. Founded in 1893 by Austrian immigrant Frank Erpeldinger, the Vienna occupied a three-story brick building downtown. It was both modern and decorative. Patrons dined at imported oak tables covered by fine white linens while experiencing the convenience of electric lights and the comfort of ceiling fans. The building's front façade was decorated in an art nouveau style that announced the name of the restaurant in colorful ceramic tile and stained glass. Only the elite could dine at the Vienna.[3]

Such restaurants were also predominately male spaces. Most of them explicitly solicited businessmen. Robert G. Thompson announced in a newspaper advertisement for his Atlanta restaurant that "New York gentlemen . . . 'stepped over from the hotel'" for dinner because his place was "equal to any first-class establishment in New York." In another advertisement, a fictional character named Polly Peablossom complained that her husband never came home for meals because he ate at Thompson's every day. The Gate City Bank Restaurant in Atlanta advertised itself as a "Business Man's Retreat" and offered wild game to tempt urban businessmen. The *Atlanta Constitution* ridiculed the practice of women patronizing eating establishments. One article condemned New Yorkers who had taken up the "Parisian custom of . . . taking meals at the restaurants." The newspaper noted, "You may see women and girls sitting at the same table with men and ordering their meals with the nonchalance of old habitués." Women dining at restaurants continued to be a cause of concern for southerners into the early twentieth century. In restaurants and cafés, it was thought, white women could be exposed to any number of activities deemed vile and inappropriate, including drinking, gambling, violence, foul language, sexual innuendo, race mixing, smoking, and cursing.[4] For these reasons, restaurants often featured adjoining "ladies' cafés," which offered service to the wives and daughters of the New South elite. Such spaces allowed women to participate in the consumer experience of dining out without being exposed to a predominately male environment. Ladies' cafés promised "neatly furnished . . . quiet, retired [dining rooms] . . . with every home comfort." Thompson's Ladies' Cafe allowed women to bring male companions, but other ventures, such as Allen's Palace Restaurant's Ladies' Dining Room and Ice Cream Saloon, also in Atlanta, advertised "for ladies only." Both proprietors put these facilities under the charge of their wives.[5]

Although an elite woman might eat out for a variety of reasons, ladies' cafés targeted shoppers. Atlanta restaurateur O. L. Pease and his wife solicited the patronage of women who needed a respite "after fatiguing walks" or shopping trips. They promised a "safe and pleasant retreat" where women could "refresh" themselves with "oysters or any other delicacy." Department stores also opened cafés that catered predominately to a female clientele. Richmond's Miller and Rhoads advertised a "light luncheon" for its customers. The convenient location ensured that patrons could eat without neglecting their shopping. The menu included salads, light meats, hot rolls, sandwiches, and soda fountain specials. Piano music accompanied lunch.[6] Such places emphasized femininity, offering the amenities and lighter fare considered appropriate for a woman's supposedly more delicate tastes.

Although restaurants were geared toward the elite, the lower classes could eat out in other types of public spaces in the New South. Hotels, for example, offered dining facilities for residents and travelers alike. In the late nineteenth century, most hotels served patrons under the American plan: meals were included in the price of the room. The lower classes also could access meals at saloons. In early urban areas, the local saloon provided a preferable and convenient site for working men to eat. In an effort to entice midday customers, many saloons offered free lunches. For the price of a glass of beer or whiskey—generally five cents—patrons devoured impressive spreads.

From around 11:00 a.m. to 1:00 p.m., saloons set out buffets described as "a first-class lunch in every respect," which could include hot turtle soup, roast beef, potato salad, olives, pork and beans, or barbecued pig—the same fare served at many of the finer restaurants.[7] Saloonkeepers competed to attract the most customers, and many proprietors used up their profits to keep pace. These spaces, too, were gendered because city ordinances generally prohibited women from patronizing saloons.[8]

The Changing Urban Foodscape

As urban environments developed in the New South, eating practices evolved to better fit city life. In the countryside, the midday meal was the largest repast of the day. Rural women labored over dinner, as it was called, from the time the breakfast dishes were put away, and families gathered for a leisurely meal and a break from agricultural work at the height of the day's heat. Leftovers from that meal usually formed a small evening supper. But urbanization changed those food habits. Early twentieth-century home economics instruction gave housewives the choice to serve a light meal, or luncheon, with a heavy dinner in the evening, or to have a heavy dinner at midday with a light supper to follow.[9]

The growing class of manual laborers and office workers in southern cities and towns, however, generally did not have time for a leisurely midday meal. In a letter to a former employer, Joseph R. Smith, who had clerked at a Birmingham office supply company in 1915, recalled his typical workday: "Went to work at 7:30 and worked until 6 with a 30 minute break for lunch."[10] As Smith's memories indicate, urban lifestyles ran according to the clock. Most working men and women had little time to prepare meals and only a short break to eat during the workday. As a result, a quick lunch came to define the midday meal for most urbanites. Many workers prepared their own lunches and took them to their shop or office. For others, like Joe Christmas and his foster father, cafés provided convenient spaces for a quick meal.[11]

At the turn of the twentieth century, a series of unrelated but concurrent circumstances changed the way that urban-dwellers accessed the public table. Although most southerners continued to eat at home primarily, these changes ultimately made eating out more accessible for the broader popula-tion. First, saloon proprietors, with support from restaurateurs and temper-ance advocates, lobbied local legislators to end the free lunch. In June 1897 a group of Atlanta saloonkeepers petitioned the city council for legislation prohibiting the practice. They resented the expense involved and the lowly status of those attracted to the buffets. The Kimball House Hotel's saloon reportedly abolished the custom and, as a result, experienced an improve-ment in the class and behavior of its lunch patrons. Although he did not halt the practice, saloon owner John P. Buckalew lamented the cost and "the lower classes of trade" that free lunches attracted to his establishment, Buck's Place. Some proprietors, on the other hand, defended the practice as an aid to digestion or as charity. "The lunches attract a poorer class of trade," Ernest Naylor of the Opera Saloon agreed, "but it does me good to see the hungry ones eat." Naylor's was a minority opinion among Atlanta's saloon community. Most barkeepers maintained open buffets only because they feared losing business. By 1898 the anti–free lunch forces prevailed, and the city council limited bar food to pretzels and crackers.[12]

The free lunch controversy galvanized smaller southern towns as well. In 1901 a group of saloon operators in Macon, Georgia, petitioned their city council to abolish the practice. As in Atlanta, Macon proprietors differed on the issue. One barkeeper vowed to continue the practice even if the legisla-tion prevailed: "They say that if council should grant the petition and forbid the serving of free lunch they will sell lunch for 5 [cents] and give away a glass of beer with each purchase of lunch." Although patrons insisted that they saved money and made strong friendships "over the bar rails," Macon, like many other southern communities, banned the practice.[13] By the sec-ond decade of the twentieth century, temperance advocates threatened the existence of the saloons themselves. The end to the free lunch and to saloons more generally meant that many middle- and lower-class men lost access to an inexpensive midday meal.

Corresponding with the end of the free lunch, southern hotels adopted the European plan of service, and meals were no longer included in the cost of the room. Under this new scheme, patrons purchased meals separately at either the hotel dining room or another eating place. Hotels across the South advertised the European plan as a modern, upscale amenity. At the turn of the century the Arlington, the newest hotel in Montgomery, Alabama, advertised the European plan along with its "new and fresh" architecture and furniture. In Norfolk, Virginia, the Lynnhaven, touted as the city's "latest and largest fire-proof hotel," noted its use of the European plan. As another modern amenity, the Lynnhaven encouraged visitors to book reservations via telegraph. By 1913 Louisville had only one hotel, the Willard, which still advertised the American plan. The Willard Hotel, an older establishment that catered to in-state travelers, promised it was the "Best in the City for the Money," but it offered no modern conveniences or advancements.[14] For the modern, upscale southern hotel at the turn of the twentieth century, the European plan prevailed.[15] Again, this left a significant portion of the South's urban population, including both travelers and residents who lived permanently at hotels, without an affordable, convenient, and reliable source of sustenance.

At the same time, a demographic change helped to fill the void left by saloons and hotels for inexpensive, everyday food service. Around the turn of the twentieth century foreign immigrants to the South found a niche in the food industry. Although the percentage of immigrants in southern cities and towns was quite small, especially compared to national demographics, immigrants nevertheless had a significant influence on regional foodways. They settled across the South and opened various food-service businesses. In small Mississippi Delta towns, for example, Chinese immigrants opened grocery stores and Lebanese immigrants built cafés. In places like Montgomery and Atlanta, European Jewish immigrants peddled fruits and vegetables.[16] By interrupting the black-white dichotomy generally associated with southern society, immigrant communities had the potential to threaten white supremacy as practiced by native-born white southerners. This tendency is apparent in the reaction to the cafés opened by Greek immigrants across the American South. Sometimes, native-born whites identified the capitalist-oriented Greek immigrants as models of Americanism, but at other times they considered Greek businesses to be threats to the southern social structure.

Greek proprietors often moved around after immigrating to the United States in order to gain experience, make contacts, and save the money to open their own businesses. Birmingham restaurateur Nicholas Christu emigrated from the island of Megisti in Greece to Ellis Island on October 30, 1910. He traveled to Ashland, Ohio, where a Greek acquaintance hired him to work at a candy store and soda fountain. Christu worked for friends in different cities in Ohio until he could afford to open his own business. After World War I, Christu's new wife, also a Greek immigrant, heard that a community from their home village had settled in Birmingham, Alabama. The couple moved to Birmingham, where Christu worked at a restaurant until he could afford to purchase a small sandwich shop. In Birmingham, Christu found a vibrant Greek community made up largely of fruit peddlers, restaurateurs, lunch-stand operators, café proprietors, and their employees.[17]

Wherever they settled, Greeks tried to open their own businesses because entrepreneurship provided more financial and personal independence than wage work.[18] In establishing eateries, the Greek communities helped to build southern urban areas. They helped to define how food would be prepared and served in the public sphere, irrespective of the designs of the predominately native-born, middle-class, white urban authorities. Their presence ensured that public spaces where food was served, regardless of the exact nature of the establishment, would become more diverse venues where people of different backgrounds and life experiences met and intermingled.

Contested Eating Space

As a result of these concurrent developments, the number of public eating places advertising their services in southern cities increased dramatically at the turn of the twentieth century. This increase occurred primarily in the quick-service segment of the industry, with significant consequences for the process of urbanization in the twentieth-century South. The vast majority of these new public eating places were owned by immigrants, African Americans, and non-elite whites and were patronized by the middle and lower socioeconomic classes. These lower-end eating places took the form of stands, lunchrooms, cafés, and "cookshops" (cafés operated by African American women). They tended to be ephemeral establishments, in business for only a year or two. They specialized in foods such as sandwiches or soups, which could be prepared quickly and cheaply.

Although the interiors of such spaces might differ, as a group they looked

FIGURE 3. A lunch counter connected to a grocery store operated by the Duke family on Hill Street in Atlanta, ca. 1925. Vanishing Georgia Collection; courtesy of Georgia Division of Archives and History, Office of Secretary of State.

little like Louisville's decorative Vienna Restaurant. A 1925 photograph of a lunch counter in a small grocery store run by the Duke family in Atlanta reveals an interior that resembles the description of Faulkner's unnamed restaurant, with a simple wooden counter and backless stools. Pots and pans simmer on a stove behind the counter, and signs advertise national brands of soft drinks and manufactured foods.[19]

These establishments had no direct nineteenth-century antecedents. They did not cater to an elite clientele; they did not bother with expensive décor or extensive menus; and they did not provide separate facilities for women. The cultural diversity and novelty of these spaces prompted concern over their suitability and respectability. As more people depended on such eateries for their sustenance, cultural anxieties over their influence on public health and morality entered public discourse. Poor southerners continued to lack sufficient nourishment. But as food practices evolved to fit the different pace of an urban environment, concern over eating the wrong types of food became a more common public-health fear. One Galveston, Texas, newspaper suggested that constantly eating out caused a myriad of contradictory digestive problems, such as overeating, undereating, extravagance, frugality, indigestion, eating at odd hours, eating too quickly, eating too much meat, and other unwise food choices.[20] National consumer markets offered solutions specifically designed for the working man forced to eat lunch out. The Natural Food Company, for example, advertised the fiber in its shredded wheat as the solution to digestive problems caused by fast meals at the lunch counter.[21]

Such anxieties extended beyond the body as these public spaces came to be identified with immoral activities. Café proprietors would not, or could not, control activities in their establishments in the same way one might order one's home—or in ways deemed appropriate by white urban authorities. As public spaces, restaurants and cafés sometimes served as scenes of crime. In particular, Atlanta authorities often arrested Greek proprietors and employees for nonviolent offenses. In April 1909 Atlanta police arrested Jim Hanjaras, Jim Poulos, Tom Poulos, and Charlie Dordas for gambling in the basement of Hanjaras's eatery. All four either owned or worked at a café.[22] In February 1912 Atlanta police arrested Jim Favors and John Poulos for selling whiskey in contravention of local prohibition laws. Favors, the owner of a local restaurant, was convicted of running a "blind tiger," a term used to describe a lower-class establishment that sold illegal liquor.[23] In May 1914 Nick Caccans, Jim Poulos, George Poulos, and five others were arrested for gambling in the basement of Caccans's restaurant.[24] These arrests reveal more about the status of public eateries in the southern urban environment than they do about the alleged morality of any particular café owner or employee. As sites of legal consumption with a regular urban customer base, cafés made convenient locations for offering extralegal goods and services as well.

Urban authorities worried that eating places might provide public spaces for acts of supposed moral degradation, especially drinking. After Atlanta's city council ended food service in local saloons, eateries established push-button systems with nearby saloons so that patrons could continue to have a drink with their meals. When Jim Brown, a Greek café owner in Atlanta, wanted to order drinks for a patron, he pushed a button to contact the saloon and placed the order. Every restaurant in the city reportedly used a similar system until 1906, when the city council prohibited restaurants from serving alcohol. Officials enforced this ordinance by refusing business licenses to restaurants located near saloons.[25]

The struggle that southern cities had to reconcile eating and drinking in public places reveals the complicated merger of various value systems in a diverse urban environment. The governing, salaried classes worried that working-class whites, African Americans, and foreigners might use these spaces as unregulated saloons. If drinking were allowed, an assortment of patrons of both sexes might linger in restaurants, becoming intoxicated and perhaps indulging in further public immorality and debauchery. City councils worried especially about eating places frequented by lower-class whites and African Americans.

The desire to separate eating and drinking by restricting alcohol service in restaurants had class and racial implications.[26] In Atlanta, for example, the city council admitted that a new regulation against drinking in restaurants specifically targeted black establishments. Nevertheless, the broad ordinance covered all public eating places. This more general application caused some white councilmen to initially oppose the law. One council member argued that men who did not frequent saloons nevertheless drank alcohol with their meals and joked that restaurant service "was the only way the prohibitionists could get a drink." The mayor opposed its wide applicability, stating that "there can be no harm in serving beer in such [eating] places as are in the center of the city [where the white restaurants were located]." Despite such protests, the council passed the law unanimously.[27]

Atlanta also tried to do away with alcohol entirely. One month after it took alcohol out of city restaurants, the Atlanta city council closed the city's saloons and limited the purchase of alcohol to a low-alcohol beverage nicknamed "near beer." The mayor recognized the incongruence of this action, commenting in late 1906, "The council recently refused to license certain restaurants because they were next door to saloons and then later closed up the very saloons which adjoined the objectionable restaurants."[28] For Atlanta, prohibition represented only the latest in a series of legislative attempts to govern the use and sale of inebriants in the city. The discourses and actions surrounding these events reveal white middle-class anxieties over the consumption of alcohol in public spaces. But despite the council's best efforts, closing the saloons failed to solve the problem of drinking in public eating places and encouraged the emergence of cafés intended to circumvent the laws. Atlanta authorities continued to spend time and energy regulating the sale and consumption of alcohol in public eateries. The city licensed near-beer purveyors. Atlanta went through various stages of prohibition and temperance in attempting to end crime and disorder in public spaces.

In the absence of traditional saloons, many observers considered lower-class eating places to be fronts for the service of alcoholic beverages, legal or otherwise. White middle-class authorities, some of whom no doubt served whiskey at home, believed eating places that continued to serve alcohol attracted lower-class elements and that this combination led to trouble. In 1908, two years after Atlanta closed its saloons, the local columnist J. Francis Keeley noted that he would rather see "a respectable saloon than a so-called café, selling 'near beer' and given to rowdyism."[29] Although the city passed more prohibition laws, authorities continued to struggle with eating places and near-beer saloons that sold alcohol illegally or served near beer to their customers in contravention of local licensing provisions.

Controversy stemmed from these attempts to ban a substance that had a long connection with consumption and eating. In Montgomery the connection between eating and drinking alcohol was so common that proprietors assumed that having a business license to serve meals also allowed them to serve alcoholic beverages. In 1875 the Montgomery authorities convicted a local restaurateur named Nicrosi for selling alcoholic beverages without a license. Nicrosi apparently sold drinks to patrons eating on-site and argued that his restaurant business license implied the ability to serve alcohol with meals. The Supreme Court of Alabama disagreed and affirmed Nicrosi's conviction, but this did not end the controversy.[30] In 1904 Montgomery's chief of police complained that a local ordinance allowing restaurants to conduct business on Sunday enabled the sale of alcohol despite laws against the practice. The connection between the sale of food and drink was so strong that the city's blue laws were threatened "where saloons are allowed to have restaurants attached and keep open all day Sunday to serve meals."[31]

The struggles of urban areas such as Atlanta and Montgomery reveal the difficulties of regulating morality in eating establishments.

Drinking in public spaces, illegal or otherwise, led to other alleged moral infractions. Alcohol in public spaces often coincided with sexualized conduct between men and women. Again, cafés served as sites for these alleged transgressions. Unlike the higher-class restaurants and their ladies' cafés, quick-service eateries did not separate men and women. In fact, the ability to interact with the opposite sex might have been an enticement for some patrons, as it was for Joe Christmas. These spaces offered opportunities for men and women to meet, mingle, converse, and engage in sexualized activity that encompassed everything from drinking together to public displays of affection to sexual intercourse.

Atlanta police often raided cafés to halt sexual interactions considered to be improper. In May 1914 the College Inn was the site for such a raid. Its proprietors faced charges related to illegal drinking and sexual mingling. The judge accused the café of circumventing local prohibition laws by purchasing near beer from black merchants, who delivered drinks to the College Inn in violation of city ordinances. Worse still, men and women reportedly drank together at the College Inn, leading to a variety of different types of "disorderly conduct." Among other things, reports indicated that women sat in the laps of male companions and "embraced" them.[32] These eating establishments violated local laws and cultural conventions that attempted to control sexualized conduct in the public sphere by separating men and women. Unlike ladies' cafés, these eateries failed to respect these principles in favor of more liberal interactions among men and women.

In addition to the relatively innocent intermingling of the sexes in legitimate eating places, southern authorities worried that an eatery could serve as a front for a brothel. In 1903 black prostitutes arrested on vagrancy charges in Atlanta inevitably reported working at "Old Lady Brown's Restaurant." Sarah Brown, a sixty-year-old African American woman, operated a café that authorities assumed was a front for prostitution. Police often visited her establishment for unspecified complaints of "disorder," and reportedly "drunken men [visited] at all hours of the day and night." Brown's café was located on Decatur Street, an area of Atlanta notorious for drinking, prostitution, and other vices. She reportedly hired around forty women to work at her restaurant. In 1900 Atlanta authorities had charged Brown with running a disorderly establishment. The judge let her go with the promise that she would keep her customers in line. Despite this warning and the apparent illegal activities undertaken at Brown's café, there is no evidence that police shut her down. But the police did begin arresting any woman who reported working for Brown on "vagrancy" or prostitution charges.[33]

The fact that Brown hired African American women as supposed waitresses illuminates another complicating factor with regard to public spaces designated for eating. For white southern authorities, the potential for race mixing in quick-order public eating establishments increased the potential threats associated with illegal drinking and illicit sexual interaction. Although southern eating places tended to implement some form of racial segregation even before formal Jim Crow laws, interracial interactions nevertheless took place. The fact that many café proprietors came to the American South unfamiliar with the region's racial mores may have increased the threat to white supremacy. Albert P. Maurakis, the son of a Greek café operator, recalls his confusion over racial segregation when he moved from Pittsburgh to Danville, Virginia. He relied on family members with longer tenures in the South to elucidate the region's racialized eating rituals. He recalls, "Uncle Steve explained the Southern Jim Crow practice of segregating the races in the use of all public facilities and that the 'colored' must enter back doors to eat in restaurant kitchens." The Maurakis family acquiesced to segregation culture. Although his uncle's restaurant had no rear entrance, he served black customers through a window. When Maurakis's father opened the Central Café, he included separate entrances and an eight-foot partition to separate the black and white dining areas.[34]

Despite such concessions, evidence reveals that some Greek immigrants, perhaps because of their own experiences as the object of discrimination, never accepted southern racial mores thoroughly. In Durham, North Carolina, the Lincoln Café, an African American eating place operated by Greek immigrants, reportedly received a threatening letter from the Ku Klux Klan alleging that white men and black women met at the café and left together in automobiles. "You are fraternizing with the Negroes," the letter warned, "and allowing a low element of whites to meet Nigger women in your place." The threatening letter expressed the Klan's concerns that the Greek immigrants were socializing with African Americans and that white men and black women were using the café as a meeting place for dates or sexual liaisons.[35]

The 1920s Klan's notorious nativism further complicated its overt anxieties regarding so-called race mixing. In this case, the apparent financial success of the immigrants may have provided fodder for the organization's xenophobic beliefs. The name of the café was an explicit reference to Abraham Lincoln and, by implication, to black emancipation. The notion that immigrants and African Americans had the freedom to act independently in a public space may have exacerbated the white anxieties that the Klan expressed through concerns about miscegenation. The Klan's attitudes toward race and morality sometimes went beyond mere rhetoric, of course. In many parts of the South in the 1920s, the Klan held a significant amount of political power, and its ideology informed some official decision making.[36]

The recollections of Greek café owners reveal a certain amount of ambivalence toward southern racial mores on the part of the immigrant. In his memoir, Greek immigrant and South Carolina restaurateur John Katsos recalls an African American acquaintance asking him if he was Jewish. "No," Katsos responded. "I thought you knew I was a Greek." The African American man answered that he was not aware of Katsos's ethnicity, "but I figured you ain't been no white man."[37] This story, assuming its truth, suggests that Greek immigrants may have treated African Americans subtly better or with more respect than did native-born southern whites. At the very least, Katsos's presence interrupted the racial dichotomy that normally defined both black and white lives in the region. In these ways, the important status of Greek immigrants in the public food culture in the South may have served as a threat to white supremacy and to the cultural system of racial segregation.

For southern white authorities, a potentially volatile situation could be ignited when illegal drinking and illicit sexual activity combined with race in the public sphere. City authorities across the South implemented programs in the early twentieth century to do away with "negro dives." A dive could take the legal form of a restaurant or saloon, but city authorities rarely made a distinction. Throughout the day and night, the *Atlanta Constitution* reported, black men and women hung out at one such "restaurant" supposedly to eat, but really to drink and mingle. The *Constitution* noted that this marked one way in which black women circumvented the city ordinance that prohibited women from patronizing saloons. In addition to the drinking and sexualized activity, Atlanta authorities also complained about crime, which they associated with black restaurants.[38]

The question of black dives in early twentieth-century southern cities points to many of the race, class, and gender issues that existed in the broader society. Southern white authorities took issue with several aspects of these inexpensive restaurants. First, although some black restaurants were operated by whites, these establishments provided public spaces for African Americans to congregate without the oversight of white employers or white authorities. Second, these public spaces implicated much broader concerns about social control in the urban environment. Every day, new people came into town who did not have any history in the area and about whom city authorities had no knowledge. Urban routines differed from the daily and seasonal rhythms and traditions of the agrarian lifestyle. In particular, racialized rituals were less determined in young southern cities. For African Americans, negotiating the urban consumer landscape could bring escape from the normality of racial difference and prejudice. But such escape threatened white supremacy. White urban authorities strove to ensure that emerging consumer markets, which included cafés and restaurants, did not undermine racial difference in their cities.

Other southern cities joined Atlanta's crusade against the supposedly demoralizing effect of black dives and to mitigate the threat these establishments posed to white supremacy. In 1902 white Montgomery residents complained about "negro dives" operating just outside the city limits and violating the Sunday liquor laws. Newspaper reports variously refer to these public spaces as saloons, stores, and cookshops. According to reports, these establishments, located in what the *Montgomery Advertiser* referred to as the "dive district," experienced good business on Sundays with patronage from black men and women, and white men.[39] The presence of white men implicated the common trope of so-called race mixing. Fear of miscegenation was no doubt at the heart of many food consumption issues with which urban authorities wrestled, from alcohol sales to women's presence at cafés. In this case, Montgomery residents worried (as the Durham Ku Klux

Klan would two decades later) that black eateries provided public spaces for lower-class white men and black women to mingle and date.

But it was not just the presence of black women in public eating spaces that caused concern, or even the most concern, for southern white authorities. In the early twentieth century the presence of women of both races, even white women otherwise considered to be respectable, was becoming an ordinary sight in common eateries that did not feature a separate ladies' café. This occurrence reflected the more public daily activities of southern women who lived in cities and towns. Women bore the primary responsibility for their family's shopping, and stores were often located in downtown areas. Also, on occasion, professional men might take their wives out for a special treat. The *Atlanta Woman's Club Cook Book* advised that the women who took primary responsibility for preparing the family's meals deserved a "half-holiday" on Thursday afternoons and a "dinner out."[40] Working-class women often could not return home in the short amount of time allocated for their lunch break. In the late 1930s Mississippi's leading home economist, Dorothy Dickins, found that female workers purchased lunch in town when their factories were located too far from home.[41] In addition, some young women frequented public eating places for leisure and entertainment. When dating became a popular form of gendered interaction in the 1920s, women often visited soda fountains, cafés, or restaurants with their male companions.[42]

Even though they did not feature ladies' cafés, some lunchrooms attempted to provide a limited amount of protected space for female patronage. The Albert Restaurant in Birmingham offered to serve lunch to white women "at the tables." This condition implies that men had an option of eating elsewhere, perhaps at a counter or a bar where they presumably would come into close contact with others as they ate. White women apparently had no such options, or perhaps Albert's simply meant to assure them that they would have access to a meal "safe" from close contact with unknown men dining beside them.[43] Such accommodations, however, still would not have protected white women from contact with smoking, cursing, racial interactions, or similar activities.

The unease over accommodating white women as customers paled in comparison to the concerns prompted by white women as servers. Despite their traditional role as the purveyor of food at home, or perhaps because of it, white women did not serve in public spaces in the South. In 1915 an unnamed northern restaurant chain brought its practice of hiring white waitresses to its location in Atlanta. White Georgia natives initially refused to take the jobs, and the chain hired northern migrants to wait tables. The *Atlanta Constitution* compared the practice to Sherman's march, "shelling Dixie's hurtful menial traditions with a sweeping fire that is crumbling them as fast as they come under the range of the guns."[44] In this case, Atlanta's "hurtful menial traditions" referred to white women working in factories. As many white clubwomen recognized, some white Atlantans did not want to see poor white women performing factory work.[45] But they did not want to see them serving in public eating places either. The author of the *Constitution* article, on the contrary, advocated white female service over textile labor.[46]

By the 1930s the use of white female servers was more common, but it remained controversial because of the inherent sexuality that many southern men perceived. At the Peabody Hotel's grill room in Memphis, a visiting North Carolina journalist, Jonathan Daniels, commented on the attractive face of his waitress. His companion, a Mississippi planter, compared female food service to prostitution by noting that when poor white women were pushed off the farms, "the weakest and the dumbest go into the whore houses . . . but the pretty and smart ones get [waitressing] jobs like these."[47] The somewhat novel practice of white women serving food in public eating places threatened some white southern sensibilities and revealed the anxiety over the greater white female presence in such spaces.

Regulating Public Eating Space

As the alcohol issue revealed, the anxieties and concerns of white authorities over the "appropriate" use of public space designated for consuming food generated a call for regulation at the state and local levels. Prohibiting the consumption of alcohol was one of the many ways in which southern white authorities regulated restaurants, cafés, and other public eating places over the course of the twentieth century. These regulations addressed many of the issues that frustrated white urban authorities—especially the emerging presence of white women in public eating places. Because more white women were frequenting local eateries and because of the casual nature of most new eating places, separate spaces for men and women became impractical.

The increasing presence of women in public eating places and the increasing racial diversity in quick-service cafés encouraged politicians to craft protective legislation. In 1914, for example, South Carolina governor Coleman L. Blease asked the state legislature to prohibit smoking in public eating places frequented by women. Blease's concern involved secondhand smoke that might harm white women, who did not receive any particular protections in common eateries. The governor based his appeal on vivid imagery, describing the bodily pollution inflicted on women exposed to smoking. "People in South Carolina (I will not say gentlemen, nor will I say true men)," Blease began, "sit in our public dining rooms, restaurants and cafés and smoke cigars . . . and whiff and puff and blow the smoke out through their nostrils, and this smoke is carried either by the natural breezes or the current of an electric fan into the eyes, mouths and nostrils of refined women." His proposed law was not intended to be a general public health measure. Rather, this legislation was specifically designed to protect white women who participated in the leisure activity of eating out.[48]

Blease's speech reveals a southern culture transitioning from one that was based on private conduct, where behavior considered to be inappropriate could be regulated by family or community censure, to one that was much more public and therefore in need of official regulation. He longingly remembered "the time . . . when, if a gentleman smoked a pipe . . . while walking along the street by the side of a lady he was not regarded as well reared, and such a thing as smoking while riding in a buggy with a young lady would not have been tolerated." The opinions of family and community served as sufficient deterrents to actions that a cohesive class agreed were inappropriate—in this case, smoking in the presence of white women. In restaurants, the ladies' cafés had protected women from such activities, but they were disappearing. Blease recognized that public censure could no longer regulate places of public accommodation. He specifically berated those from outside South Carolina "who have no respect for us or our ladies." Such individuals, according to the governor, "should be made to respect them," as should any residents "who are not decent enough to respect

[South Carolina] women."[49] Here, Blease specifically referred to the proprietors and customers who operated and patronized the new quick-order cafés. Such individuals might have come from a rural area, from the North, or from another country. They might have been native South Carolinians. In any of these cases, their behavior failed to reflect the governor's personal values. Blease called out such individuals as cultural "others" because they exhibited cultural norms different from his own. The governor correctly understood that only legal requirements could force a motley urban assortment to respect a single set of cultural standards.

Smoking served as a metaphor for Blease's greater anxieties over the racial purity of white women. Although he did not explicitly implicate race in this instance, Blease certainly intended to limit the term "refined women" to whites. The descriptive imagery the governor used to describe the alleged source of the bodily pollution—the "whiff[ing] and puff[ing] and blow[ing]" of smoke out of the male body and into the various orifices of the female body—constituted a thinly veiled sexual reference that was bolstered by his additional claim that women might be exposed to syphilis, among other diseases, through such contact.[50] Although Blease did not specifically say anything about race, southern whites of the period commonly blamed African Americans for spreading syphilis. In particular, whites accused black men of spreading the disease by raping white women, and accused black female domestic servants of carrying syphilis into white homes.[51] By referencing this common theme, Blease not only relied on a well-defined southern trope to support his cause, he connected white cultural fears of bodily contamination and racial impurity to activities taking place in the relatively new consumer sphere of public eating places.

The anxieties reflected by Blease's speech informed legislative efforts across the South aimed at regulating public eating spaces, especially at the municipal level. City leaders implemented health codes that regulated sanitation, required inspections, constrained employees, and circumscribed patrons. Considering its early struggles over saloons and its aggressive policing of eating places, Atlanta's first health code emerged rather late. In 1924 the city council passed municipal ordinances that required restaurant inspections. The law required restaurants to keep walls and floors clean, to ensure access to a clean water supply, and to locate bathrooms and sleeping quarters away from the kitchen. The code required employees to wear clean, washable clothing and to be free of communicable diseases.[52]

Such laws suggest the types of activities taking place in public eating establishments—or that city officials thought were taking place. Memphis and many other cities prohibited sleeping in eateries (some cities specified kitchens). The health code required sleeping quarters to be separate from the restaurant with a complete wall that reached to the ceiling.[53] The fact that this law frequently appears in early city restaurant codes suggests that workers, probably in quick-service eateries, regularly lived in the restaurant, perhaps even sleeping in the kitchen. This might have been a common way for café workers or proprietors, native-born and immigrant, to survive on the low wages in food service. It no doubt enabled immigrants and proprietors from other marginalized populations to assist their family members by providing a cheap place to live, and many Atlanta café owners listed their eatery's address as their home address in city directories.

Additional Memphis ordinances, less common in other southern cities, explicitly prohibited prostitution in restaurants and barred bringing women into a restaurant for the purpose of prostitution.[54] These laws seem to have targeted exactly the type of activity Faulkner portrays in *Light in August* when Max, the owner of the back-alley restaurant, brings the waitress Bobbie to Jefferson for the real purpose of engaging in prostitution.[55] Although the sexual intercourse takes place in their apartment, the transactions no doubt begin in the restaurant. Although the existence of such laws cannot confirm that prostitution took place in cafés in Memphis—the largest city near Faulkner's hometown of Oxford, Mississippi—these ordinances nevertheless suggest that local authorities feared such activity. They indicate the white middle-class anxieties over sexual activities that may or may not have taken place in public eating places.

The most telling municipal ordinances, however, related directly to race. In 1914, the same year the South Carolina governor expressed his concerns over bodily pollution from tobacco smoke, the city of Birmingham added racial segregation ordinances to its restaurant health code. Birmingham's was a relatively typical law for the period. It prohibited proprietors from "conduct[ing] a restaurant or lunch counter at which white and colored persons are served in the same room." The Birmingham Board of Commissioners

FIGURE 4. Segregated café near the tobacco warehouse district in Durham, North Carolina. Photo by Jack Delano, 1940. Library of Congress, Prints and Photographs Division.

passed the law unanimously with very little explanation or public commentary.[56] The *Age-Herald* reported that the police commissioner, Judge A. O. Lane, introduced the ordinance to improve "the peace and happiness of the community"—even though cafés regularly sat the races on different sides of the dining room.[57] Because Birmingham included this racial segregation law as part of its health code and because de facto segregation already existed in many cafés, the Board of Commissioners seemed to be reflecting fears similar to those of Governor Blease—in this case, that interracial eating might contribute to racial mixing and thereby challenge racial purity. In the second and third decades of the twentieth century, legislators in cities and small towns across the South responded to these same fears by passing racial segregation laws.[58]

African American Cafés

Jim Crow laws offered the opportunity for some African American proprietors to profit by opening their own cafés. Even before formal segregation laws made the practice necessary, African Americans opened and operated eating places that catered to the black community. In the American South, city directories consistently treated black businesses (and residences) differently from those of white people. The directories generally used a symbol— either an asterisk before the name or "(c)" for "colored" after the name—to indicate race. In Birmingham, late nineteenth-century directories generally intermixed black and white businesses by listing them alphabetically in the "Restaurant" section. The 1884–1885 *Birmingham City Directory*, for example, includes black proprietors Nancy Miller, J. R. Richardson, Mattie Robinson, and Sam Scoggins along with white restaurateurs. After the turn of the twentieth century, however, this practice changed. The "Restaurant and Lunch Rooms" section of the 1904 *Birmingham City Directory* first listed white businesses alphabetically, and then listed black businesses at the end.[59] In this way, the *Birmingham City Directory* formally separated restaurants by race ten years before a municipal ordinance required physical segregation. Beginning in 1901, the *Atlanta City Directory* practiced a similar policy by listing most white eating places as "Restaurants" and all black establishments as "Lunch Rooms," regardless of their style of service—suggesting an inherent status differentiation between the two.[60] These sources indicate an increasing number of black and white establishments but also suggest that city authorities (and white directory publishers) viewed black public eating places as distinctly different from white ones by the early twentieth century.[61]

In spite of the fact that white city officials disparaged black cafés, or perhaps because of it, black newspapers encouraged African Americans to patronize "race enterprises," including black restaurants and cafés. Black entrepreneurs profited by filling this need for the community. Birmingham's first black millionaire, Mitchell Edwards, began his career by opening Mitchell's Café. He reached out to the city's black community, asking people to patronize his café by using his race as a positive endorsement. He advertised his establishment as "absolutely the finest Cafe in the South run by colored men." Food service offered social mobility to African Americans, just as it did for Greek and other immigrants. Café ownership propelled Edwards, part of the first generation of black southerners to be born into freedom, to a prominent position in Birmingham's black business community. The

Jordan F., 2012½ 1st ave

Land Department L. & N. R. R , R. W. A. Wilda, gen agt, Alabama State Bank blg

Richardson J. T. (notary and ins), 1913½ 2d ave. See page 129

Shepherd C. D

Smith Dr. Joseph R., cor 1st al and 20th st

Smith T. W., ns 4th ave, 2 h s 22d st

Smith W. F. & Co. (ins.), 1918½ 1st ave. See first paster

Sorsby W. E., 1st ave, bet 19th and 20th sts. See page 162

Terry R. J. (ins.), Terry blg

Thomson & Berry (ins.), Roden Block

Towers John (lumber). Alabama State Bank blg

Warren Ed (ins.), ns 2d ave. bet 20th and 21st sts

Wheeler H. L. (ins.), National Bank blg. See first cover

Wilson & Ingram (ins.), ws 21st st, bet 1st and 2d aves

Wilson W. L. & Co., Alabama State Bank blg

Restaurants.

Bates W. E. (groceries), ws 20th st, 3 h s Powell ave

Beaty J. (saloon), sw cor Powell ave and 20th st

Buice Elisha & Son (groceries), ws 20th st, 1 h n ave A

Daniel Daniel, ws 1st ave. 4 h w 14th st

Dozier A. B., ws 4th ave, 3 h n 19th st

Dude Restaurant, E. Lesser, mgr, sw cor 2d ave and 20th st

Dunn Robert (saloon). ws 20th st, 2 h s Powell ave

Gale A., Iron City Exchange

Gassers (baker), 2016 2d ave

Gelders Louis, Palace Royal Saloon

Hay J. Y., cor 18th st and 1st ave

Johnson L. N., es 4th ave, 1 h n market house

Miller Nancy (c). ss 3d ave, nr 19th st

Passazan N. S. (fruits), 19th st, nr Morris ave

Richardson J. R. & Co. (c), (confections. and shoe-mkrs), 19th st, bet 2d and 3d aves

Robinson Mattie (c), ss 3d ave, bet 19th and 20th sts

Rowlett Daniel (bakery), 2d ave, bet 19th and 20th sts

Ruehle Mrs. Elizabeth, 2d ave, bet 19th and 20th sts

Scoggins Sam (c), cor 2d al and 19th st

St Clair Wm, & Co., nw cor 1st ave and 20th st

FIGURE 5. Restaurant listings in the 1884–1885 *Birmingham City Directory.* Black-owned businesses, marked with (c), are mixed with white establishments. Courtesy of Birmingham Public Library.

RESTAURANTS AND LUNCH ROOMS.

Albert Restaurant, 213 N 20th
Balabonas Gust, 2128 2d av
Balabonas T N, 9 N 20th
Campbell A E Catering Co, ground floor 1st Natl Bank bldg
Chicago Restaurant, 308 N 20th
Cocalis John, 24 S 20th
Colias Gus, 2129 1st av
Costellos Mitchell, 120 N 20th
Coveles George, 311 N 19th
DAIRY DEPOT CO THE, 310 N 19th (See right top lines)
Day W H & Co, 1724 2d av
Dudley Thomas, 2124 2d av
Easonville Creamery, 303 N 20th
Ellis Restaurant, 2016 2d av
Fidger Wm, 225 N 20th
Fisch Wm & Co, 1815 1st av
Fish & Bosman, 2219 2d av
Gatoras J & Co, 210 N 20th
Gelders Louis, 110 N 20th
Gilardoni Paul, 215 N 19th
Govatos Anton, 124 N 20th
Hobson Cafe, 9 N 20th
Hruza J F, 308 S 20th
JOHNSON PETER, 11 N 20th (See right bottom lines)
Kanakis George, 2202 2d av
Lewis J F, 409 N 20th
Little Home Restaurant, 2003 2d av
Manfredo Valentine, 113 N 20th
McLanahan B E, 116 S 18th
METROPOLITAN CAFE, Metropolitan Hotel Blk (See left inside lines)
Moransas J P, 1730 2d av
Morris Hotel, 1907 1st av
National Cafe The, 106 N 18th
Nicholas George, 402 N 20th
Pantaze C D, 14 N 20th
Pappageorge Gus, 1814 1st av
Paris & Govatos, 221 N 19th
RELIANCE RESTAURANT, 218 N 20th (See page 8)
Rymarkiewicz James, 1105 Av B
Solomon Tom, 1810 1st av
Stratte John, 1328 1st av
Ward W P, Union Station
Washugas Christopher, 122½ N 20th
WHEELER JOE, 11 N 20th (See right bottom lines)
Woman's Exchange, 2026 1st av
*Ammons G W, 226 S 21st

*Black George, 2627 2d av
*Brown Samuel, 818 N 24th
*Burns Elizabeth, Tennessee Pike, N B'ham
*Cole Kate, 1718 2d av
*Colston John, 2708 1st av
*Crawford Jesse, 2209 2d av
*Davis Wylie, 222 N 18th
*Diffay George, 208 N 18th
*Dunn Wm, 2212 2d av
*Edwards P M, 1915 3d av
*Ferrell Arthur, 207 N 22d
*Foster John, 2304 Av C
*Freeney Zylphia, 228 S 22d
*Glenn G R, 417 S 20th
*Gould Robert, 2620 2d av
*Harris Fannie, 202 N 14th
*Harris W C, 213 N 18th
*Hiram Alexander, 204 N 24th
*Jackson Georgia, 1410 2d av
*Jackson Wright, 2116 1st av
*Jones Frank, 425 S 20th
*Lee C W, Tennessee Pike, N B'ham
*Lewis Walker, 2125 Av B
*Moncrief Charles, 416 S 20th
*Moore Katie, 1910 4th av
*Newsome George, 1404 2d av
*Oliver Alice, 1406 2d av
*Pearson Ellis, 2603 2d av
*Peterson Annie, 2201 Av B
*Powell John, 2615 2d av
*Shepperd George, 2501 2d av
*Shields Love, 2303 Av C
*Steele Samuel, 1704 1st av
*Strickland Wallace, 1921 3d av
*Taylor Hattie, 909 N 16th
*Taylor Sallie, 2027 Av B
*Walker Louis, 2127 Av B
*Walker Newton, 2104 Av B
*Wiley James, 1915 3d av
*Williams J W, 2423 2d av
*Wilson Ella, 206 N 16th

*ROOFERS—GENERAL.

HEAVEN GEORGE & CO, 109 N 24th (See back cover)

*ROOFERS—SLATE.

HEAVEN GEORGE & CO, 109 N 24th (See back cover)

*ROOFERS—TIN AND IRON.

HEAVEN GEORGE & CO, 109 N 24th (See back cover)

FIGURE 6. Restaurant listings in the 1904 *Birmingham City Directory*. Black-owned businesses, marked with *, are listed after white establishments. Courtesy of Birmingham Public Library.

son of a sharecropper from Greensboro, Alabama, Edwards labored on a farm from a very young age. As a young man, he moved to Birmingham, where he worked for the railroad. By 1889 Edwards had opened his first business, probably a sidewalk stand. He struggled on his road to success, waiting tables for a white restaurant at one point, but his persistence paid off. By 1900 Edwards owned Mitchell's Café and held shares in the Alabama Penny Savings Bank. He dealt in local real estate and served as an officer for several fraternal organizations. In 1906 he constructed a new building to house his restaurant and other ventures. Despite an increasingly antagonistic southern white attitude toward African Americans in the Progressive era, Edwards thrived in the business community.[62]

African American women, in spite of white perceptions that associated them with prostitution, also used café ownership for social mobility—especially to escape domestic service. In 1900 Dora Edwards opened a lunchroom at her home on Twentieth Street South in Birmingham. Before that, Edwards had worked as a cook for prominent white families. In 1898 she had worked for John O. Cross, a manager for the Birmingham Brokerage Company. The following year, she had cooked for James D. Moore, the president of the Moore and Handley Hardware Company. In both cases, she lived at the home of her white employer.[63] We do not know how Edwards perceived her experiences working for white families, but her frequent relocations suggest that the working and living conditions were unsatisfactory. In response, Edwards used many of the skills developed as a domestic servant to live independently. In addition to operating a lunchroom in her home, Edwards also took in laundry. Although she did not support herself entirely on the profits of her café, Edwards no doubt gained many intangible benefits from operating an eatery. She lived in her own space, independent of her white employers. She gained autonomy over her body without constant worry that her white employer might violate her physical security. She had independence in her own kitchen without the oversight of another woman.

By 1902 the Birmingham city directory listed Dora Edwards as a laundress.[64] Her café business had lasted only two years—similar to other quick-service establishments, which were often ephemeral in nature. Café proprietorship may have served as a bridge occupation for Edwards—a means of support using skills she developed cooking for white families while she built the clientele for her laundry business. She may have chosen to close her lunchroom because of difficulty keeping up with the ever-increasing health regulations the city applied to food establishments, which may have had a disproportionate effect on black businesses. But despite the overregulation, black cafés generally thrived in the early twentieth century, providing space for African Americans to access profits, experience independence and social mobility, and participate in community development.

The early twentieth century found the American South in transition. Although the region remained predominately rural, more southerners began to live apart from agricultural routines and customs. In towns and cities across the region, new lifestyles necessitated different eating habits. People ate new types of foods, at different times of the day, and in new public eating spaces. Among these developments a quick lunch, as opposed to a leisurely midday dinner, created a need for lunchrooms and cafés.

As more public consumer places opened to serve growing urban appetites, customers and civic authorities realized that eating might not be the only activity that took place in these spaces. Regulation was difficult because, unlike finer establishments, quick-order eating places attracted a diverse population of different ethnicities, races, classes, genders, marital statuses, backgrounds, and occupations—with cultural mores that differed from those of the predominately middle-class, white, male urban governments. Moreover, the new proprietors did not exercise strict control over their patrons as did those who owned more elite restaurants. The cultural conflict that ensued in the saloons, cafés, and lunchrooms where the middle and lower classes dined led to cultural conflicts in the public sphere.

Controlling alcohol, gambling, and sexual propriety (among other activities) often put city officials at odds with café regulars of different genders, ethnicities, and races. Regulations included racial segregation codes that limited access to public eating places for African Americans. Black southerners responded to segregation in part by creating opportunities for themselves. Despite the negative feelings that white urban authorities had toward these spaces, in most cities and towns, black cafés emerged to provide financial profit and enhanced social standing for proprietors as well as opportunities for eating, drinking, and social interaction for patrons.

PART 2
Democratizing Southern Foodways, 1936–1959

THE NEW DEAL and World War II were turning points in southern foodways. Government initiatives involving extension services, agriculture reform, housing, and electrification, among others, offered a greater number of Americans access to modern kitchens. War rationing encouraged Americans to become more educated food consumers. As government initiatives created greater standardization in foodways, southern white women continued to practice modern culinary techniques—using electric stoves, relying on standard measurements, and eating out in increasingly uniform eateries. At the same time, these women used their culinary power to create a distinctive South in a region that increasingly resembled the rest of the country. As modern cooking techniques became more common and rising standards of living after World War II boosted the middle class, many home cooks professed to reject the scientifically based cooking of the previous generation in favor of a "traditional" southern fare that was more of an art. They revered as "natural" artists the black cooks that many of their mothers and grandmothers had criticized as unfit and unsanitary. Starting in the Great Depression, white southerners would re-create southern cuisine as fare properly prepared by black hands, which God had supposedly imbued with special skills.

After World War II, southern foodways would take further steps in the public sphere toward uniformity and standardization. Inspired by the McDonald brothers in California and their successful experiment in streamlining the drive-in, fast food would spread across the region. Early fast-food restaurants reflected all the qualities of the postwar Sunbelt. Cooks and servers implemented the concept of an assembly line to provide quick and easy service. Customers walked up to a window to order and pick up their food. They ate outside or in their cars. This new type of service took advantage of the region's temperate weather, the postwar popularity of suburbs and automobile culture, and the Sunbelt's emphasis on technology. Fast food represented the culmination of the twentieth century's trend toward democracy in public dining culture. Yet in an era in which white southerners held fiercely to Jim Crow, this most egalitarian of institutions still provided unequal service for African Americans.

CHAPTER THREE

Southern Norms and National Culture

The Woman's Auxiliary of the Olivet Episcopal Church in Franconia, Virginia, opens its 1957 cookbook with a recipe collection attributed to the Robert E. Lee and George Washington families. *Virginia Cookery—Past and Present* includes recipes for yeast, blackberry wine, and calves' head soup; medications for curing rheumatism, sprained ankles, and head colds; and instructions for cleaning alabaster. The cookbook's connection to the Lee family seems genuine. The manuscript reportedly started as a collection of handwritten receipts by Lee's aunt Elizabeth Collins Lee. Direct associations with Washington's family appear more tenuous. The editors point to a mincemeat recipe attributed to "Martha" and emphasize the close relations between the two families. Yet, as historian Karen Hess points out, it is unlikely that a cookbook would refer to a woman of Martha Washington's prominence by her first name, especially since the collection gives last names for other contributors. The "Martha" who offered her knowledge of mincemeat was more likely a slave than the nation's first First Lady. The editors probably stretched Martha Washington's connection to the collection to amplify its historical significance.[1]

Regardless of whether the cookbook had a direct connection with Martha Washington, however, a more appropriate question might be why a mid-twentieth-century housewife in Fairfax County, Virginia, needed a recipe to make her own yeast. Chances are good that the women of the Olivet Episcopal Church purchased bread at their local supermarket—or, more likely, that their black domestic servants did the grocery shopping, giving the white women of Franconia more time to participate in civic activities like the woman's auxiliary. By the 1950s Franconia and the surrounding communities in Fairfax County had transformed from a rural, agrarian area reliant on the tobacco trade to a suburban enclave interconnected with the nation's capital. The population of Fairfax County grew very little in the nation's first 140 years (from 12,320 in 1790 to 25,264 in 1930). Over the next three decades, however, the county grew exponentially. In 1940 it had a population of just under 41,000. By 1957, when the Woman's Auxiliary published *Virginia Cookery*, Fairfax County's population had approached the 275,002 residents reported in the 1960 Census.[2] This increase was partly a result of significant in-migration from other regions of the country, the result of federal employment in nearby Washington, D.C.[3] The changes in population were also accompanied by many significant changes to the ways of life in northern Virginia.

By 1950 longtime residents and newcomers to Fairfax County conspired in civic organizations and local historical societies to save the history of the region from the forces of progress. They founded the Historical Society of Fairfax County in 1950 and the Fairfax County History Commission in 1969. Both organizations offered private- and public-sector support for preserving the county's history through publications, conferences, historical markers, and cultural resource management.[4] But other organizations also worked to protect the county's heritage—especially for white Virginians. At the Olivet Episcopal Church, the Woman's Auxiliary participated in this process with the publication of *Virginia Cookery*, which was intended to create a historical memory of the culinary traditions of the state. This is typical of southern cookbooks across the region at this time. Whereas regional cookbooks of an earlier era tended to emphasize science and to disseminate useful information to promote social reform, later southern cookbooks such as *Virginia Cookery* relied more on white southern nostalgia to create and communicate historical memory.

Several practical reasons account for this transformation. By the late 1930s the foundations of domestic science, especially the use of exact measurements and modern technology, had become standard in cookbooks, schools, and all but the poorest kitchens. Many white women no longer felt the need to constantly promote these advances with missionary zeal. But culturally, as the Franconia example reveals, as the South modernized and became more in line with national norms in all aspects of society, some southerners—especially whites—thought that more had been lost than gained. They responded to this perceived loss in a variety of ways, in particular by creating historical tributes. Many women across the region, much like the Woman's Auxiliary of Olivet Episcopal Church, used cookbooks to serve as historical connections to the past, regardless of how tenuous those connections might be.

Although the modernization of the region's food systems started at the turn of the twentieth century, it accelerated in the 1930s and 1940s. The New Deal and World War II changed the ways in which southerners cultivated, prepared, served, consumed, and thought about food. Most of these changes signified the growth of a more national consumer culture, especially as the federal government played a larger role in the sustenance of ordinary southerners. White southerners responded to these changes by intermittently embracing and rejecting the national norms. At home, white women generally adopted the national standards related to obtaining, preparing, cooking, and serving food to their families. But their discourse around such standards evolved. Starting around the mid-1930s, although the fundamental features of scientific cooking remained standard and continued to spread through education, many women began to criticize and reject domestic science as the essence of home life. Many white women no longer used cooking as a basis for social reform. Instead they saw it as a way to promote southern history and local memory.

Such women pined for a time when cooking was considered to be an art. Most white women who experienced this longing did not have to look beyond their own kitchens to find their image of the ideal in domesticity. As they had in the Progressive era, white women connected food prepared by black hands to the intuitive and artistic. Instead of condemning black women for this, however, white women of the New Deal era and beyond tended to praise black artistry in the kitchen. Because white supremacy interpreted black practices to be unchanging and immutable, white women who valued history over progressivism saw great value in African American domestic labor. The result was the same: to denigrate African American women and thereby validate the common white trope that connected blackness to service and common labor.

In an earlier generation, some Progressive-era white urban southern women had considered African American women to be poor cooks, but they continued to rely on black domestic servants because white women refused to take the jobs; because they considered the labor of black women in white kitchens to be an economic necessity; and because a servant helped white women of means to maintain their class and race privilege. Over the course of the 1930s and 1940s, however, such perceptions slowly changed. The adaptation of southern practices to national norms and the nascent civil rights activity during World War II signaled threats to white supremacy and segregation in the South. A more generalized dismissal of the idea of domestic science, even without rejecting its underlying precepts, encouraged white women to reinterpret black domestic service as a boon for both races because African American women supposedly were natural artists in the kitchen. This view served the needs of white supremacists because it reinforced the notion of Jim Crow as a purportedly natural institution.

This subtle change in the characterization of black cooking skills by some white women occurred as white southerners transitioned from the necessity to reestablish white supremacy in the new urban environment to the struggle to maintain and defend Jim Crow at all costs. By the 1930s racial segregation was a well-established—but still contested—concept. Nostalgia for an imagined past of grand white ladies who offered recipes for yeast and mincemeat, as well as for the servile black cooks who prepared such dishes, gave credence to the notion of Jim Crow as an ancient institution. Although the "mammy" image had long been used to sell foodstuffs, such characters began to play leading roles in more southern cookbooks and newspaper articles as the authority on homemaking and cooking skills. In an earlier generation, many white middle-class women had used culinary education to promote social reform by depicting domesticity as a science. This new cohort, on the other hand, used food to communicate cultural and historical memory in an attempt to bolster a regional distinctiveness that national consumer markets seemed to be eroding.[5]

A New Deal in Food

Greater standardization in foodways encouraged by the government is evident in the New Deal South. Depression and later war encouraged the movement of people and ideas, and the modernization of homes and kitchens. Increased federal funding for extension services and other initiatives spread national standards from the cities into the southern hinterlands. The postwar period brought even more change to the South because Cold War spending, among other factors, encouraged the movement of people to the West and the South, where suburbs and automobiles became the norm for most white Americans.[6] All of these changes enabled and encouraged southerners, especially whites, to consume foods in new and different ways.

At home, economic and technological changes enabled women of different lifestyles and socioeconomic levels to access more modern culinary techniques. New Deal projects encouraged funding for electricity, indoor plumbing, modern homes, and extension services for southerners who had previously lacked access to modern amenities. Franklin D. Roosevelt's administration sponsored many building projects that enabled disadvantaged white and black southerners to move into homes with modern kitchens. In Atlanta, the Public Works Administration constructed the region's first public housing projects, Techwood for whites and University Homes for African Americans, to replace the "ramshackle hovels" in which the city's lower classes had lived. The federally funded apartment buildings and homes, intended for lower-income workers of both races, included indoor plumbing and electricity, access to which many of their residents had not had previously.[7] Such amenities, including electric stoves and other appliances, no doubt allowed residents to implement more modern food preparation practices.

Other New Deal projects, such as the Tennessee Valley Authority (TVA), which had its primary impact on the infrastructure of several southern states, allowed rural women to access electricity and the kitchen appliances that required it. Lower-class rural women responded by acquiring these modern kitchen accoutrements, either voluntarily or through compulsion by government administrators. Tressa Waters, a Tennessee homemaker, recalls that the TVA required her family to get an electric stove: "When we got electricity . . . I got my stove right away. . . . every family had to sign up for so many appliances . . . we just got what we had to have in order to get the electricity."[8] Despite the economic hardship and physical dislocations of the period, the changes fashioned by New Deal financial, technological, and government expansion allowed, and even required, access to more modern systems of procuring and preparing food.

Cooking as an Art

As more southerners gained access to modern food preparation methods and moved away from the Progressive-era imperative of reform, the commitment to domestic science as a means of gender and racial progress declined among many white women. This transformation was evident in home economics education at George Peabody College in Nashville, Tennessee. Mary S. Hoffschwelle argues that from 1914 to 1939, domestic science changed from "a reform program that promised women professional and social importance to a training course in domestic skills."[9] Although the program continued, and even expanded, it did so with the express intention to train women in their gender-specific roles rather than to use women's supposedly unique place in society to initiate and further reform. The New Deal, Hoffschwelle argues, provided an optimal time for George Peabody College to revisit the social improvement goals that initially propelled its domestic science department—as had been the case at Montevallo and Georgia College as well. But administrators failed to pursue such a path. "They continued to train their students to be better wives and mothers and to teach homemaking skills to others," Hoffschwelle notes, but educational imperatives no longer included the "vision of regional social uplift" that had once guided such instruction.[10] The situation at George Peabody College reflects a broader regional departure from the Progressive idea that homemaking should be used to improve society.

Although, as the George Peabody College example illustrates, home economics education continued and its fundamental principles remained viable, the late 1930s nevertheless witnessed a visible rejection of the understanding of cooking as a science—even among the white, middle-class, southern women who had once embraced such ideas. In 1938 the Alabama native and *New Yorker* magazine culinary writer Sheila Hibben announced, "Cookbooks aren't sacred!" a statement that might have been considered heretical among culinary experts of the Progressive period. In her *Atlanta Constitution* article of that title, Hibben declared it "humiliating [and] aggravating . . . never to be trusted with the amount of parsley or pepper or salt" to use in preparing a dish. The well-known food expert and author suggested that "taste and imagination" as well as "guess or inspiration" must play a significant role in the everyday preparation of food. Hibben's own recipes illustrated this point. She created "imitations" of quality restaurant meals and encouraged her readers to experiment in a similar manner.[11]

Southern cookbooks published during and after this decade reveal a similar shift toward an understanding of southern foods as a vehicle to transmit cultural and historical memory. In 1938 Kay Burdette, a white southerner, published *Cookery of the Old South (Translated from Southern Lore)* that made no claim to scientific dogma and offered no endorsements from home economists. Instead, similar to the women at Olivet Episcopal Church two decades later, Burdette attributed her recipes to the personal "hand printed guides" that southern women might have once kept in their kitchens. Burdette's subtitle, "Translated from Southern Lore," demonstrates this supposed genesis of her recipes—handed down through the generations. The cookbook's design conveys this notion as well. The publishers used a font that resembled handwriting, paper that was treated to appear yellowed with age, and a woven cover made to look homemade and bound with leather ties. The text romanticized the antebellum kitchen where, Burdette explains, recipes had been carefully guarded secrets handed down orally through generations of "artistic" cooks.[12]

Cookbooks inspired by domestic science focused on a commitment to standardized principles and conformity among households, towns, and regions. Burdette's contribution to culinary literature encouraged the independent judgment of individual cooks. Each recipe suggests spices to enliven the dish but, like Sheila Hibben, Burdette trusts her readers to use the spices according to their own tastes and imaginations. Burdette also presents southern foodways as distinct from other regions in a way that more scientific cookbooks failed to capture. She even suggests that different cooking styles led to the Civil War. Discussing the cause of the war, Burdette claims, "It was more than likely because the South wanted hot breads and the North insisted upon cold light breads." Burdette insists that "a vast difference [exists] between the two sections" at the table and pledges her allegiance to the South.[13]

Burdette creates a myth to perpetuate the distinctiveness of the South, but her cookbook itself is a myth. She claims, "Every detail of this edition has been designed to conform with the antiquity of the recipes."[14] But the recipes are not genuine. Burdette relies on the standardized measurements and recipe formats (with ingredient listings up front) propagated by home economics. This method suggests that, despite Burdette's claims otherwise, she accepts the movement's fundamental concepts. She builds her imaginary South, with its faux handwritten recipes, on the modern culinary techniques that had become standard nationwide.

This attempt to generate and perpetuate myth through foodways can be seen in southern women's club cookbooks of the period as well. In 1935 and 1941, the Ginter Park Woman's Club issued two slightly different versions of *Famous Recipes from Old Virginia*, which presented cooking as a feature of cultural memory instead of science. Organized in the 1890s by General Lewis W. Ginter, an industrialist who wanted to provide professional men with a country retreat to which to return at the end of the day, Ginter Park was one of the South's earliest suburbs. In 1895, an extended streetcar line connected the neighborhood to downtown Richmond, Virginia. Early residents, including doctors, lawyers, executives, and other high-salaried professionals, left their offices in the city each evening to return to their homes in a safe, clean, and attractive community. These white professional families were among the first southerners to adopt a suburban lifestyle—a setting that became normal for white southerners after World War II. The Ginter Park Woman's Club had a tradition of advocating Progressive-era reforms, such as starting the area's first kindergarten.[15]

The modern clubwomen of Ginter Park had little direct connection to the plantation era of the Old South. Yet by the mid-1930s, as New Deal programs modernized the region, the wives of Ginter Park professionals looked back to the plantation as the proper standard by which cooking and homemaking should be judged. There are many differences between the cookbooks published by the Ginter Park Woman's Club in the 1930s and the Atlanta Woman's Club a decade and a half earlier. Instead of using the cookbook as a forum to spread domestic science principles, as the Atlanta clubwomen had done, the Ginter Park group attempted to disseminate their idealized understanding of historical and cultural memory through the use of recipes and food-related images. The title, *Famous Recipes from Old Virginia*, establishes the cookbook's theme as a tribute to early Virginia history. In the first chapter, the club offers recipes copied from early southern cookbooks that, like the cookbook published later by the women of the Olivet Episcopal Church, would have been of little practical use to white women living in an upper-middle-class suburb in 1935. They include "To Make Excellent Bread without Yeast," originally published in a 1795 Virginia almanac, and instructions for roasting a pig or turkey on a spit, from Mary Randolph's 1824 household manual. The Ginter Park Woman's Club provides these instructions directly from the original sources with no attempt to update them with standardized measurements or for modern technology.[16] These twentieth-century women, whose lives revolved around streetcars and modern kindergartens, certainly had no need or desire to roast a pig on a spit in their fireplace.

By contrast, in the more modern sections of the cookbook, the editors use precise measurements and include a discussion of proper meal planning and nutrition called "Needful Knowledge." These features demonstrate that the club bought into more modern modes of cooking and communicating recipes, even if the members did not emphasize the science of their cooking. The primary purpose of the cookbook was not to spread this scientific knowledge. Instead, this group of white Richmond women desired to transmit their understanding of Virginia's place in the nation's cultural history. In one chapter, they include recipes from important national and international figures, such as First Lady Eleanor Roosevelt and several foreign ambassadors to the United States.[17] Such inclusions imply that the club members were a cosmopolitan, politically oriented, well-placed group of women living in the new type of American community.

Some of the more important contributions, however, are not the recipes but the accompanying notes and comments, which emphasize the importance of instinct, experience, or simple trial and error in the kitchen. A memo accompanying the recipe for "Lydia's Wine Jelly," contributed by the pianist John Powell, reads, "You have to know just how Mr. Powell likes it to get it right. Some lemons are more sour than others, and the sweet must agree with the sour. Better taste it often."[18] Powell's cook, Lydia, who wrote the note and the recipe, clearly did not rely on scientific precision to prepare the wine jelly to her employer's taste. Instead, she depended on experimentation and an intimate knowledge of Powell's palate. By including her note, the women of Ginter Park recognize Lydia as an expert in preparing wine jelly, who gained her skills through experience. They respect her opinion on this point—although they fail to respect her autonomy as an individual separate from her identity as Powell's cook.[19]

The admiration that the white Ginter Park clubwomen reveal for Lydia's improvisational approach to cooking reflects the tendency, changed in many ways from the first two decades of the twentieth century, of white women to attribute a natural cooking ability to black cooks. By 1935, segregation culture had become established across the South. White women, like those who joined the Ginter Park Woman's Club, no longer had to fear that a black presence in white kitchens threatened racial purity or white supremacy because a set of well-established rituals, customs, and laws now regulated racial interactions in the domestic and public spheres. By this time, cooking instinct was often attributed to black cooks as an organic part of their nature. Although white women might lay claim to this talent as well, they did so in ways that did not diminish the notion that a black woman's natural place was in kitchen service. In the note that followed another recipe, Mrs. Robert B. Tunstall, a white woman and self-described poet, explains that her recipe for almond cake came from her cousin, who "had an especial 'knack,' which is the extra touch that all recipes need." Tunstall also includes the following excerpt from a nineteenth-century poem written by the white Alabama author Maria Howard Weeden:

> Kaze cooking's like religion is—
> Some's 'lected, and some ain't!
> And rules doan no mo mek a cook
> Dan sermons mek a saint![20]

Although Tunstall's cousin was most certainly a white woman, Tunstall relied on this poem, written in a stereotypical African American dialect, to express the importance of intuition and talent in the kitchen. The poem compares a good cook to one of John Calvin's "elect," suggesting that this status has already been decided regardless of the person's education or knowledge. The stanza suggests that cooking is a talent bequeathed by God, and not a skill learned in domestic science classes. By affirming her under-standing of cooking as a practice of instinct and artistry, Tunstall rejects the rigidity of domestic science, which had dominated much of the culinary discourse of the previous decades. By referencing a poem written by a white woman with the supposed articulation of a black cook, she also reinforces the notion that black women have an inherent ability to cook and that their service to whites is preordained by God. The common white perception that African Americans had organic cooking skills fostered a broader white understanding of black cooks and other African Americans as inherently servile and helped to maintain white supremacy and segregation culture.

In addition to the recipes and their accompanying comments, the Ginter Park Woman's Club reinforced white supremacy through images that re-vealed racial interactions within and outside of white southern homes. These images, sketched by Richmond artist Margaret Dashiell, complement the cookbooks' text by displaying allegedly typical scenes of Richmond life that set forth supposedly appropriate racial patterns in the home and on the streets. Every chapter of the 1935 edition opens with a small image that il-lustrates certain racial interactions. The section of colonial recipes opens with a picture of the "Kitchen at Stratford," the ancestral home of the Lees of Virginia. An older, bow-backed African American woman greets two finely attired white women and a white girl in front of a large cooking hearth. The black woman wears a plain dress and head wrap; the white women wear large-hooped colonial dresses; and the caption reads, "Ash cake, sweet 'taters, an' meat on de spit, / In de ole Lee kitchen dey sur' did cook a bit." Both the image of the black cook in the Lee kitchen and the use of stereotyp-ical African American dialect reinforce the notion of black southern women as "natural" cooks and as subservient.

The 1941 edition of *Famous Recipes from Old Virginia* relies even more heavily on these images. Along with the text, they construct a historical memory that reinforces the racial interactions considered to be appropriate in segregated Richmond. In this edition, the editors added a chapter that featured antebellum recipes. The image that Dashiell drew to represent the antebellum period shows old Confederate veterans, dressed in uniforms and propped up with canes, milling about a park. Several young white girls enthusiastically greet them. A rebel battle flag hangs in the background, and an old African American woman stands in the foreground to watch over the white children. "'Fore de war on de ole plantation, mammy was de cook," the caption reads. "She give 'em den de bestest food and never used a book." Although the image reveres the Confederate veteran, the caption memorializes the old enslaved plantation cook, who learned her craft orally without the need for written recipes.

According to the chapter introduction, the editors wanted to include a section of Civil War recipes, but the scarcities and substitutions of the war made that objective difficult. Instead, they focus on recipes that were popular prior to 1861, "when cooking in the South was such an art," with the desire to resurrect "a glorious period" of Richmond's past. The Ginter Park Woman's Club uses an imagined historical past to manage the homogenizing effect of modernization on regional identity and to emphasize their understanding of the servile nature of black women to aid in maintaining segregation culture.

Although earlier twentieth-century cookbooks sometimes exalted the South's antebellum and Civil War history, historical memory did not define such tomes. The Ginter Park Woman's Club, on the other hand, used images and recipes from a past era to preserve and impart the region's "history" in a way that served the white interests of a segregated Richmond. The recipes supposedly represent the antebellum period, but individual foods and contributors proudly display their Confederate credentials. Several recipes reportedly hail from the Lee kitchen at Stratford, including one for an orange and coconut sponge cake that "tradition says . . . was the favorite recipe of General Robert E. Lee." The recipe is simply named "Lee's Favorite Dessert," with no indication as to whether it is a cake, pie, or some other sweet. The importance of this recipe is not based on its potential as a dessert but on its storied past. Throughout this section, the cookbook variously describes contributors as the "Wife of [a] Confederate soldier," "Wife of General Pegram who was fatally wounded at the Battle of Hatchers Run," or "Daughter of Mrs. Norman Randolph, one vitally interested in the Confederate Cause and the days that followed." Another contributor is described as the wife of a cousin to General Lee.[21] Testimony to the contributors' Confederate bona fides is intended to situate them as appropriate conduits of an antebellum history preserved through recipes and memories attributed to—but not necessarily prepared by—the white elite.

In addition to communicating memories of the South's Confederate "tradition," the second edition of the Ginter Park cookbook uses foodways to describe a more recent imagined past based on dependable black servants and knowledgeable white women. One Dashiell drawing in the 1941 cookbook depicts the assembly of a Christmas pudding. "The mixing of the Christmas puddings," the caption explains, "was for many years a ritual in the South." The image shows a kitchen bustling with activity. An old black woman sits with a large bowl on her lap and stirs the pudding while white children hang over her. In another chair across the kitchen, another black servant holds a young white toddler. Standing in the center of her kitchen with a commanding air, a white woman reads from a book, presumably a cookbook, to instruct the servant on the correct preparation of the pudding. Although the white children surround the black domestic servants, they rivet their attention on their white mother in the center of the kitchen. Dashiell has illustrated the supposedly appropriate domestic roles for each woman based on her race. The black women perform the manual labor associated with feeding and otherwise caring for healthy white children. The white woman provides the leadership and knowledge necessary for this endeavor. The image's presumptuous title, "Any Richmond Kitchen of Not Many Years Ago," assumes that every kitchen in the city belonged to an upper-middle-class white woman who could afford several servants and had the time to personally oversee and instruct her kitchen help as they worked.[22]

The images and history supposedly preserved in the two editions of the Ginter Park cookbook reveal more about elite white Richmond in the 1930s and 1940s than they reveal about "Old Virginia" or its culinary legacy. The cookbooks expose a white female population that understood black service as a static institution intrinsic to the foundations of southern domesticity. They are unlike many of the southern white middle-class women of two decades earlier, who worried about the quality of their servants.

These cookbook images are instructive as to the supposed timelessness of racial roles in the region—where whites progress with the times while maintaining an interest in their so-called heritage, but African Americans are considered to be unchanging. In Dashiell's drawings, the images of the white women evolve across time. For the colonial picture of the Lees' kitchen, the white women wear low-bodiced hoop dresses. Images set in later time periods reveal more contemporary styles on the white women and children. But the images of the black women remain constant and time-less. They always wear plain dresses and head wraps. They work in white kitchens or urban marketplaces and constantly mind white children. The drawings show many healthy, rambunctious white children, who are always the center of the black servant's attention. Many images reveal one African American girl as well, but she is always off to the side and never the focus of anyone's attention. Her only role seems to be to wait and watch as she learns about her own future as a domestic servant. Certainly the Ginter Park Woman's Club did not represent all white women, or even all white middle-class women of the World War II era, but these images reflect a changing culture among many southern clubwomen as a result of greater nationalization during the New Deal and World War II eras.

Domestic imagery in cookbooks and culinary literature attempted to define southern distinctiveness in terms of a unique food tradition. White southern women created an imagined antebellum past of black women as artists in the kitchen, preparing meals for their white employers based on proprietary recipes handed down across the generations. African American cooks served important roles in these myths as the holders of innate culinary talents and, by implication, as "natural" servants to whites. These myths helped to sustain southern white supremacy and segregation in an American culture that was quickly becoming homogenous.

CHAPTER FOUR

Restaurant Chains and Fast Food

Before World War II, Wilber Hardee ran a snack shop behind a family gas station in rural North Carolina. The venture offered a way for his family to survive the economic depression without leaving their farm. After the war, Hardee entered the food-service industry full time. He operated another snack shop at the Robersonville, North Carolina, bus station, which he sold to his brother-in-law in order to open a full-service restaurant in Greenville called the Port Terminal Inn. Hardee recalls, "Our 40-seat dining room was full every night." Two years later, he sold the Port Terminal Inn for a profit and designed Greenville's first drive-in restaurant, which he named the Silo Restaurant because of its round building. He later enlarged the Silo to add a dining room that served Carolina-style barbecue, steaks, seafood, hamburgers, and fried chicken.[1]

The Silo Restaurant prospered in the postwar economic boom. More North Carolinians had the money to dine out, and entrepreneurs like Hardee profited as a result. Hardee recalls living a "comfortable lifestyle" with his wife and their four children. He didn't need to invest in a new restaurant concept. But when he first heard about a drive-in called McDonald's, one of the many "postwar fads and fashions" that had moved eastward from California, Hardee was intrigued. He recalls, "Probably everyone in the restaurant business began about the same time to hear stories of the new hamburger chain that served hamburgers instantly for only fifteen cents." North Carolina's first McDonald's franchise was in Greensboro. Although it was a two-hundred-mile drive for Hardee, he had to see it for himself. One Sunday, he drove to Greensboro and witnessed a long queue of customers

FIGURE 7. The McDonald's in Greensboro, North Carolina, was the first in the state. This site encouraged Wilber Hardee to start his own fast-food chain. Courtesy of the *Charlotte Observer*.

who parked their cars, stood in line dressed in their Sunday best, and purchased bags of hamburgers at the walk-up window. Within an hour, Hardee estimated, the small drive-in took in about $140.

As he drove home, Hardee planned the restaurant he would open based on the McDonald's concept and the charbroiled hamburgers he already served at the Silo. He chose a site in Greenville with a large parking lot near East Carolina College to take advantage of the automobile traffic. Following the McDonald's model, he constructed a small building with no dining room. A façade covered with ceramic tiles gave the structure a clean, modern look. On September 3, 1960, the first Hardee's fast-food restaurant opened. Because there were no other fast-food restaurants in the vicinity, the grand opening was an event. Customers traveled as far as fifty miles to visit the new restaurant. Hardee later recalled it as "one of the proudest days of my business career."

Hardee's career reflects the evolution of southern foodways in the post–World War II period. As the region began to prosper, more southerners could afford to eat out. Hardee was one of the first southerners to recognize and capitalize on the future of food service—the fast-food chain. The rise of fast food was part of the broader economic and demographic changes that were affecting the entire nation, including national migration into the Sunbelt and the growth of national chains. These changes may have represented a threat to the white privilege in southern eating spaces that white southerners had carefully constructed during the first part of the century. Yet white supremacy—specifically, the privileging of white consumption—was a component of the business models adopted by white southern entrepreneurs like Hardee.

Increasingly after World War II, national chains—both stores and restaurants—became standard features of the southern landscape. National chains fed southern appetites and imaginations. Although the fast-food concept did not originate in the South, southerners recognized its potential to fit the region's environment. As Hardee's story indicates, southern entrepreneurs understood that the low-price, high-turnover concept would be particularly marketable in the South. The Cold War spending that flowed into the region helped to economically enfranchise most white southerners. The region's temperate weather, commitment to the automobile culture, and suburban migration contributed to an atmosphere in which fast food thrived. Hardee was one of many white southern entrepreneurs who opened fast-food establishments modeled after McDonald's. Although many of these southern chains struggled or failed, others would go on to become well-known national names. The region's adoption of fast food became one thread that tied it to the Sunbelt, and the growth of this new democratic style of cuisine mirrored how the region's influence spread across the nation.

The emergence of fast food in the South after World War II, from the spread of western chains like McDonald's to homegrown versions like Hardee's and Burger King, created new democratized public spaces in which the cooking, serving, and eating of food took place. Unlike any type of eating place before them, fast-food chains were spectacles of modernity that irrevocably tied southern consumers to national economic and cultural patterns. With its national presence, simple design, and inexpensive fare, fast food should have represented a threat to white privileged eating space. After all, in its earliest years, fast food had no dining rooms to segregate based on race. These spaces, however, built white privilege into the key features of the fast-food concept: the automobile, the hamburger, and the national chain. As a result, white southerners in particular embraced the new concept, and fast food became a reflection of the increasingly significant role the region played in the national culture.

The Automobile

The automobile enabled fast-food culture. Early on, proprietors tended to locate these spaces away from city centers. But even before the development of the concept, the greater availability of automobiles and the expansion of southern roadways encouraged the construction of eateries in the South's countryside and emerging suburbs. The connection of a more mobile population of southern consumers to national food markets changed the nature of public food consumption. In theory, automobiles provided a new mobility and freedom to all southern consumers. Neither train schedules nor Jim Crow railcars restricted them. For those who could afford transport by automobile, new types of consumer sites emerged in the form of roadside cafés and food-service stands. According to one estimate, tens of thousands of food stands existed along the nation's roadways by the 1930s. The South's temperate weather allowed for outdoor service and dining throughout much of the year, making such stands particularly popular in the region. Southern roadside stands often served barbecue, a regional specialty that thrived especially in more rural areas.[2]

Barbecue stands took different forms. Some establishments, modeled after urban cafés, allowed customers to sit down at counters or tables. Others took the form of drive-ins, where waitresses called "carhops" served customers in their automobiles. Some stands more closely resembled a city sidewalk stand, with no interior seating or car service. Architecture varied as well. Some proprietors created elaborate, decorative exteriors intended to attract the attention of drivers.[3] The entrance to a barbecue roadside café located near Harlingen, Texas, during World War II took the form of a large black-spotted pig. Patrons entered through a doorway under the pig's massive snout. Despite the elaborate entryway, parking consisted of a simple gravel lot with no landscaping or gardening out front. The building's ostentation attracted drivers who would then stop, if only out of curiosity, and have a bite.[4]

Other roadside stands and cafés preferred functionality over spectacle. One operator near Corpus Christi, Texas, in 1939 constructed his stand with sheets of corrugated metal that may have been scraps. There was no on-site dining room. The stand needed no name—just the word "Barbecue" emblazoned in large capital letters so it could be identified from the road. Large tin signs posted on the front and sides advertised 7-up and Royal Crown Cola.[5] In another example, Big Chief Barbecue, located near Fort Benning in Columbus, Georgia, around 1940 provided a place for customers to sit down in a simple structure constructed of cement blocks. The proprietor covered the outside of the building with signs that advertised, among other products, Dr. Pepper and Atlantic Ale and Beer.[6] Large signs by national advertisers allowed roadside cafés to announce their wares in ways that captured the attention of passersby, but they also gave independent eateries a more common appearance from one region to another. They allowed consumers to participate in the national consumption of popular soft drink brands, even at the most out-of-the-way places.

Rural proprietors often opened roadside cafés at gas stations or hotels to provide one-stop accommodations for the needs of travelers.[7] Behind the pumps at a Texaco station near Yulee, Florida, in 1941, for example, a wooden building served a quick lunch.[8] In the 1920s and 1930s, a national increase in automobile ownership had coincided with low crop prices, and southern farm families like Wilber Hardee's added to their income stream by selling food to travelers. Rural entrepreneurs could add a café to a gas station with minimal investment by constructing a small structure with scrap lumber. Like urban cafés, the menus at these roadside stands emphasized convenience and simplicity over indulgence. They generally featured items such as hot dogs, sandwiches, and barbecue. Farm families thus did not need to leave the countryside or quit farming in order to supplement their incomes. In 1937 the proprietor of a small roadside café and gas station near Ennis, Texas, celebrated the optimism that his small brick eatery engendered with the name "Nu Deel Sandwich Shoppe."[9] In this way, some southern farmers helped themselves toward recovery through food-service entrepreneurship.

Despite the freedom represented by the automobile and a newfound ability to access roadside dining, all southerners did not participate in this new culture equally. Roadside dining involved a great deal of uncertainty for African Americans. Eating on the road was one more potentially dangerous situation that, for black travelers, required careful planning and negotiation. While the automobile freed African Americans from the Jim Crow car on southern trains, it exposed them to other, sometimes more insidious, dangers on the roadways.

Unlike in railroad dining cars, where the rules were more or less understood, African Americans looking for a meal along southern highways were in a much more perilous situation. Around 1954 Barbee William Durham, an African American man from Columbus, Ohio, wrote about traveling in the South. "The most difficult problem that confronts Negro American citizens when they travel by automobile," Durham explained, "is finding a place to stop for the night and a place to eat."[10] African Americans did not necessarily know the rules at unfamiliar roadside cafés. A more mobile African American population could face significant troubles when they traveled away from areas they knew, where the local racial policies were well understood.

The Negro Motorist Green Book was a tool to help alleviate the uncertainty. Starting with its first edition in 1936, the *Green Book* provided black motorists with information about accessible hotels, restaurants, and amusements in all parts of the country. Created for the black middle class, the guide included a section called "Important Convention Dates," which listed, for example, the annual meetings of the National Medical Association and fraternal organizations. Having the names of restaurants and hotels that accepted black business enabled African Americans to travel for work and pleasure. Still, the *Green Book* was incomplete. For instance, the guide listed only one restaurant for the entire state of Alabama—Bonnie's on Jeff Davis Avenue in Montgomery. This does not mean there were no other restaurants that catered to African Americans—Birmingham and Montgomery had several other black cafés—but only that the *Green Book* lacked complete knowledge of every part of the country.[11] Such a resource helped African Americans to negotiate the dangerous territory of eating out when they traveled away from home. Still, the incomplete nature of the *Green Book* highlights the many uncertainties and inherent dangers of Jim Crow dining culture.

The Hamburger

The second key ingredient of the success of fast food in the South and across the nation was the common hamburger. Like the automobile, the hamburger claimed no particular regional affiliation and became popular among Americans in general. Most national quick-order establishments came to depend on it. Hamburger steak can be found on earlier menus, but it developed into its full, portable potential in the early 1920s. Edgar Waldo "Billy" Ingram, who founded the modern hamburger stand, recalls that early twentieth-century American consumers actually distrusted hamburger meat. "When Mother wanted hamburger," Ingram recalls, "she would innocently buy a pound or two of a certain cut of beef and then, as the butcher started to wrap it up, say, 'Would you mind grinding it for me?' and stand and watch him do it." In the aftermath of the 1906 muckraking novel, *The Jungle*, which encouraged the regulation of the U.S. meatpacking industry, the nation understandably remained wary about a product composed of an unidentifiable meat and any number of unknown additives or impurities.[12]

In 1921 Ingram and his business partner, Walter Anderson, set out to change the negative image of the hamburger sandwich, which is what they called a hamburger steak served between two pieces of bread. They stocked their stand in Wichita, Kansas, with the same type of beef they imagined American mothers buying and had butchers grind it to their specifications. They encouraged confidence in the quality, purity, and sanitation of their kitchens and pantries by arranging tours for local women's clubs. They selected the name of their new hamburger chain, White Castle, to symbolize safety and trustworthiness. According to Ingram, "'White' signifies purity and cleanliness and 'Castle' represents strength, permanence and stability."[13]

Although it may not have been Ingram's explicit intent, the name White Castle also suggests white privilege. The fact that Ingram specifically chose the word "white" to denote good hygiene complemented the tendency of white Americans to conflate whiteness with cleanliness. The word symbolizes more than simple sanitation; it implies racial purity. Moreover, the imagery of the castle implies the strength of European, or white, culture. Not only did the name of the chain that popularized the common hamburger privilege whiteness, but the word "hamburger" itself, with its Germanic origin, is similarly suggestive. This is not to suggest that white Americans deliberately connected the hamburger or White Castle to race. But the symbolism no doubt spoke to a race-conscious society. Although the hamburger is not a food particularly associated with the South, its earliest history referenced white privilege, which facilitated the new food's acceptance in the racially segregated region. As the simple, inexpensive product at the center of fast-food cuisine, the common hamburger expanded the availability of a more democratic style of eating to southerners in a way that privileged white consumers.

The Fast Food Chain

A final important ingredient of post–World War II dining in the South was the fast-food chain. National chains standardized nearly all aspects of their operations, from the structure of their buildings to the food they served. The first chain eateries probably entered the South through the five-and-dime variety store. Frank Winfield Woolworth originated this low-cost, high-volume store concept with his first successful shop, which he opened in 1879 in Lancaster, Pennsylvania. Woolworth instituted food service in all of his stores between 1910 and 1925 by adding "refreshment rooms," which mostly resembled high-end restaurants in their look and service. Later, these rather elaborate restaurants took on the appearance of a modern lunch counter with plastic counters and vinyl bar stools. Woolworth entered the Atlanta market in 1915, the first entrance of a national chain's food service in the city.[14] But Woolworth's and its competitors in the variety-store lunch-counter business were only the first wave of chain restaurants to hit the South. After World War II, chains became a leading segment of the southern foodscape.

Although they had antecedents in prewar lunch counters, fast-food chains expanded across the nation, including the South, after World War II. Automobiles, suburbanization, and—because many new chains targeted children and families—the Baby Boom spurred both the success of quick-lunch chains and their evolution into modern fast food. Entrepreneurs designed the fast-food concept to feed people cheaply and efficiently. McDonald's epitomizes the post–World War II incarnation of fast food.

Two brothers, Richard and Maurice McDonald, developed the fast-food concept in San Bernardino, California. Initially, they operated a traditional drive-in with carhops serving barbecue, hamburgers, and other menu items to a customer base dominated by teenagers. In 1948, in an effort to increase their sales volume, the McDonald brothers streamlined their operations. They eliminated the carhops, popularizing a new style of self-service drive-in where customers walked up to a service window. They also reduced the menu to five items: hamburgers, cheeseburgers, french fries, milk shakes, and soft drinks. Menu prices ranged from ten cents for an order of fries or a Coke to fifteen cents for a hamburger to twenty cents for a milk shake.[15]

The new McDonald's Hamburgers focused on sanitation, affordability, and speed. The brothers arranged their kitchen so customers could view the clean, tiled interior. White male cooks wore crisp uniforms and paper hats. The McDonald brothers designed the grill and other preparation surfaces for maximum efficiency. They cooked hamburgers by hand using "a specially built polished steel griddle," and they could prepare forty hamburgers in less than two minutes. They served hamburgers with mustard, ketchup, chopped onions, and pickles, allowing no substitutions or special orders. They peeled and cut potatoes to make fresh french fries, but peelers and slicers eased the labor involved. They created an "assembly line" to manufacture milk shakes. Standardization in product and preparation allowed the brothers to keep prices down, to work efficiently, and to quickly serve the lines of customers who gathered in front of their establishment. Despite long queues, customers only waited a short amount of time. That time could be spent admiring the new spectacle of modern, efficient, inexpensive food service developed by the McDonald brothers.[16]

In 1954 an Illinois businessman, Ray Kroc, sealed the future of McDonald's as the standard for fast-food franchising when he visited the San Bernardino drive-in. At that time, Kroc was traveling the country selling milkshake machines, each with the capacity to mix five shakes simultaneously. The McDonald brothers owned eight machines at their little hamburger stand. Kroc wondered why any one restaurant, especially one located in the "quiet town" of San Bernardino, needed to make forty milk shakes at one time. Once there, he witnessed the crowds that gathered to consume the brothers' hamburgers. "Soon the parking lot was full," Kroc recalls in his memoir, "and people were marching up to the windows and back to their cars with bags full of hamburgers." In particular, he noticed the diversity of the clientele, from the construction workers who ate lunch there every day to the "demure" young blonde eating a hamburger in her convertible. Kroc left California with a contract to franchise the brothers' operations. In April 1955 Kroc opened the first national franchise in Des Plaines, Illinois, and it became an immediate sensation. Restaurateurs from all over the country traveled to California to copy the original design and to carry the modern fast-food concept to their hometowns.[17]

Over the next decade, McDonald's spread across the country and throughout the southern states. As population growth shifted from the Northeast to the South and Southwest, Kroc recognized the potential of the Sunbelt for the success of the national chain.[18] By 1963 the South boasted 122 out of roughly 550 McDonald's locations, with the largest southern presence in the states of Florida, Georgia, Maryland, Virginia, North Carolina, and Alabama.[19] One of the earliest McDonald's franchises in the region may have been in Sarasota, Florida, where builders struggled with local health officials. The standardized McDonald's structure, covered with red and white tile and dominated by two parallel golden arches on either side, failed to gain approval. The local health department refused to allow McDonald's to prepare milk shakes and hamburgers in the same room. The issue may have been a deal killer. Fast food depended on efficiency and economy, and McDonald's kitchens had been designed with these particular goals in mind. The company and local officials compromised on a simple redesign, but the incident reveals the potential challenges when a national chain restaurant moves into a new area with different notions of health and sanitation.[20] But the Sarasota incident failed to inhibit the chain's movement throughout the South. In 1965 the corporation opened a regional office in Atlanta.[21]

McDonald's influence on southern eating places, however, greatly exceeded its own presence in the region. From the very beginning McDonald's served as a model for other fast-food chains.[22] Southern entrepreneurs like Hardee recognized how well the concept suited the postwar southern marketplace by providing a relatively inexpensive meal for an increasingly suburban population no longer concentrated in downtown areas. As a result, Hardee's and most other southern fast-food chains explicitly modeled their restaurants on the McDonald's design.

Burger King, founded in Jacksonville, Florida, in 1953, encountered some difficulties along its course to becoming McDonald's best-known rival. The entrepreneur Matthew L. Burns experienced trouble when he attempted to duplicate and improve on the McDonald brothers' success. Burns discovered fast food on a trip to California, where he visited McDonald's Hamburgers in San Bernardino and also purchased two machines, the Insta-broiler and the Insta-shake machine, intended to bring food service into the factory age.[23] Burns carried his discoveries back to Jacksonville, where he and his son-in-law, Keith G. Cramer, opened the first Insta–Burger King, expecting the new devices to make the fast-food system more efficient.

The Insta-broiler simultaneously cooked twelve hamburger patties in individual baskets that carried the raw meat through two electrical heating units. A wire screen kept the patties in place until the baskets rotated back to the operator, and then a stainless steel slide pushed each cooked patty into a pan filled with a special sauce. Hamburger buns ran along a conveyor belt below the patties, where they collected juices from the meat cooking above. Similarly, the Insta-shake machine automated the preparation of milk shakes. With the flip of a switch, an ice-milk mixture of either chocolate or vanilla froze instantly into a shake so thick that customers had to eat it with a wooden spoon.[24] Such innovations seemed to be the culmination of a century-long effort to make food service more efficient.

Despite the success of McDonald's and similar chains, Insta–Burger King reveals that fast food still had much to prove in parts of the Sunbelt in the late 1950s. A year after Cramer and Burns opened the first Insta–Burger King in Jacksonville, two Miami entrepreneurs, David R. Edgerton Jr. and James W. McLamore, opened four franchises.[25] For a variety of reasons the fast-food concept took time to become established in some areas. Insta–Burger King, in its original formation, never appealed to the Florida populace and suffered financially. McLamore recalls several Florida chains, including Golden Point, Henry's, Red Barn, Burger Castle, and Biff Burger, that failed in fast food's early years. Lack of enthusiasm from Florida customers and lack of experience on the part of the proprietors contributed to these failures. "In 1954 Miami," McLamore says in his autobiography, "[fast-food service] was unproven, unfamiliar, and unpopular."[26] Continued concern over the quality of the meat in the hamburgers may have plagued these chains as well.

McLamore recalls that Floridians believed that an "inexpensive hamburger couldn't possibly be wholesome."[27]

In Burger King's case, the Insta devices, intended to improve on the McDonald's system, were unreliable and contributed to consumer dissatisfaction. In attempting to automate the system, Burger King's founders had actually weakened a key ingredient in fast-food success—the ability to serve customers quickly and efficiently.[28] The franchisees, Edgerton and McLamore, saved Burger King from failure by replacing the inefficient Insta machines with new flame broilers. The broilers operated with a speed and efficiency that enabled Burger King to gain the confidence of South Florida consumers. All Burger King franchises soon implemented these changes. In 1957 Burger King added the Whopper, made with a quarter pound of meat, which turned the typical fast-food hamburger, usually one-half that size, into a larger, heartier meal.[29]

By its nature, fast food had the potential to be a more democratic mode of consumption. First, the food was inexpensive. The McDonald brothers and Kroc purposefully established the McDonald's system to scale down the process of eating out. "What we have attempted to do is eliminate those things that people don't eat," Kroc explains in a 1961 *Time* magazine article. "You can't eat a 20% tip, a perfumed finger bowl or a waitress."[30] Second, Kroc's philosophy theoretically offered access for all. There was no drive-in, no drive-thru, no dining room, no lunch counter, no waiters or waitresses. Everyone walked up to the window and ordered. Then, customers took their food to the car or elsewhere to eat. McDonald's did not implement indoor seating until 1963, when the corporation enclosed the buildings to provide air conditioning, heating, and small dining areas in an effort to increase sales.[31] The industry relied on low prices and high volume. It was not in the nature of fast-food enterprises to discourage consumption by anyone.

What's more, unlike the restaurants and cafés of an earlier time, which were controlled by individuals, these new spaces relied on franchises by regional or national corporations. By definition, individual franchises were steeped in the corporation's identity and economics. Again leading the pack, McDonald's became the first fast-food chain to engage in national advertising. The chain placed its first national ad in *Reader's Digest* in October 1963, a half-page advertisement showing a typical McDonald's structure at the top and announcing McDonald's as "Everybody's Favorite! Coast to Coast." In the same year, a national public relations campaign celebrated the chain's billionth hamburger sold with newspaper articles and television appearances.[32] In 1965 McDonald's sponsored a float in the Macy's Thanksgiving Day parade and hired a national agency to oversee its print, radio, and television advertising.[33] National advertising helped to build a uniform public identity for these spaces and to familiarize potential customers with the chain's iconic structure for easy recognition.

Fast food thrived on uniformity in its menu offerings and operations. From the beginning, the existence of national chains depended on standardization. "Our aim," Kroc recalls, "was to insure repeat business based on the system's reputation rather than on the quality of a single store or operator."[34] Signs, architecture, logos, and other identifiable symbols required homogeneity and consistency so that potential consumers could recognize the business from one location to another. The regular standards of chain businesses also ensured brand loyalty. When a customer became familiar with a particular chain, she could expect the same products and quality in Columbus, Georgia, that she received in Springfield, Massachusetts, and everywhere in between. In theory, creating a national corporate identity for a fast-food chain should have made the existence of varied service policies—especially discriminatory policies—difficult, unreasonable, and embarrassing. White southerners should have had to work hard to maintain white supremacy and segregation in these public spaces.

White supremacy and racial segregation nevertheless prevailed, especially in the South, in the earliest years of fast food. At that time, national corporations tended to leave policies related to the human interactions in these public spaces to the discretion of the local manager or franchisee and to community law or custom. In his 2001 critique, *Fast Food Nation*, Eric Schlosser points out that even today McDonald's regulates all aspects of its operations, down to the diameter of the pickles on the hamburgers, but nevertheless allows local managers to handle employee-related issues, such as wages, hours, and benefits. According to Schlosser, this lenience allows local wage rates to prevail, virtually eliminates overtime for most hourly workers, and inhibits union influence.[35]

In the 1950s and 1960s the chain used the same laissez-faire approach to customer relations, allowing local law, custom, and manager preference to dictate service to African Americans. No doubt, white southern entrepreneurs who started fast-food chains and purchased national franchises recognized the propensity for such spaces to maintain the well-established racial mores. There is little evidence of how black southerners might have negotiated the walk-up service windows that all customers used in the early years of fast-food service. But discriminatory customs that had prevailed for decades in southern stores, dictating that whites be served before black customers, may have also regulated the racial interactions at the McDonald's service counter.[36] Also, automobiles and suburban shopping centers encouraged proprietors to build away from downtown areas. In the postwar era, white southerners tended to move away from the cities into the suburbs. The locations of the restaurants and residential segregation thus may have limited black access to these public spaces. Wilber Hardee located his first Hardee's hamburger restaurant near the whites-only East Carolina College.[37] From the beginning of Kroc's expansion, McDonald's focused on suburban areas for franchise locations.[38]

There is no doubt that segregation and discrimination existed at McDonald's locations and at other chains in the South. Three years after activists, merchants, and city officials negotiated to desegregate the downtown lunch counters in Greensboro, North Carolina, students staged a stand-in demonstration at the local McDonald's, which—despite lacking a dining room—refused to allow equal service.[39] When McDonald's implemented indoor seating, in the midst of civil rights sit-in activism, many southern franchisees insisted on racial segregation even when other local eateries had abolished the practice. In Pine Bluff, Arkansas, during the summer of 1963 local civil rights activists called for a national boycott of McDonald's when the local franchisee obtained an injunction requiring them to cease their direct action campaigns at the restaurant. According to the periodical of the Student Nonviolent Coordinating Committee, the *Student Voice*, most Pine Bluff business leaders had already integrated downtown lunch counters.[40]

Segregation had been a feature of chain dining across the country, as Woolworth's and other variety-store lunch counters had demonstrated, although these spaces undoubtedly created a conundrum for the well-established segregation laws and racial customs that governed dining in public places in the South. By the 1960s Woolworth's slogan was "Everybody's Store," and in fact the retailer did allow African Americans to shop in its stores.[41] Black southerners spent their hard-earned money on toiletry items, home décor, and similar low-cost products at Woolworth's and other five-and-dimes. Yet they could not dine at the lunch counter alongside white customers. In these chains, local control over service policies allowed segregation to prevail wherever local law or custom—or the discretion of local management—dictated discrimination. As early as the 1940s, the civil rights group the Congress of Racial Equality (CORE) attempted to use the national reach of these lunch counters to force desegregation, but CORE soon recognized the strength of local custom.

In Baltimore, CORE tried to influence racial policies by pressuring stockholders and officers of national chains and by encouraging picketing at locations in African American neighborhoods. In 1953 CORE conducted months of sit-ins at the lunch counter at Grant's variety store in Baltimore. Several Grant's locations changed their policies in light of the protests, apparently with some interference from the national offices, but the manager of at least one location remained "hostile." In an effort to end the stalemate, the CORE leader Bayard Rustin met with a corporate officer, who maintained that lunch counter service was "completely a local matter." Rustin also suggested a sympathy boycott of Grant's in Harlem to support the Baltimore desegregation effort.[42] Efforts such as these were arduous, and contacting national offices had little impact on desegregation efforts. Like the five-and-dime lunch counters, the local franchisees of modern fast-food chains retained autonomy over service issues, which allowed segregation to continue.

Exacerbating the discriminatory effect of laissez-faire policies at the national level, many fast-food chains constructed national identities that reinforced white supremacy. McDonald's, for example, represented its target customer as a white, middle-class, Protestant family. From the start of his operations, Kroc prohibited pay telephones, jukeboxes, and vending machines in order to discourage loitering or disruptions that he thought would "downgrade the family image."[43] Corporate portraits illustrating McDonald's idealized operations reveal the significance of the white middle-class family to the company's identity. In 1963 the inside cover of McDonald's first annual report depicted a colored drawing of the original drive-in as conceived by the brothers in the 1950s. The image portrays the red-and-white tiled structure and its large, overhanging golden arches on either side. The customers consist entirely of white, well-dressed, well-behaved families, who park their modern automobiles at the side of the building and walk to the service window.[44] Later, the chain increased the family feel of the company by introducing the new slogan "The Closest Thing to Home."[45] Yet, at least in the South, only whites would be entirely welcomed into this home.

A more nationalized southern food culture combined with a population mobilized increasingly by automobiles could have contributed to more democratic foodways even in the South. But in spite of the great changes that followed World War II, or perhaps because of them, white southerners worked hard to maintain segregation culture in public eating places. The lower prices and accessibility of fast-food franchises implied egalitarianism, but the chains maintained the exclusivity to which white southern diners had grown accustomed. Changing social mores, including suburbanization and the automobile culture, assisted this process—as did corporate cultures that respected local customs in their service policies and imagined their ideal customer as white.

Still, in the economic expansion of the postwar period a growing number of African Americans achieved the middle-class milestones of car ownership and dining out. Black restaurants and cafés continued to serve this market, but locating them in unfamiliar areas remained a challenge. Seeking service at the wrong restaurant in the wrong area of the South could be a dangerous error for black travelers. For many reasons, dining among them, African Americans did not get to enjoy all the benefits of middle-class status. This situation, as well as a desire to expand democracy in the public sphere, contributed to a rise in civil rights activism in the postwar period. In the 1960s much of that activism played out in the region's public eating places as dining out became more overtly political.

PART 3
The Civil Rights Revolution, 1960–1975

IN 1954, WHEN AN Alabama native and high school freshman named John Lewis read about the Supreme Court decision in *Brown v. Board of Education of Topeka*, he was elated. "No longer would I have to ride a broken-down bus almost forty miles each day to attend classes," he recalls in his memoir. "Come fall I'd be riding a state-of-the-art bus to a state-of-the-art school." But he searched in vain for news of Alabama's plans to desegregate its public schools. The next year, he followed a more tragic story—the murder of Chicago teen Emmett Till, who had been tortured and killed in the Mississippi Delta for transgressing racial norms by allegedly whistling at a white woman.[1]

These two events profoundly influenced the collective memory of a generation of young black men and women. *Brown* represented the hope of a better life and future for African Americans, who would no longer be limited by the constraints of Jim Crow. Yet Till's murder the following year reminded all that the culture of segregation could not be changed with a stroke of the Supreme Court's pen. Six years after *Brown*, Lewis and his generation had graduated from the same Jim Crow schools. As college students, they pooled their collective frustration with the slow pace of progress and released it in a long-term, broad-based movement to eradicate racial segregation.

Segregation, however, would not end easily. In many restaurants, the culture of race-based eating practices proved strong. Many white proprietors called on their constitutional and providential rights to discriminate based on race. These entrepreneurs recognized that their white customers received certain intangible benefits from the exclusivity—eating their barbecue with a side order of segregation. They openly worried that white southerners would stop eating out if the restaurants took discriminatory practices off the menu. This contrast—between activists who interpreted equality in the consumer sphere as a citizenship right and white supremacists who considered segregation to be a property right—set the basis for the construction of whiteness in the American South in the latter part of the twentieth century.

CHAPTER FIVE

The Politics of the Lunch Counter

In November 1959 a group of black Nashville college students approached the Harvey's department store lunch counter, where a white waitress refused to seat them. The group's leader, a Fisk University student named Diane Nash, asked to speak to the manager, who reiterated the store's policy against serving black customers. After a polite exchange, the students left the store. This brief incident was a test. The students knew the lunch counter would deny them service, and they did not plan to push the issue at that time. Testing the equality of service at downtown lunch counters was the first step in a long-term plan by the Nashville Student Movement, a well-organized group of determined activists from area colleges, to end racial exclusion at Nashville's lunch counters. Before starting these tests, the students trained for almost a year by analyzing the fundamental tenets of nonviolent protest, learning the processes of direct action campaigns, and role-playing the use of nonviolence in real-world scenarios.[1]

The tests confirmed that, although these stores eagerly accepted black trade at their cash registers, the managers of the lunch counters refused to provide equal service to African Americans. Some stores served African Americans at a stand-up counter, but they could not sit down at the main counter, which was available exclusively to whites. In January 1960, after the students returned from their semester break, the Nashville Student Movement planned a full-scale assault on lunch counter discrimination. Such an initiative would take time. They had to train hundreds of volunteers in the principles and practices of nonviolence. They had to organize the students into groups. Each group needed a leader who could speak for the movement. They had to decide which lunch counters to target and how to react to white resistance. They needed to make dozens of decisions: Would arrested students accept bail? Would they pay fines for violating unjust laws? Who would put up the money? Who would represent the students in court? The preparations would take months.[2]

Then, on February 1, 1960, four students at the historically black North Carolina A&T State University—unrelated to the Nashville Student Movement—demanded service at the Woolworth's lunch counter in Greensboro, North Carolina. Franklin McCain, Ezell Blair Jr., Joseph McNeil, and David Richmond purchased several small items at the register and then sat at the counter to order a cup of coffee. Unlike the Nashville students at Harvey's almost three months earlier, when white waitresses refused to serve the Greensboro Four, they refused to leave. As news of the events at Greensboro spread, so too did the newly coined term "sit-in" to describe this type of protest. During the first week of February 1960, more students held sit-ins in nearby Winston-Salem and Durham.[3]

These developments changed the Nashville Student Movement's plans. Greensboro and its aftermath reflected a strong desire among young people for equality at the table and a commitment to fight for these rights. The Nashville Student Movement fast-tracked its program and began sit-ins immediately.[4] The Greensboro sit-in had a similar effect on students all across the South. What had been a slow, methodical process for the Nashville students turned into a rather spontaneous popular uprising across the region as student activists from Richmond to Miami to Austin took their seats at downtown lunch counters.

Although most southern cities discriminated against African Americans in public accommodations—including parks, theaters, restaurants, and hotels—the fact that these first publicized sit-ins took place at lunch counters was not happenstance. Discrimination at downtown lunch counters represented an immediate problem for black communities in the South. Black women, especially, spent a lot of time and money in stores with lunch counters. Proprietors gladly accepted their money for consumer goods, but black customers had no place to rest their feet, grab a cup of coffee, or eat a quick lunch. A trip to the store was a lesson in the region's racial hierarchy since the discrimination forced black mothers to explain to pleading children why they could not stop for a treat.

Lunch counter activism symbolized more than access to a tasty snack, however, for those who met in Raleigh in April 1960 to form the Student Nonviolent Coordinating Committee (SNCC), a new organization designed to coordinate the student sit-ins. The civil rights veteran Ella Baker encapsulated the greater meaning of lunch counter sit-ins when she famously informed the new members of SNCC that their mission was "bigger than a hamburger." For Baker, SNCC, and black southerners in general, consumer equality was the means by which they would claim their rights as Americans.[5] After World War II, as American incomes grew and consumerism expanded, national citizenship became increasingly identified with the ability to consume goods and services.[6]

Sit-ins illuminated a conflict between two different visions of citizenship and two opposing views of southern culture. Civil rights activists believed in a common humanity that gave all Americans the right to participate in consumerism and politics, both of which they connected to democracy. White supremacists, on the other hand, held an understanding of African Americans as inherently different and resisted, often with violence, any action toward dismantling the racial hierarchy on which this difference was constructed. Southern whites often displayed their views in counterdemonstrations that used the Confederate battle flag as a symbol of white supremacy and hostility toward sitters-in.

By 1960 this conflict had already played out publicly in other contexts, including at schools in Little Rock, Arkansas, and on buses in Montgomery, Alabama.[7] As two of the earliest southern institutions to establish formal, or de jure, segregation, education and transportation were touchstones for segregation culture. But the attempt to desegregate public eating places moved African Americans forward in the quest for equal access to southern spaces and consumer culture. The students involved in the sit-in activism were often well trained, well organized, and well aware of their place in the history of peaceful dissent. But they were also reactive and unconstrained by established rules—or the risks involved in breaking them. Their activism was an important step in deconstructing the laws and culture that sustained racial discrimination in all aspects of southern life.

Deciphering a Lunch Counter

The lunch counter is a distinctly urban space that allows a server to wait on many individual customers quickly and efficiently. Department stores and five-and-dimes located in downtown business districts featured lunch counters prominently in their spaces. The staff, usually white waitresses wearing starched uniforms and aprons, worked behind the counter, where they had easy access to the kitchen or grill, beverage dispensers, and other service items. Patrons perched on stools anchored to the ground in front of the counter. The counters physically separated servers from their customers while still allowing waitresses to take orders, answer questions, and serve patrons promptly by reaching across with food and drinks. Display cases often tempted customers with appetizing desserts.[8] The convenience and speed of lunch counter service accommodated a variety of urban workers, who needed to fit lunch into a thirty-minute break.

Lunch counters ranged from large U-shaped (or double U-shaped) arrangements that accommodated dozens of customers to simpler, straight bars that had room for fewer diners.[9] This structure meant that individual patrons came into intimate contact with each other at the lunch counter as they vied for elbow room, competed for servers' attention, and shared communal condiments. Lunch counters often appeared in cafés that also featured separate tables for larger parties. But most lunch counters were in department stores or five-and-dimes, where the shopping public could, all things being equal, sit down for a quick meal.

In the 1960s in the American South, however, all things were not equal. By 1960, thanks to decades of activism and the resilience of Montgomery's African American community, federal law required city buses to offer equal service.[10] But lunch counters resisted. Segregation is an imprecise term in all cases but especially when talking about lunch counters. Although generally defined as "separation," few segregated spaces involved a true separation of the races. Instead, the term segregation implies a careful performance of race-specific roles within the space. By the 1960s, white women staffed most downtown lunch counters, serving as the public face of the establishment as they took orders, served food, and accepted payment. Black women often prepared food in the kitchens in the back. White customers, who included businessmen, working girls, shoppers, students, and laborers, occupied the stools in front of the counter. Black customers, for the most part, stayed outside of the space of the lunch counter as they selected and completed purchases at the store's registers. Some stores offered a stand-up counter where African Americans could eat, maintaining their distinctly differentiated status.

Despite this segregation, black urbanites came into direct contact with the downtown lunch counter as a matter of course. African Americans, particularly women and their children, saw the lunch counter every time they shopped at the department store or five-and-dime—a near inevitability in post–World War II towns and cities. They had access to the shopping space and the main register to purchase goods from the store. They might be able to walk through the eating space to a stand-up counter or order takeout. But they could not sit down with white customers. At lunchtime, the alleys and curbs of southern downtowns were often filled with African Americans sitting outside to eat food prepared at home or purchased as takeout.[11] Such public lounging, necessitated by Jim Crow, reinforced the stereotype created by whites that African Americans were lazy.

A common theme of black southern memoirs is the efforts of black parents to shield their children from the indignities of segregation culture. W. Ralph Eubanks recalls that his college-educated parents raised their family on a farm rather than living in one of the designated black neighborhoods of Mount Olive, Mississippi, because the rural area better protected their children from Jim Crow. Eubanks writes that his parents created "a world of their own" on their eighty-acre farm. He refers to it as "an idyllic place where racism and intolerance had no place." Unlike the children growing up in the town's black neighborhoods, which white townspeople insulted with such racialized names as "The Quarters" and "The Jungle," Eubanks encountered the horrors of racial segregation only when he went to town. Because of his isolation and because his educated parents satisfied many of the family's needs on the farm, Eubanks grew up to consider the perception of racial inferiority to be the "exception" and not the harsh rule that it actually was in the American South.[12]

Yet most African American parents could not isolate their children from Jim Crow. The segregated lunch counter served as a constant reminder of the region's racial politics. As consumerism became a necessary part of urban life, black and white southerners shopped at downtown stores to satisfy their wants and needs. The low prices at the five-and-dime enabled the lower economic classes to purchase necessities and inexpensive luxury items. No one, of course, was required to visit the lunch counter. But the lunch counter's prominence in a space that had become so essential to urban life meant that black consumers came across it on a regular basis, even though race-based policies prohibited them from sitting down. Black mothers who shopped at the five-and-dime could not guard their children from this indignity. For young African Americans growing up in a southern town or city, the weekly shopping trip turned into a regular civics lesson on the politics of subordination.

At the same time, the nature of the lunch counter epitomized the more democratic character of post–World War II consumerism—for whites. Its purpose was to accommodate shoppers, workers, and professionals who had only brief lunch breaks. Waitresses simultaneously waited on multiple customers without having to move around the room. Menu items required little preparation and could be passed quickly across the counter. The low prices allowed lower-income workers to afford the fare. The combination of widespread accessibility mingled with racial exclusivity created a space committed to white consumer democracy.

"A Community within a Community"

No lunch counters epitomized these democratic tendencies more than those located at the Woolworth's five-and-dimes. Woolworth's relied on high volume and low margins. By the turn of the twentieth century, Woolworth's was a thriving national chain selling low-cost factory goods to an increasingly consumer-based society. Food service at the five-and-dime started with a highly popular candy counter, where patrons could get a quarter of a pound for five cents. Early attempts to sell snacks and non-alcoholic beverages were unsuccessful. In 1910, however, the New York City store opened the first "refreshment room." It boasted marble and glass tables, fine china, and linen tablecloths. Soon, every Woolworth's store offered food service in the form of either a sit-down restaurant or a stand-up counter.[13]

After World War II, the introduction of cheap, durable plastics changed the face of the Woolworth's lunch counter. Plastic counters and red plastic stools replaced the fine tables and chairs. Grilled hot dogs and chicken soup replaced fried oysters on the menu. These lunch counters, like those at other five-and-dimes, had greater meaning to some diners than simply a cheap meal. In her book about personal reminiscences of Woolworth's, *Remembering Woolworth's: A Nostalgic History of the World's Most Famous Five-and-Dime*, Karen Plunkett-Powell describes the ritual and ceremony of dining at the lunch counter: "For many families . . . eating at Woolworth's on Saturday afternoon was a tradition. It was part of the weekly lifestyle, right up there with Sunday church and Monday wash day. Often, the lunch counter took on the role of a central meeting place for members of the community, or a place of solace for the elderly. Across America . . . the local Woolworth's luncheonettes became a community within a community."[14] The inverse of these wistful memories, of course, is that anyone who did not have access to this urban space was explicitly left out of the "community." In the South, Woolworth's followed the local laws and customs that excluded African Americans. Plunkett-Powell's account lacks the voices of these southerners who could view, but not access, this privileged space.

That the sit-in movement started in 1960 at the Woolworth's lunch counter in Greensboro, North Carolina, is a result of the store's egalitarianism (for whites) and its ubiquitous nature in the mid-twentieth century combined with the commitment by the black community to access American democracy through their consumer power. The Nashville Student Movement deliberately based its decision to target lunch counters on the placement and function of these spaces. In the year leading up to the sit-ins, the Nashville Christian Leadership Conference sponsored coffee hours with local African Americans to discuss the needs of the community. Black women in particular identified segregation at downtown lunch counters as a critical hardship, because of their regular shopping trips. Unlike the earlier rural culture, when women manufactured necessities at home, made seasonal visits to the store, or did without, the modern consumer culture demanded frequent trips to purchase food, toiletries, clothing, school supplies, and other consumer goods. Although the black community remained disproportionately poor compared to whites, African Americans made significant contributions to downtown economies with their purchases at these stores.[15] The frequent presence of African Americans, particularly women, in and around these spaces of racial exclusivity positioned lunch counters as an appropriate place to initiate activism.

Sit-In Precedents

Although Greensboro spawned a new energy among college students for equal rights, the sit-in movement had precursors. In the 1930s labor activists developed the sit-down strike as an alternative to picket lines. In a sit-down strike, workers occupy the factory floor but refuse to perform any work. In an era when labor unions remained illegal in many states and received little protection from the federal government, this tactic gave employees greater physical security than picketing outside the plant and limited the employer's ability to bring in new workers to break the strike. Also, unlike a picket line, the sit-down strike did not rely on the participation of every single worker.[16]

The best-known sit-down strike took place in Flint, Michigan, from December 1936 to February 1937, when workers occupied several General Motors plants. The turning point came when union leaders used diversionary tactics to hold manufacturing plant No. 4, which supplied motors to all Chevrolet automobiles. Leaders leaked the news that they planned to occupy manufacturing plant No. 9, one of many factories that supplied autobody parts. When General Motors moved its security forces to protect plant No. 9, the strikers successfully occupied plant No. 4 and shut down General Motors' operations. Almost two weeks later, the company ended the strike by agreeing to recognize the union.[17]

The success of a sit-down strike required significant discipline. Opponents of this strategy—including company officials, community members, and some workers—attributed the tactic to communists and criticized it as a violation of property rights, but there is no evidence that any actual communists promoted or participated in the Flint strike. One former General Motors employee, Floyd Root, compared the strategy to entering a person's home, throwing the owner out, and refusing to leave. Sit-down strikes also required a lot of organization. Participants formed committees that attended to strikers' personal needs, furthered union objectives, and protected company property.[18]

The successful sit-down strikes throughout the automobile industry encouraged other workers to implement this strategy. In Detroit, Woolworth's female sales clerks—referred to as "counter girls"—whose responsibilities included maintaining the display counters, making change, and looking pretty, went on strike with a list of demands. They wanted union representation, seniority rights, free uniforms and laundering, shorter hours, and higher wages. These working women, whose labor contributed to Woolworth's success, had previously presented these demands to the store manager in a less formal manner, to no avail. They worked hard for little remuneration: fifty to fifty-five hours per week for miniscule wages. The store's founder, Frank Woolworth, had purposely hired an all-female sales force in order to keep labor costs low. A male manager often dictated a counter girl's career path based on whether he considered her to be attractive or charming.[19]

The Detroit Woolworth's strike commenced on a Saturday in February 1937 during the store's busiest hours, with many customers mid-purchase. Organizers barred the doors and offered management their demands. Female strikers occupied the store. Woolworth's upper management initially responded with defiance. The district superintendent for Detroit refused to negotiate and threatened to lock out employees at Woolworth's other stores in the city. Union organizers responded by closing down a second, smaller store with a sit-down strike as well. The strikers slept on the sales floor—three to a mattress under brightly colored blankets provided by the union. After a week of the strikers occupying the two stores and threatening to expand the strike, Woolworth's capitulated. Management agreed to all the strikers' demands—a forty-hour work week, pay raises (including time and a half for overtime), free uniforms and laundering, and union recognition. Woolworth's agreed to extend these benefits to every store in the city and even to the hourly male cooks, who had not participated in the strike.[20]

The success of sit-down strikes as a labor strategy encouraged the Congress of Racial Equality (CORE), founded in 1942, to adapt this technique to civil rights activism. Many of CORE's early leaders had backgrounds in labor organizing, so they understood the power of the sit-down tactic. CORE focused especially on using the sit-down strike technique to desegregate restaurants outside the South. Although northern states generally lacked formal racial segregation laws, segregated eating had emerged as African Americans migrated to northern cities. A combination of local management, community custom, and general apathy supported segregation outside the southern states. But without the same history of vicious racism and without the urgent need to uphold white supremacy at all costs, northern eating places tended to be less rigorous in their application of racial segregation.

In 1949 members of the CORE affiliate in Appleton, Wisconsin, called downtown eating places to determine each establishment's racial policies. They found that every café discriminated in some way, but no absolute rule prevailed. Some places refused to serve African Americans altogether; one café offered to serve black customers at the back door; and others conditioned their acceptance of black customers on the manner and occupation of the individual in question, agreeing to serve the "well-bred . . . member of an orchestra," for example.[21] In some ways, Appleton resembled a southern town because its café operators identified race as an important point of differentiation in the consumer sphere. But the flexibility demonstrated by Appleton's café owners in this survey did not exist in the South. This pliancy, common in many northern communities, allowed CORE to pursue equality in eating places outside the South with some success, but with relatively little publicity, in the postwar period.

CORE adopted different methods of direct action, all of which had been common to labor disputes up until that point, and applied them to the campaign for civil rights in public spaces. These actions provided important precedents for later civil rights activism. The first step in a direct action campaign included testing local restaurants by the use of integrated groups of customers. CORE would send into a restaurant two or three groups with different combinations of black and white, male and female, to ascertain whether a particular eatery would serve the group. A single white customer or a white group usually followed to observe. If the testing revealed racial discrimination, CORE would attempt direct negotiations with the owner or manager and, as a last resort, organized boycotts, pickets, and sit-down strikes (only later referred to as "sit-ins"). Later, SNCC adopted these techniques to pursue equal opportunity in the southern consumer sphere.

CORE's early experiences were in many ways similar to SNCC's later activism. Both organizations identified downtown, quick-order eating places as important spaces in which to pursue consumer equality. Although the organization was committed to ending racial segregation wherever it existed, CORE's annual surveys reveal that local affiliates tended to focus on the desegregation of public eating places. In Denver, a CORE affiliate reported, "Most of our work had been concentrated on breaking racial discrimination in restaurants." Philadelphia CORE identified as that year's "greatest specific accomplishment" the testing of fifty restaurants in the city center and the "distribution of the results."[22]

Because no consistent patterns of segregation existed in northern eateries, CORE found a wider range of conditions than activists would encounter a decade later in the South. CORE activists might find a number of eating places that practiced no discernable discrimination; they might find a segregation stronghold; or, more likely, the circumstances fell somewhere in between. In Columbus, Ohio, for example, a group of three African Americans and seven whites tested two restaurants. They experienced no discrimination in the first, but the second eatery refused to serve the black customers. The waiter attempted to close the restaurant. When the group protested and refused to leave, the waiter called the police. Two black police officers responded to the call. The policemen listened to the activists' account and suggested they sue the restaurant for discrimination.[23]

CORE also attempted negotiation as a step toward desegregation outside the South. Describing efforts to integrate the White Coffee Pot chain, Helen W. Brown explains, "In accordance with our usual practice, we first met with Myles Katz, the owner of the chain to try to effect a change in policy through negotiations." When this approach proved unsuccessful, CORE began a series of sit-down strikes and pickets in and around the restaurant's locations.[24] At other times, negotiation worked. In 1948 CORE successfully desegregated the Tea Cup, a Chinese American restaurant in Berkeley, California. CORE activists had realized by talking with the manager that he refused to serve African Americans because he worried about losing white trade. After two months of negotiations and testing with varying degrees of success, the manager capitulated and changed his discriminatory policies. The process took the time and effort of dedicated activists, but did not require mass demonstrations. CORE focused on communicating with the manager and reassuring him through a combination of reason, demonstration, and persistence that he could maintain his business with an integrated customer base.[25]

The negative consequences for activists escalated as lunch counter protests moved southward. In 1950 the CORE affiliate in Bartlesville, Oklahoma, focused primarily on equal employment. A small cadre, including the town's white librarian, Ruth W. Brown, and two of her African American friends, decided to integrate the local drugstore's lunch counter. The waitress refused to serve the group, and they left peacefully. After the attempt, CORE's Bartlesville membership decreased to only five white members. Only a few CORE members agreed to participate in the "drugstore project," as Brown termed it, likely because they feared retribution. They had good reason to fear. After the town council confronted Brown, asking whether she had accompanied black women to the drugstore—"where they weren't supposed to be"—they fired her.[26] The Bartlesville project reveals that lunch counter protests farther south put CORE members in greater jeopardy than did demonstrations in other sections of the country. Brown's dismissal foreshadowed the struggles that activists faced after Greensboro. Everywhere in the South, the sitters-in risked their educations, positions, and physical security as the result of their direct action campaigns at lunch counters and cafés.

The Sit-In

CORE created the model for sit-in activism, and the student members of SNCC adapted it for the southern environment. Knowledge of the sit-ins spread through firsthand accounts and newspapers. The Nashville students learned of the Greensboro sit-in within days of its February 1, 1960, occurrence. The Reverend Douglas Moore, the minister at Durham, North Carolina's Asbury Temple Methodist Church, called James Lawson, a Vanderbilt seminary student, to discuss the Greensboro situation. Both Moore and Lawson had been holding nonviolence workshops for college students in their respective cities. Moore drove the fifty miles to Greensboro to witness the students gathering at the lunch counters. By February 3, under Moore's leadership, students began sit-ins at Durham's downtown lunch counters.[27]

John Lewis followed the events in Greensboro and elsewhere through the *Nashville Tennessean*'s coverage. He describes the moment in his memoir: "I felt a rush—not one of those 'I can't believe it' responses, but rather a feeling of 'Well, of *course.*' I *could* believe it."[28] He could believe it because he shared the feelings of the Greensboro students: something had to be done to eliminate Jim Crow and, as omnipresent symbols of oppression and disfranchisement, lunch counters were the place to start. Nashville students began sit-ins at local lunch counters on Saturday, February 13.

Although more organized than most other communities, especially in the beginning, Nashville's sit-in experience was typical. Students gathered at the First Baptist Church, which had served for more than a year as the site of Lawson's workshops and would continue to serve as a civil rights headquarters in the city. Students dressed in their nicest clothes. Lewis wore the light blue suit he had purchased for his high school graduation, which he recalls would become a "trademark of sorts for me in the years to come."[29] The students traveled to lunch counters in groups of twenty-five, each with a designated leader to serve as the spokesperson. On the first day, Nashville students targeted lunch counters at Woolworth's, McLellan's, and Kress—all located along Fifth Avenue, Nashville's busiest shopping corridor. The activists made small purchases. Then, they sat at the lunch counter. The middle-aged white waitresses noticed the new customers but refused to serve them. Lewis recalls that the waitresses seemed nervous and scared but not hostile. A few minutes after the activists sat down, a waitress placed a handwritten sign reading "Counter Closed" on the lunch counter. They turned off the lights and left. The same thing happened at all three lunch counters. The students pulled out schoolbooks and studied. They stayed for several hours, suffering only a few racial taunts from whites. At 6 p.m. a runner from the church brought a message to the activists at each of the three department stores, telling them that it was time to leave.[30]

As the students continued their sit-ins, the black community supported their efforts by boycotting downtown stores. The boycott was a common civil rights tactic in streetcar and bus demonstrations. Over the next four years, it became a useful strategy for communities attempting to desegregate public spaces and advocating for racially fair hiring practices. Boycotts were a great tool for black communities because downtown economies depended on black money for their survival—especially after whites began to leave downtown areas for the suburbs. In Nashville, one estimate suggested that black trade was worth $10 million at downtown stores in 1960. In this case, economic withdrawal was the "best weapon they had at their disposal," according to an NBC report. As the primary buyers in their families, black women in particular provided significant support in the boycott. Wearing stockings with runs, buying a coat at the thrift store, and wearing old clothes at the Easter church service that year represented political statements to demonstrate solidarity with student sit-ins.[31]

Civil rights activists demonstrating at southern eating places also attempted diplomacy with store managers and city officials, but negotiations did not always take place smoothly or cooperatively. The actions of white and black mediators were more inhibited in the South. The threat of violence against activists and of retaliation against white moderates often constrained negotiations. In 1960 activists attempted to meet with Birmingham mayor James Morgan to discuss lunch counter desegregation. City officials ejected them from city hall before they could state their case.[32] It would be another three years before the civil rights movement brought Birmingham officials to the bargaining table—and that was in the midst of massive demonstrations by African Americans and retaliatory violence on the part of white authorities. After months or years of dedicated sit-in activism in southern localities, negotiations often helped to ameliorate discrimination in isolated situations and led to localized desegregation. In Greensboro, the city that triggered the sit-in movement in February 1960, store managers agreed to desegregate downtown lunch counters the following autumn. But citywide, the process was incomplete. In 1963 students continued protests against segregated eating places elsewhere in the city.[33]

White city officials worried about white reactions to desegregation. In Atlanta, after more than six months of active demonstrations at downtown lunch counters and grills, Mayor William B. Hartsfield and student activists agreed to a thirty-day "truce," during which the mayor agreed to work with store managers to find "an ultimate solution" to the problem of segregated eateries. Other cities, like Birmingham during the demonstrations in the spring of 1963, formed biracial committees to consider desegregation. In Nashville, the students recruited well-respected white women in the community to eat at desegregated downtown lunch counters to show that whites would continue to patronize these spaces. The mediated desegregation of southern eating places often took place quietly to avoid white counter-demonstrations and violence. The African American students did not mind such discretion. Their goal was justice and equality, not public victory.[34]

Legal Challenges

Students who participated in sit-ins risked their safety and their educations. This latter threat was significant, especially for the many first-generation college students and scholarship recipients who advocated for justice at the lunch counter. In some states, white authorities threatened the funding of state-financed black colleges that failed to take a hard line against student protestors. The sit-in movement led to complicated showdowns among students, college administrators, and state officials. These conflicts had enduring implications for student rights in higher education. In the short term, however, they affected the path of the movement, the lives of the students involved, and the civil rights of the larger African American community.

The circumstances surrounding the lunch counter activism of students at the historically black Alabama State College in Montgomery exemplify these tendencies. On February 25, 1960, Alabama State students staged a sit-in at the whites-only grill at the Montgomery County courthouse. In response, the grill closed for the day. But Alabama governor John Patterson attempted to quash further protests by threatening to close the school if Alabama State did not expel the participating students. Undeterred, the students warned school officials of a mass walkout in the event of any expulsions. They informed state officials that they would apply for admission to tax-supported white institutions if the state closed their school. Students reportedly chanted, "If we can't go to Alabama, we'll go to Auburn," referencing the all-white, publicly funded Auburn University.

Despite such threats, the Alabama Board of Education, with Governor

Patterson at its helm, expelled the nine sit-in leaders and suspended another twenty participants. Patterson justified the disciplinary action as a matter of public safety, but his language revealed his antagonism toward the activists and his racial animosity. Patterson described the protestors as "arrogant"—coded language for African Americans who stepped outside the places that white culture constructed for them. The Montgomery police chief, L. B. Sullivan, criticized the college faculty for encouraging "hate and racial bitterness." Press reports contributed to the negative, racialized depictions of the participants by describing the well-organized activists as "frenzied" and "wildly cheering."[35] Such characterizations by the governor, police officials, and the press contributed to a mainstream understanding of the students as "others" who should be excluded from public eating places because, in Patterson's words, they "couldn't behave." Patterson suggested that further demonstrations could lead to "riot, injury, and possible death."[36] He apparently did not consider that the simpler act of desegregating the grill could eliminate these possibilities as well.

Despite white southern antagonism, their fellow students, the local black community, and national activists supported those who had been expelled. Approximately one thousand students at Alabama State boycotted classes to protest the expulsions. Student demonstrations related to the boycott resulted in around thirty arrests. At nearby Tuskegee Institute, traditionally considered a more conservative black college, students staged a sympathy walkout. At the end of the winter term, when the expulsions became effective, Alabama State reported that around nine hundred students, almost 40 percent of the student body, had not registered for the next quarter.[37]

In Montgomery, the Dexter Avenue Baptist Church, which had served as the headquarters for the bus boycott four years earlier, organized a prayer meeting at the state capital to oppose the expulsions. State troopers, local police officers, sheriff's deputies, and white civilian counter-protestors disrupted the peaceful demonstration. National backers pledged tuition support for the expelled students to attend other colleges. Local activists encouraged the Alabama State students to register to vote and to encourage their parents to do the same.[38] The words that Ella Baker would speak at a meeting the following month were foreshadowed in Montgomery: lunch counter activism was "bigger than a hamburger." These were not the actions of the "outside agitator" of the white supremacist imagination. Nashville and Montgomery show how a localized student sit-in led to widespread activism among the local black community.

The Alabama State incident also reveals the slow expansion of rights initiated by the sit-in movement. Bernard Lee, one of the student leaders expelled from Alabama State who later worked closely with Martin Luther King Jr. at the Southern Christian Leadership Conference, and five of the other expelled students filed suit against the state university. The students asserted that they had been denied notice of the reasons for the expulsions, were refused a hearing to determine the state's right to expel them, and were denied the right of an appeal. A federal circuit court decided in the students' favor. In *Dixon v. Alabama State Board of Education*, the court ruled that the state should have held a hearing before expelling the nine students. The enduring importance of the *Dixon* decision is the due process rights it conferred on college students in their relations with a public university. As a result of this case, universities cannot expel students for any reason without the benefit of a hearing and an appeals process. In 1961, however, *Dixon* was the first public recognition of rights for student activists. The federal circuit court acknowledged that students participating in sit-ins had rights that state officials could not abridge.[39] Although the decision did not stop white officials from using taxpayer dollars to pressure historically black colleges and universities to end student activism, it did force the state to work within different parameters.

After *Dixon*, southern authorities looked for more creative ways to punish student activism at predominately black institutions. In December 1961 Baton Rouge authorities made mass arrests of activists demonstrating against local segregated lunch counters. Among those arrested were several Southern University students. Despite pressure from white lawmakers, officials at the historically black college wavered on expelling the students, in part because the ruling in *Dixon* required a hearing first. The white Louisiana State Board of Education responded with a harsh and far-reaching tactic designed to circumvent this legal requirement: it closed Southern University until an unspecified date—at which time it would require all students to reapply for admission. This drastic measure was a roundabout way to expel the activists without a legal process and was an attempt to generate a general student fear of activism. The state forced every student off campus by 5 p.m. on the day of the announcement, leaving thousands of young people with no food, lodging, or transportation. The university reopened a month later and denied admission to the demonstration leaders.[40]

The threat of violence from white segregationists was another risk of sit-in activism. The 1963 sit-in at the Woolworth's in Jackson, Mississippi, became dangerous when white counter-protestors threatened the activists. In her memoir, Anne Moody recalls that she, Memphis Norman, and Pearlina Lewis, all students at the historically black Tougaloo College, entered the store through the rear entrance. They made small purchases at the register and sat down at the whites-only lunch counter. The Woolworth's in Jackson had a lunch counter in the back of the store for black customers, and a waitress directed the three activists to that location. They refused to move. By the time the waitresses closed the counter, television news crews had arrived to record the event. White students from a nearby high school came into the store. Several of the white students formed a noose with the rope that closed off the lunch counter and tried to put the noose around an activist's throat. As the activists bowed their heads to pray, Moody recalls, "all hell broke loose." White students threw Norman to the ground and kicked him in the head until blood ran from the corners of his mouth. Joan Trumpauer, a white Tougaloo student, took Norman's place at the counter. Several white counter-protestors dragged the activists from their stools, but Moody and her fellow activists made their way back to the lunch counter. The white segregationists attacked the African American students by pouring ketchup, mustard, sugar, and other condiments from the counter over their heads and smearing their clothing. Moody recalls that she and the other activists endured three hours of such violence while ninety Jackson policemen watched through the window. The president of Tougaloo College finally ended the melee by escorting the activists out of the store.[41]

In Jacksonville, Florida, the violence did not stop when activists left the store. The NAACP Youth Council organized sit-in demonstrations in Jacksonville in August 1960. After two weeks of sitting-in at a downtown Woolworth's, they chose to demonstrate at the W. T. Grant department store, several blocks away from the city center. Like the Woolworth's in Jackson and in Jacksonville, Grant's had a "colored" lunch counter located away from the space designated for whites. The young demonstrators sat at the whites-only counter. After the sit-in, the activists exited Grant's and saw a white mob armed with heavy ax handles approaching them. The white seg-regationists swung the ax handles at every African American on the street—regardless of whether they had participated in the demonstration. "We had tried to prepare for most scenarios," sit-in leader Rodney L. Hurst recalls in his memoir, "but nothing prepared us for an attack as vicious as this." Most of the African Americans on the street ran for safety. Hurst believes that the Jacksonville police knew about the segregationists' attack beforehand.[42]

In addition to school expulsion and violence, sit-in activists faced arrest and conviction because of their violation of state and local laws. In the long run, the legal cases that arose from these situations brought about the end of segregated eating practices, but the process was difficult. The earliest sit-ins tended to target national chains and department stores, such as Wool-worth's, S. H. Kress, or Rich's, in which store managers had no proprietary interest.[43] The managers generally refused to serve African Americans based on community customs and local laws. Most managers responded to sit-ins by closing the counter, ordering all customers to leave the premises, and calling the police. At that point, local authorities often charged the nonvio-lent activists with criminal trespass or disturbing the peace.

On August 9, 1960, the arrest of ten black students at the local Kress de-partment store in Greenville, South Carolina, followed this pattern. James Peterson, Doris Wright, and the other students requested service at the lunch counter. G. W. West, the Kress store manager, closed the dining area. Three Greenville police officers arrived shortly, arrested the activists, and charged them with violating a state trespass law. Unlike racial segregation laws, criminal trespass did not explicitly refer to race. South Carolina's tres-pass law, amended in 1960, prohibited anyone from remaining on private property after being asked to leave. In reaction to sit-in activism, many states had amended their trespass statutes to give white authorities greater power to arrest activists. Convictions under South Carolina's trespass law subjected violators to thirty days in jail or a $100 fine.[44] Racial segregation laws, in comparison, were generally categorized as business licensing ordi-nances or health codes, not as criminal laws.

Sit-in arrests were problematic in the South because racial segregation ordinances represented "state action," which, unlike the "private conduct" of individual restaurant owners, implicated the activists' equal protection rights under the Fourteenth Amendment. The distinction between state action and private conduct stems from the *Civil Rights Cases* (1883), which invalidated the Civil Rights Act of 1875. Congress had passed this Reconstruction-era law to require equal service in theaters, railroads, and other places of public accommodation pursuant to its power under the newly enacted Fourteenth Amendment. Among other things, the Fourteenth Amendment requires states to provide equal protection under the law. It was intended to ensure that emancipated slaves shared the rights of citizenship. The *Civil Rights Cases* were a group of lawsuits, each brought by an African American plaintiff who had been denied service in a place of public accommodation in violation of the 1875 act. The Supreme Court decided against the black plaintiffs and invalidated the law because it regulated the "private conduct" of independent business owners to select their customers. The Court ruled that constitutional principles did not regulate such private actions.[45]

Almost eighty years later, in a 1961 case brought by an African American customer against a Delaware eatery, the Court applied this distinction to restaurant discrimination and held that only state action, and not private conduct, violated the equal protection clause of the Fourteenth Amendment.[46] Two years later, in *Peterson v. City of Greenville*, a case resulting from the Greenville, South Carolina, trespass charges, the Supreme Court clarified that the existence of a city ordinance requiring the racial segregation of public eating spaces was sufficient to categorize any such discrimination by private restaurants as "state action," and therefore unconstitutional, because the proprietors could not act on the basis of their personal discretion.[47] This decision effectively dismantled legally sanctioned racial segregation in southern restaurants.

Individual restaurant proprietors, however, remained free to discriminate based on race so long as no state or local law compelled the practice. In Birmingham, the city moved to repeal the racial segregation ordinance, relying on a strong segregation culture to preserve the status quo at local eateries. Three days after the Court issued the *Peterson* decision, Birmingham's city attorney, J. M. Breckenridge, recommended repealing the restaurant ordinance "so it cannot be used to take away from private café, restaurant and lunch stand operators their freedom of choice in the selection of customers."[48] On July 23, 1963, the city council repealed its segregation laws.[49]

In *But for Birmingham: The Local and National Movements in the Civil Rights Struggle*, the historian Glenn T. Eskew interprets this repeal as an attempt to work toward desegregation. According to his research, black activists and white moderates cooperated in efforts that led to the slow, and sometimes awkward, desegregation of many eateries in and around the city following the city's violent reaction to the protests there in the spring of 1963.[50] Yet if effective desegregation had been the city's motive, there would have been little reason to act so quickly to repeal the ordinance. In a companion case to *Peterson*, the Court explicitly invalidated Birmingham's racial segregation law, making the repeal a moot point.[51] Breckenridge's memo identifies another motive for the repeal. The refusal to desegregate by many white Birmingham restaurateurs, like the McClungs, confirms that the repeal of Birmingham's ordinance served Breckenridge's stated purpose of placing the decision, at least temporarily, with white restaurant owners. Repealing the racial segregation law primarily represented a last-ditch effort by the city to sustain the practice of segregation in some local eating places.

Civil Rights Act of 1964

By 1964 segregation in the South's public eating places was an ambiguous concept. Many downtown areas had desegregated lunch counters as early as 1960. Some establishments had agreed to quiet desegregation on a limited basis to test the reaction of the white community. In other areas, especially in the Deep South, activists began to target some of the most intransigent restaurants with demonstrations. Black citizens negotiated dangerous terrain on a daily basis in order to identify which spaces they could safely occupy. Sit-in arrests had thousands of court cases pending. Business disruptions, threats of violence, and negative international publicity began to worry federal officials.

In response to all this, particularly the violence leveled at the demonstrators in Birmingham, President John F. Kennedy submitted a civil rights bill to Congress in June 1963.[52] Among the many provisions in the new bill, which would become the Civil Rights Act of 1964, Title II prohibited discrimination based on race in places of public accommodation. The act covered any public eating establishment if "a substantial portion of the food which it serves" moved through interstate commerce.[53] Although the Fourteenth Amendment gave Congress the power to legislate to ensure equal protection under the law, pursuant to the *Civil Rights Cases* Congress could not use that authority to regulate private businesses. To get around that restriction, Congress used its power to regulate businesses engaged in interstate commerce and removed the discretion the Supreme Court had left with white restaurant owners to discriminate based on race.

After Kennedy's assassination in November 1963, his successor, President Lyndon B. Johnson, called on Congress to pass the civil rights bill as a tribute to the slain president. In his 1964 State of the Union speech, Johnson recognized the interconnection among blacks and whites in the American polity. "Today, Americans of all races stand side by side in Berlin and in Viet Nam," the president noted. "They died side by side in Korea. Surely they can work and eat and travel side by side in their own country."[54] The House of Representatives already had the votes to pass the bill when Johnson came to office, but his personal intervention in the Senate and his unwavering certainty that the bill would become law helped to push it through Congress.[55]

Many civil rights activists, who had been harassed, beaten, and arrested for the past four years, criticized the act because it did not go far enough to ensure equality and justice. The sncc chairman and former Nashville Student Movement leader John Lewis declined an opportunity to witness the president sign the act and instead chose to continue his work in Greenwood, Mississippi, where county officials had cut off federal food assistance to the black community. Lewis describes his reaction to hearing that the bill was now law: "There was no sense of celebration. We were still in the middle of a war [in Mississippi]. . . . The news from Washington felt as if it were coming from another country, from a very distant place."[56] Nevertheless, this legislation represented the legal culmination of the sit-ins and the downtown boycotts. The law finally gave federal recognition and protection to the right of African Americans to equality in public eating establishments.

The Greensboro sit-ins were not the first time that civil rights activists used direct action to pursue equality in the public consumer sphere. Not only did

CORE use sit-ins as one of the tools in its arsenal to desegregate public eating places outside of the South in the 1940s, but a local civil rights group made up predominately of high school students had desegregated Oklahoma City lunch counters two years before Greensboro.[57] The sit-in was a shrewd tactic for this type of activism because occupying the lunch counter's seats demanded that the downtown stores pay attention to demonstrators. More important, however, student activists gained the attention of the local black community, who supported their efforts in many ways, such as boycotting downtown merchants.

The significance of Greensboro was that black, and some white, students across the nation recognized that they shared a similar desire to pursue equality. Students in Nashville and elsewhere not only shared this goal, but they had been actively planning to pursue sit-ins when the news of Greensboro broke. Lunch counters were an obvious target for this activism because of their ubiquity in the urban sphere. Students' sit-in activism caused a resurgence in civil rights activity that had an effect on every aspect of life in the South.

The Civil Rights Act of 1964 marked the culmination of these efforts. Criticized by some war-weary activists for failing to fix all the civil rights problems in the region, the Civil Rights Act went further than many would have thought possible just four years earlier. Title II of the act was a broad attack on segregated eating spaces across the country. It ended the uncertainty that had existed as the result of episodic successes in desegregation. Yet many white restaurateurs believed that the Civil Rights Act went too far and continued to resist desegregation in flagrant defiance of federal law.

CHAPTER SIX

White Resistance in Segregated Restaurants

John G. Vonetes, a white native of New York state, owned and operated two eating places near Petersburg, Virginia. Of Greek heritage, Vonetes had served as a U.S. intelligence officer during World War II. Although he did not grow up in the South, he acquiesced to the region's racial practices easily and suggested that other northern transplants in the area did so as well. Testifying before Congress against what would become the Civil Rights Act of 1964, he stated somewhat cryptically that white northern soldiers at nearby Fort Lee had "quickly come to enjoy the freedom, the collective privacy, the customs and the social safety of protective southern eating establishments." In other words, many white men enjoyed the elevated status and exclusivity they found in segregated restaurants. During questioning by the senators, Vonetes admitted that he regularly made exceptions for some black soldiers in uniform and did serve them, especially if they were eating with a large group.[1]

Vonetes ran the Lee House Diner, a white restaurant, which he described as "a modern, family-type facility." He also owned the Playboy Buffet, an establishment with "a collegiate-party type atmosphere," which specialized in pizza. According to his testimony, Vonetes had considered investing in a diner that catered to an all-black customer base but decided it would not be profitable. He resented the civil rights activism that had dominated the region in recent years and opposed the proposed legislation. Despite the overwhelmingly peaceful nature of civil rights activists, Vonetes imagined that the civil rights law would encourage black militancy. He imagined an outrageous scenario of an African American soldier at the door of the Lee

House Diner demanding, "Let me in or I shall return in full battlefield dress with my bayonet fixed, and show you."[2] Clearly, Vonetes, like many white segregationists, relied on the myth of the dangerous black man to support his political position.

Throughout his testimony, Vonetes relied on stereotypes of African Americans common to the white imagination, particularly the white southern imagination. He hired all black cooks but claimed that his African American employees could not stand the smell of the garlic they put in the Playboy Buffet's pizza sauce: "They cover their nostrils and they squirm." Vonetes used this characterization to justify his claim that the pizza joint would not survive with an integrated customer base. In his opinion, African Americans would not order pizza. Again relying on a racial stereotype, he suggested that "chitterling pizza" might be more profitable for a black establishment. He further claimed that desegregation would destroy the financial health of his businesses and "trammel [his] constitutional rights."[3] Vonetes offered no support for these claims other than racial stereotypes and white supremacist rhetoric.

Vonetes's racialized sentiments are surprising coming from a man who, as an assistant to Supreme Court justice Robert H. Jackson in the aftermath of World War II, witnessed the Nuremberg trials and therefore saw firsthand the tragic effects of racism and discrimination.[4] But his testimony as a whole is not unusual compared to the many similar claims of white southern restaurateurs, who feared and defied the public accommodation provisions in Title II of the Civil Rights Act of 1964. Across the South, many of the white male proprietors, who had mostly avoided sit-ins before 1964 because their establishments were located outside the city center, shared Vonetes's opinions. They used the U.S. Constitution and the Bible to advocate for what they considered to be their God-given property right to discriminate based on race.

For proprietors like John G. Vonetes and Ollie McClung, the co-owner of Ollie's Barbecue, the lunch counter sit-ins also brought into question an important aspect of white southern mythology: the maintenance of racial purity. Some of the most vocal defenders of restaurant segregation connected it to notions of miscegenation and racial purity. The white supremacists who clung to segregation the longest tended to own and operate family restaurants, which they treated like their own homes. For this reason, they made little distinction between the public and the private in their business practices. They interpreted civil rights victories as personal assaults on the white southern home and as a threat to the nature of whiteness. Civil rights activists, on the other hand, attacked segregation at lunch counters and other public eateries, confronting the decades-long connection between public food consumption and whiteness.

Massive Resistance

When the Birmingham city council repealed the city's segregation law in 1963, it did so with the express intention of allowing de facto segregation to continue. Ollie's Barbecue was among the many establishments that did not disappoint. The most virulent defenders of racial segregation in public eating places were independent white restaurant proprietors, like Ollie McClung Sr. and his son, who conducted business outside the city center. Ollie's and similar establishments continued to discriminate after most downtown eateries had agreed to desegregate through negotiation or force. They continued to segregate after the city repealed the segregation ordinance. They continued to segregate after Congress specifically prohibited racial discrimination.

Vonetes and the McClungs were not alone in their antagonism toward civil rights legislation. They were part of a significant segment of white restaurant owners who served as staunch defenders of racial segregation in public eating places, including Lester Maddox, who used the notoriety he received from resisting the civil rights law to catapult himself to the Georgia governor's mansion, and Maurice Bessinger, who flamboyantly resisted federal power and continued to sell barbecue in South Carolina until his death in 2014.[5] Exploring the lives and businesses of these three white supremacist restaurant owners provides insight into the intransigence of lesser-known but like-minded proprietors.[6]

The McClungs claimed that desegregation would destroy their business but did not go into detail about how this might happen. If all the nation's restaurants accepted black customers equally, as the law required, then it would seem that white customers, regardless of their inclinations, would have no choice but to patronize integrated restaurants. Nevertheless, the McClungs took great pride in controlling the human interactions in their restaurant as "stewards" for their white patrons. Their target customer base included white "business people and family trade." They did not allow alcohol or profanity on the premises and did not open on Sundays. At the trial opposing the civil rights law, Ollie McClung Sr. testified that he tried to maintain "a religious environment." He expressed his refusal to provide equal service to African Americans as a moral issue. "I would refuse to serve a drunken man or a profane man or a colored man or anyone who I felt would damage my business," he testified at the trial, "and I run a good, clean place there."[7] Such testimony suggests that the McClungs considered racial segregation to be a religious imperative.

The Atlanta cafeteria owner Lester Maddox professed a similar commitment to religion as his justification for refusing to serve African Americans. Maddox grew up in a working-class section of Atlanta. When the Great Depression hit, Maddox dropped out of high school and picked up various odd jobs to help support the family. He worked as a delivery boy, soda jerk, dental technician, and steel worker before deciding that his future lay in entrepreneurship. During World War II, he opened Lester's Grill, which served ice cream, sandwiches, soft drinks, and candy. He sold the grill for a profit and in 1947 opened a cafeteria called the Pickrick in a white blue-collar area of Atlanta. The specialty of the house was fried chicken. Maddox hired sixty-five employees, including forty-five African Americans. The Pickrick was located along a federal highway. In its early years, the cafeteria survived through the patronage of interstate highway travelers. When the state proposed rerouting the highway, Maddox battled Georgia officials to halt the plans. His actions saved the highway route and his restaurant business.[8]

Maddox refused to knowingly serve African Americans in any capacity at his restaurant. For its white customers, the Pickrick was an odd combination of impersonal cafeteria self-service and homey conviviality and welcome. Customers stood in line and placed their orders as they passed by employees who loaded the food onto trays. Sitting in the dining room, patrons might meet Maddox himself as he drifted around to refill coffee cups and iced tea glasses and to talk casually with his customers. Long-time patrons recall Maddox sitting down at dining room tables with patrons to visit and pass the time. After the midday rush, he and his wife, Virginia, ate lunch in the dining room. Maddox sponsored games and contests to encourage business and to make his customers feel at home. One time, he offered a $50 prize to the family who brought the youngest baby to the Pickrick. A young couple won when they stopped to eat with their three-week-old daughter.[9]

Throughout his ownership of the Pickrick, Maddox made little distinction between his personal political beliefs and his restaurant business. In 1949 he began running ads in the Saturday newspaper that he described as "a mix of commentary, political observations, opinions, and, of course, the Pickrick's menu and prices." He received both compliments and criticism for these ads, which he entitled "Pickrick Says." The newspaper's editors were among the ads' critics. Maddox saved his most vehement rhetoric for his fight against desegregation. Much of Atlanta's downtown was already integrated when the Pickrick experienced its first bout with activism in the spring of 1964. Seven activists, three white and four black, attempted to enter the Pickrick. Maddox physically manhandled one of the activists who, in accordance with nonviolent principles, did not resist but went limp and dropped to the floor. Maddox offered to pay his black employees $20 for each of the activists they could physically remove from the premises.[10]

Ironically, Maddox imagined himself as a freedom fighter in his battle against civil rights. He actively compared himself to the nation's founding fathers. "The men who framed our Constitution had to fight for their freedom," Maddox recalls in his autobiography, "and I was ready to fight for mine." Like the McClungs, he positioned his fight as one for private property rights and free enterprise, but he was not satisfied to confine this battle to the court system. On the afternoon of July 3, 1964, the day after President Johnson signed the Civil Rights Act, three African American ministers attempted to exercise their right to eat at the Pickrick. Lester Maddox and his son ran the activists off the restaurant's property. An Associated Press photographer captured the scene, showing Maddox holding a gun behind one activist and his son carrying a pickax handle. Ever the salesman, after this incident Maddox began selling pickax handles for $2 each. In an odd version of reality, Maddox recalls the incident as one in which he protected the rights of "every citizen, including the three men I chased off my property."[11] Not only did Maddox refuse to knowingly serve African Americans in his

FIGURE 8. Lester Maddox and son chase activists from the Pickrick Cafeteria on July 3, 1964. The day before, President Lyndon B. Johnson had signed the Civil Rights Act of 1964, which required restaurant desegregation. Associated Press Photo/Horace Cort.

cafeteria, but he used his antagonism toward the civil rights activists as performances of whiteness to maintain racial exclusivity in the public sphere.

The South Carolina barbecue master Maurice Bessinger equaled Maddox in both his contempt for desegregation and his flair for salesmanship. Bessinger was born on a family farm in rural South Carolina at the start of the Great Depression. In 1939 his father sold the family cow and used the proceeds to purchase a café in Holly Hill, South Carolina. From the time Bessinger was twelve years old, he worked full time at his father's café. He opened the café at five o'clock in the morning and served customers until it was time for him to go to school at eight. After school, he worked again until they closed, sometime between nine o'clock and midnight.[12] Bessinger recalls, "[Daddy] believed that running a business was the same as running a home . . . that the Constitution of our country gave him the right to treat his home and his business alike: namely, he was king of both. . . . He would not hesitate to protect his customers, his family and his business from any outside threat."[13] Bessinger professed religious beliefs similar to those of the

McClungs and Maddox. Although the Holly Hill café served beer, his father refused to serve "drunks." Later, the Bessingers stopped serving alcohol entirely and displayed a sign that read "No Drinking, No Profanity."[14]

The Bessingers' café served African Americans on a segregated basis, although it employed many black workers. Bessinger understood his African American employees as racial stereotypes. In his memoir, he describes Martha—no last name—an African American woman who washed dishes and cooked part time at his father's café, as "the spitting image of the woman on the Aunt Jemima boxes."[15] Bessinger's memories of his father reveal a man who interacted with his black employees in much the same way that whites typically acted toward African American domestic laborers. Bessinger's father gave them food he did not think was suitable to serve to his white customers, and he fired one black cook after accusing her of theft. Bessinger recalls that his father had regularly given the woman pans full of used grease, with which she made soap. One day, his father noticed that she had hidden a good center ham in the grease.[16] "Pan-toting" was a typical practice for black domestic servants, whose miniscule incomes barely supported their families, and theft was a common accusation that whites made against black servants.[17]

In the 1950s, after his father's death and his own stint in the army, Bessinger opened a small chain of restaurants in South Carolina that specialized in barbecue. His first establishment was the Piggie Park Drive-In. The building featured a large, upright pig wearing a chef's hat.[18] By the 1960s Piggie Park Enterprises consisted of five barbecue restaurants in various locations across the state and a small sandwich shop in Columbia. Bessinger used his restaurants to display his understanding of the unchanging racial mores in the region. One location featured a sign on the rooftop that said "Old South Barbeque." In the early 1960s, when other establishments in downtown Columbia desegregated, Bessinger refused to do so. He based his actions on his late father's belief that a man could run his business with the same level of control as he ran his home. In response, activists picketed for weeks along the street outside his sandwich shop. After the passage of the Civil Rights Act of 1964, Bessinger refused to comply with the federal law. Like the McClungs and Maddox, he filed suit. The Supreme Court in 1968 ordered Piggie Park Enterprises to desegregate in compliance with federal law.[19]

The McClungs, Maddox, and Bessinger shared many similarities. They served foods considered to be local specialties, prepared according to proprietary recipes. Their fare—barbecue in the case of the McClungs and Bessinger, and fried chicken in the case of Maddox—held contradictory cultural meanings for different groups of southerners. Traditionally, barbecue and fried chicken were rural foods consumed by both races. It was not uncommon for African American cooks to prepare both dishes for white and black consumption, or for black and white homemakers to serve these dishes to their families. Black entrepreneurs often profited financially from these dishes by serving them in their own stands and cafés. Black communities found empowerment in these foods, celebrating meaningful holidays with a barbecue or serving fried chicken as a special meal on Sundays after church. In the black community, chicken is often referred to as the "gospel bird." Yet, despite the fact that both races consumed barbecue and fried chicken, white southerners conjured negative stereotypes surrounding the black consumption of these foods, especially fried chicken.[20] The McClungs, Maddox, Bessinger, and other white southern entrepreneurs repackaged these rural foods, identified them as house specialties, and sold them for consumption by white urban southerners and their families.

In addition to the similarity of their foods and service, these proprietors shared backgrounds and world views. They were white male entrepreneurs who owned restaurants oriented toward white families. They attributed their success solely to their own hard work and business acumen, with no consideration of how their family resources or the privilege of whiteness might have contributed. The McClungs, for example, inherited a successful enterprise from the family patriarch, James McClung. Bessinger's father ran a successful café at the time of his death as well. Of the three, only Maddox was a first-generation entrepreneur, but he no doubt received financing, leasing, licensing, or other assistance necessary to establish a successful restaurant in part based on his white skin. In short, these entrepreneurs' hard work and commitment to private enterprise can be said to account for their success only as two of many other factors in their favor.

All three men refused to serve African Americans on an equal basis in their restaurants and attributed their refusal to a commitment to God, country, and private enterprise. They treated their business establishments much like their own domestic spaces. Many of their actions, such as personally refilling cups, chatting with customers, and ejecting guests, resembled actions they might have taken in their own homes. This attitude became problematic, however, when it came to asserting authority over human interactions in their places of business. The McClungs claimed the right to eject customers who uttered profanity or acted inebriated. Bessinger maintained a similar policy. In his memoir, he reaches back to an incident that took place sometime before World War II, when his father expelled a wealthy white patron from his café for drunkenness, in order to support his claim.[21] With their statements, the McClungs, Maddox, and Bessinger attempted to convince themselves, the press, the legislatures, the courts, and the general population that racial segregation was only one of several supposedly valid seating policies they employed in their private spaces.

By the 1950s and 1960s, however, the notion that private owners controlled these public spaces absolutely was a fiction. Public eating places were subject to a wide range of regulations, some of which applied to all business owners and some of which were tailored specifically to the food-service industry. A combination of federal, state, and local laws required restaurants to obtain business licenses, submit to health inspections, follow standardized wage and hour requirements, make monthly tax payments, and, importantly, respect laws that required racial segregation. There is no indication that the McClungs, Maddox, Bessinger, or any other white restaurant operator ever challenged the right of any state or locality to mandate racial segregation in these spaces, which they now claimed were beyond such regulation, a point that U.S. attorney general Robert F. Kennedy made during Senate hearings for the Civil Rights Act.[22] Despite this myriad of regulations, white proprietors used the myth of private space to justify discrimination and segregation.

The essential question, though, is why these white proprietors wished so fervently to exclude African American customers from public eating establishments. The answers to this question reveal important clues about the construction of whiteness and its connection to public dining in the mid-twentieth century. White supremacist restaurant owners compared the condition of race to profanity or drunkenness, all of which they considered appropriate bases for ejecting customers. These three conditions are similar in that they are all culturally constructed to some extent. There are no universal standards that determine which expressions are considered to be profane, how much drink will make one inebriated, or which persons are considered to be black. These determinations, much like segregation itself, are formations of community customs, laws, and (to a lesser extent) independent judgment. As cultural constructions, they are subject to change over space and time. But in any specific location or time period, they place a particular status on any individual who is assumed to fall into one of these constructed categories. The accused individual is marked as profane, as drunk, as black—and is categorized for all to recognize as such. Profane and drunk also imply a certain moral judgment. By including "black" on this list, these proprietors assigned a similar moral judgment to this status as well.

Status played a significant role in the strength of racial segregation in southern eating places. The McClungs, Maddox, and Bessinger hired many African Americans to work in their restaurants, as did many other white restaurant owners. In these establishments, African Americans modeled the same positions in which black laborers served in white southern homes: cooks, servers, dishwashers, and busboys. Maddox believed that the fact that he employed forty-five African Americans to cook, clean, and serve in his restaurant proved that he was not a racist. In his memoir, he recalls a visit to the offices of the *Atlanta Constitution*, whose editors often criticized him, where he witnessed no African American workers except the janitorial staff.[23]

Yet Maddox's hiring of African Americans to cook, serve, clean, and bus tables perpetuated the white supremacist image of the servile black person. The same situation existed at Ollie's Barbecue. African Americans helped to cook the barbecue that the McClungs served to white customers. Black women took primary responsibility for serving the food. Yet, whereas his white employees could eat in the dining room alongside white customers, his black employees ate "in their own room" on the premises. Black customers could not eat there at all.[24] This contributed to the widespread white construction that situated white Americans as the proper consumers and African Americans as the proper servers of food.

The fact that these foods, specifically barbecue and fried chicken, have long histories among black and white southerners complicated the issue further. White southerners eagerly consumed the same foods that they derided African Americans for eating. One way for white southerners to enjoy these foods without actively connecting themselves to "black" foodways was to physically separate themselves from the black consumption of the same foods. Black and white southerners could eat the same foods, prepared by the same black hands, but—if white supremacists had their way—they could not do so together, thereby preserving the status of the white consumer and the sanctity of the white body.

The white body also was significant in white supremacist ideology, and its purity was an important element in the campaigns to continue racial segregation in public eating spaces. White opponents of restaurant desegregation related the consumption of food to racial purity and demonstrated concerns over the protection of white women. In response to the rising tide of civil rights activism, Georgia passed an anti-sit-in trespass law much like the South Carolina law at issue in the *Peterson* case. Defending the law in an appeal filed by convicted demonstrators, the state argued that restaurant owners could discriminate in any way they saw fit—"evict[ing] wearers of shorts [or] swimming suits or unescorted females."[25] The Georgia solicitor general's words here are revealing because they suggest a continuing concern about the many imagined threats that white women faced in public eating places.

The parallel to the image of the white woman in need of protection was the racist stereotype of the black man bent on ravishment. In correspondence opposing the Civil Rights Act of 1964, pending at the time before Congress, a former Alabama resident, Lallage Longshore, returned to the common white southern trope that linked black men to violence against white women. She referred to the college-educated, Christian minister Dr. Martin Luther King Jr. as a "savage" and informed Alabama senator Lister Hill that she would not bring King into her home.[26]

Many intractable white restaurant owners sounded a similar theme. When Ollie McClung Sr. testified, "I would refuse to serve . . . anyone who I felt would damage my business and I run a good, clean place there," it is possible that he thought African American customers threatened his "clean" restaurant in a literal, hygienic sense. But that seems unlikely, because he hired African Americans to cook and serve barbecue to his white customers.

It is more likely that allowing whites and blacks to eat together in the same dining room violated the McClungs' sense of proper racial mores. McClung did not want to transgress racial customs in his restaurant any more than he would have in his own affluent home.[27] The McClungs refused to serve "profane" men in their dining room, as the signs on their tables indicated, because they feared such men would offend the white families—especially the white women and children—who frequented his barbecue restaurant. They refused to knowingly serve African Americans in the dining room for the same reason. In their minds, eating with African Americans represented a threat to the white family.

Lester Maddox feared the interaction of African American men and white women in his establishment so much that he called the police on a black employee who allegedly asked a white waitress for a date. In 1962, in the midst of southern sit-in activism, Atlanta police arrested Tommy Lee Jordan, an African American employee at the Pickrick, after Jordan allegedly "tried to date" two white waitresses. Reportedly, Jordan had followed a Pickrick waitress into the ladies' room to ask her out. When she refused, he "had 'pulled on her coat' . . . when she brushed past him on her way out." Three weeks later, another waitress reported that Jordan had asked her to go to a nightclub with him. Atlanta police charged Jordan with disorderly conduct, disturbing the peace, and molestation. A year earlier, Maddox had accused Jordan of stealing a woman's purse, but he had not called the police at that time.[28]

Maddox had only contacted the authorities when Jordan challenged Maddox's understanding of proper racial and gender conventions—even though no crime had occurred. In a politically charged newspaper ad for his restaurant, Maddox directly connected the desegregation of eating places with the desegregation of southern bedrooms, writing, "I do hope you'll get your integration wishes—a stomach full of race mixing, and a lap full of little mulatto grandchildren."[29] Maddox aimed this statement primarily at the white moderates who negotiated with activists to desegregate downtown lunch counters and cafés. His statement makes a direct connection between eating and sexuality by implying that desegregating southern eating places would result in miscegenation.

Maurice Bessinger makes a similar connection when he expresses what he considers to be the logical conclusion to the new civil rights law. "It might be possible for a black man to try and marry a white woman," Bessinger muses in his autobiography, "and if she turns him down, he can sue for discrimination."[30] Here, Bessinger completes Maddox's thought by suggesting not just that miscegenation will result, but that it will occur between black males and white females and will be against the wishes of white women. Both men are suggesting that if the government can compel blacks and whites to engage in as intimate an activity as eating together, it may compel even more intimate interactions. This is another manifestation of the white supremacist myth that food consumption, like marriage, is a purely private transaction and that if compulsion can be applied in one case, it can be applied in the other as well. Bessinger's "forced" marriage example also uses another well-recognized white supremacist image by implying that the federal government might support the alleged atrocities of the mythical "black beast rapist."[31]

The white supremacist image of the black rapist threatening white female purity was never far away during the restaurant desegregation debate. In December 1964, while the Supreme Court was considering its decision in *Katzenbach v. McClung*, the *Citizen*, a national magazine published by the white supremacist Citizens' Councils, made no mention of the public accommodations section of the Civil Rights Act nor the Ollie's Barbecue case. Instead the magazine devoted that month's edition to the imagined threats that white women faced in the event of so-called race mixing. The common "black rapist" trope predominated. One editorial warned that "some drastic action is needed to protect whites from colored criminals—especially rapists" and continued by describing hundreds of alleged violent crimes committed by black men against white women. The list included the following examples: a "Negro gang" raped a white nurse in New Jersey; "a gang of about 10 Negro youths" raped white teenage girls in Memphis; "eight Negro youths . . . gang-raped" a white mother in Knoxville; "a Negro raped and murdered a young white housewife when she returned home from an early afternoon trip to the grocery store" in New Orleans; and in Mississippi "several white homemakers have been terrorized on their own premises by colored intruders evidently bent on rape." There is no indication that any of these alleged (and undocumented) atrocities occurred in public eating places or even occurred at all, but the timing makes the connection clear. While much of the country focused on the Supreme Court as it decided the Ollie's Barbecue case, the Citizens' Councils of America focused on the dangers of "race mixing." All of these supposed threats involved the well-being and racial purity of white women—and, by extension, white families.[32]

Some white supremacists reacted to this culture of hyperbole with actions intended to protect white women. When Jimmy's Restaurant in Montgomery desegregated, the white owner reportedly fired the white waitresses and hired black men to wait tables because he did not think that it was proper for white women to serve black men.[33] In a violent incident in Chattanooga, Tennessee, a white man shot and killed a black patron who allegedly "called a white waitress 'baby doll' . . . in a recently desegregated restaurant."[34] Like Lester Maddox's call for racial purity, these incidents demonstrate the white paranoia that interaction between blacks and whites in southern restaurants might lead to sexual relations between white women and black men. Because southern white supremacists could not comprehend that such interactions could be consensual, this ideology reinvigorated the notion of the black rapist.

After Ollie's Barbecue

As a result of *Katzenbach v. McClung*, desegregation in the nation's public eating places now had legal force. Ollie's Barbecue, like most other formerly white restaurants, capitulated and began serving African Americans equally. The McClungs announced ruefully, "We will accept customers at our restaurant without regard to race or color." Despite ceding to what they considered to be an unjust decision, the McClungs and many of their white customers retained their segregationist viewpoint. At the time, Ollie McClung Jr. publicly called the decision "a blow to the American tradition of private ownership." Later, he claimed that some white customers refused to return to Ollie's after desegregation. Like most of the white supremacist rhetoric surrounding segregation, this last claim made little sense. If all local restaurants were required to desegregate—and the federal law mandated that they were—then white patrons who wanted to eat out should have had no other option than a desegregated restaurant. But most white supremacist rhetoric had little basis in reality when it came to civil rights and food. Ollie Jr. recalled that most of his white customers were "supportive" and grateful for the McClungs' effort to maintain segregation.[35] The continued intransigence of the McClungs and their white customers reveals the persistence of white supremacy in public eating places, even after the Supreme Court ruling.

The strength of cultural segregation in the South meant that some white restaurants did maintain discriminatory practices after 1964. In Mississippi some whites barely noticed a difference because racial discrimination continued undeterred in many communities. In 1968 a federal inspector reviewing poverty programs in Woodville, Mississippi, noted in her report that although white employees often ate out at lunchtime "the black employees have to eat lunch in the office because there is no resturant [*sic*] where they can attain service." Not only did this situation seem to cause little concern when she pointed it out—at least among the white employees—the inspector, who was not native to the state, described the local office as "somewhat surprised . . . I would even notice this."[36] Across the South, many whites perpetuated the status quo by refusing to submit to the new federal law.

In some cases fear and intimidation helped spaces to remain segregated. In Statesboro, Georgia, the physical structure of a local barbecue restaurant, held over from local laws and customs that required separate dining rooms, discouraged African Americans from entering the traditionally white dining room. Since 1953 Vandy's Bar-B-Que had maintained two dining rooms, each with a separate entrance. Whites entered from the front of the building and ate in a dining room that seated forty-five patrons. African Americans entered from a side entrance and ate in the back room, which seated only twelve. A wall separated the two dining rooms. Food preparation took place on the white side, and Vandy's served black customers through a window in the wall. The only way to pass from one dining room to the other was through a narrow work area in which employees washed dishes.

In 1968, years after desegregation became settled law, a fire destroyed Vandy's Bar-B-Que. When the owners, Don and Carl Boyd, rebuilt the restaurant, they retained the separate dining rooms. African Americans understood through verbal and nonverbal cues that they would not be served in the front room. Most local African Americans feared requesting service in the front room because it was commonly known to still be the white dining room. Some African Americans had the courage to challenge Vandy's violation of the federal law, but they had little success. In one instance, Vandy's purposefully overcharged a black man who chose to eat in the front dining room. In other cases, the Boyds outright refused to serve African Americans in the white dining room. In November 1968 the Boyds refused to seat a large group of African Americans in the front dining room, as local black teenagers watched from across the street. When the group refused to go to the back, the Boyds called the police. In a blatant violation of federal law, the Statesboro police ordered the African Americans off the grounds. Such actions reveal the strength of cultural segregation among many southern whites, even after the civil rights movement and changes in the law.

The U.S. attorney general filed suit against Vandy's to enforce the federal law. Testimony revealed that, like at Ollie's Barbecue, most of the food served by Vandy's Bar-B-Que moved through channels of interstate commerce. The restaurant served baked goods from Claussen's Bakery in South Carolina. Ingredients used in its Derst Bakery breads traveled across state lines—flour from Kansas, yeast from New Jersey, and oil from Tennessee. The chickens that Vandy's slow-cooked in its barbecue pits originated in Alabama. The Pepsi concentrate came from Kentucky. Like Ollie's, this case reveals the extent to which national markets drove even local restaurants in the American South by the late twentieth century. Based on the facts of this case and the Supreme Court precedent, the federal district court not only required Vandy's to serve African Americans equally but ordered that the two dining rooms be eliminated.[37] The federal court understood the power of spatial arrangements to perpetuate the culture of racial segregation.

In other cases, white restaurants tried to find legal exceptions to avoid compliance. Because the legislation explicitly exempted private clubs, some white proprietors attempted to convert their restaurants into key clubs. These clubs often had nominal "membership" requirements but only offered membership to whites. Following passage of the Civil Rights Act, a white restaurant named Landry's Fine Foods in Bogalusa, Louisiana, allowed a few African Americans to eat in the dining room. As a result, the Ku Klux Klan disrupted the restaurant's operations by picketing the site and threatening both black and white customers who patronized the integrated restaurant. These demonstrations were a part of widespread Klan attempts to disrupt civil rights activity in Bogalusa in 1965. Landry's responded to Klan intimidation by closing its doors at the end of business on March 31 and reopening a week later as Landry's Private Dining Club. The new "club" invited white restaurant customers to apply for membership and installed a lock on the front door. Members received a key card to open the lock. Only members and their guests, all white, could eat at the new club. The club operated substantially in the same manner as the restaurant that preceded it with the exception of adding a bar.

The Justice Department filed suit against Landry's and several other Bogalusa eateries that refused to serve African Americans. This case reinvigorated civil rights marches in the town, but city police refused to protect peaceful black demonstrators from white violence. The Deacons for Defense and Justice, an African American group that believed in black self-defense, complicated the situation in Bogalusa. In 1969 the federal court ruled that Landry's was not a legitimate private club because race seemed to be the primary membership requirement. The court held that "the conversion of a public restaurant into a 'private club,' which is open to the general white public . . . for the purpose of excluding Negroes, constitutes a pattern . . . of resistance to the [Civil Rights Act]."[38] In short, a proprietor could not convert a restaurant to a private club for the purpose of avoiding desegregation. Landry's failed strategy, which resembled similar attempts by white restaurants across the South, reveals the continuing strength of white supremacy and intimidation in the resistance to the desegregation of public eating places after the Civil Rights Act.[39]

Lester Maddox attempted similar strategies to avoid complying with the federal law. He closed the Pickrick and reopened as the Lester Maddox Cafeteria in the same location with essentially the same operations. Maddox's supposedly new cafeteria refused to serve integrationists, regardless of race or color. A sign on the door read in part, "We do not discriminate because of 'Race, Creed, or Color' but because we are <u>FREE</u>." Although he claimed his "new" restaurant discriminated by not serving "integrationists," by definition any African American who attempted to patronize his white cafeteria would be considered an integrationist.[40] By using his own name to christen the supposedly new cafeteria, Maddox stressed that the restaurant and all activities taking place therein constituted his personal property and were therefore not subject to any regulation. He reemphasized this position through violent actions toward civil rights activists who continued their efforts to desegregate the establishment. A short film recorded in January 1965 shows Maddox and his son physically manhandling the Reverend Charles E. Wells Sr., a local African American minister, and several other activists at the door to the Lester Maddox Cafeteria.[41] Peaceful activists faced physical violence and intimidation throughout the sit-in movement and the uneven process of desegregation, but rarely had a proprietor been the source of such an assault.

A federal court ordered Maddox to desegregate, but he closed the cafeteria altogether rather than comply with the court's order. In his typical ostentatious fashion, he announced the closure with a display in front of the restaurant that featured an empty coffin and a large sign: "Closed, Put to Death by: My President, My Government, The Communists, the Left Wing News Media, Weak and Cowardly Business Leaders, Christian Ministers Who Teach Social Salvation Rather than Christ . . ." Maddox's notorious intransigence established the basis for a successful governor's bid in 1966. Maddox had always entangled his restaurant business with his politics, starting with the "Pickrick Says" ads published in the Atlanta newspapers. He had run for several political offices in the past, including two unsuccessful bids for Atlanta mayor.[42] His election as Georgia governor revealed the immediate support of white Georgians to maintain segregation in public eating places.

Maurice Bessinger continued his restaurant operations, but like Maddox he remained uncompromising on his segregationist views. In 2000 Bessinger infamously raised the Confederate battle flag over his thirteen South Carolina barbecue restaurants to protest the flag's removal from the South Carolina state capitol. In a well-choreographed performance of southern whiteness, he arranged for the flags to be raised over his establishments at the precise time it was lowered from the statehouse.[43] For decades, Piggie Park customers could reportedly pick up various neo-Confederate souvenirs and literature, including pseudohistorical or biblical tracts describing the benefits of slavery to the black community. In response to Bessinger's racist political philosophies, several major supermarket chains discontinued

FIGURE 9. The former Pickrick Cafeteria, Atlanta, Georgia, ca. 1965. Courtesy of Kenan Research Center at the Atlanta History Center.

the sale of Southern Gold, his mustard-based barbecue sauce. "Buying a barbecue sandwich is now a political act," a 2001 *New York Times* article announced in response to the Piggie Park controversy. "You have to declare which side you're on."[44] An obvious response to this observation is "Where have you been?" The act of consuming food has always been political.

The Civil Rights Act of 1964 failed to end the controversy over segregated eating in the short term or white efforts to define southern food as a symbol of whiteness in the long term. White restaurant owners, particularly those independent proprietors whose establishments had not been targeted during the initial tide of sit-ins, asserted constitutional and biblical principles to consciously flaunt the law. Although these restaurateurs were generally affluent, their views reflected the fears of many whites, who felt their privileged status to be threatened, regardless of their socioeconomic status. The more democratic eating patterns of the late twentieth century meant that racial exclusivity gave working-class whites in particular an elevated status in the consumer sphere.

The food that such restaurants generally served as house specialties, including southern staples like barbecue and fried chicken, were important facets of their businesses and significant to their intransigence. They fought to maintain what they considered to be appropriate racial roles in their establishments—with African Americans cooking and serving the fried chicken and white customers consuming it—to offer their white customers, regardless of socioeconomic status, elevated racial standing. Although the black cook and pit master were often lauded in the white southern imagination of the 1960s, whites' hollow esteem did not conceal the reality that such people had little real economic or social power.

Cracker Barrel and the Southern Strategy

In 1969 Dan Evins opened the first Cracker Barrel restaurant off the interstate in Lebanon, Tennessee. The Evins family was in the gasoline business, so early locations of the chain restaurant included gas pumps. The locations took advantage of federally funded interstate highways to provide travelers with one-stop shopping for lunch, gas, and the sundry items they purchased at the attached "country store." The chain grew quickly. In 1977 Cracker Barrel boasted 13 restaurants around the South. By 1996 the chain had gone nationwide with 257 locations. Today, the company's website lists over 600.[1] Founded after the Civil Rights Act of 1964, and with no legitimate argument that it did not participate in interstate commerce, Cracker Barrel never entered directly into the racial politics of the 1960s. Still, the growth of Cracker Barrel implicates many of the central themes of this book.

First, Cracker Barrel's corporate strategy to develop along interstate highways was the next step in the nationalization of southern food culture. This process started with domestic science practices that encouraged women to standardize the preparation of foods in their homes based on principles largely developed in the Northeast. In the public sphere, independent cafés and lunchrooms, as well as the immigrant proprietors that owned and operated many of these places, also originated outside the region and connected the South to national practices. Fast-food chains, which developed in the postwar era at the same time the nation implemented the interstate system that would make Cracker Barrel possible, tied the region more closely to national consumer networks. Cracker Barrel represents the culmination of this process, offering its imitation of home cooking to a fast-food clientele and, as Susie Penman notes in her 2012 master's thesis on the chain restaurant, "exporting" the American South to the rest of the nation.[2]

Second, although Cracker Barrel never formally segregated its operations, the unwritten service policies and racialized environment of its establishments continue to privilege white customers. Cracker Barrel reveals the ways that many white southerners, as part of a culinary "southern strategy," continue to use food practices to distinguish whiteness and to further the goal of racial exclusivity. The racial politics of Cracker Barrel parallel the subtler, but no less insidious, systemic racism of the late twentieth and early twenty-first century. The term "southern strategy" refers to an approach developed and articulated by the conservative political strategist Lee Atwater. It alludes to the Republican Party's attempt to woo white southern conservative voters by opposing civil rights progress—but to do so with coded, rather than blatant, racial references. "By 1968 [a politician] can't say 'nigger.' . . . So you say stuff like . . . forced busing, states' rights . . . and you're getting so abstract," Atwater said in a 1981 interview with the political scientist Alexander Lamis. "Now, you're talking about cutting taxes, and all these things you're talking about are totally economic things and a byproduct of them is, blacks get hurt worse than whites." The southern strategy has allowed the Republican Party, starting with the Richard Nixon administration, to take aim at civil rights without using race-specific terms.[3]

In a similar use of coded language, the terms "southern food" and "country cooking" continue to signify whiteness in the supposedly postracial American South. Designating fare as "southern" or "country" serves to artfully contrast it from soul food. The term "soul food" was coined in the late 1960s and has been a way for black northerners to reconnect to their southern roots and to celebrate black culture. It predominately features staple dishes long served in the South—the same foods, including black-eyed peas, sweet potatoes, pork, and fried chicken, that black and white families prepared and consumed across the region. Both advocates and critics of this cuisine interpret soul food as a food based on oppression. Its foundational dishes were the basis for the diets of enslaved blacks, sharecroppers, and other poor and marginalized southern communities. Soul food's proponents interpret the cuisine as a way to memorialize generations of African American women who labored in black and white southern kitchens preparing this food. Its critics charge that unhealthy soul food diets serve to perpetuate historical racial inequities and oppression.[4]

But soul food can be seen as an instance of culinary self-determination for African American communities. After generations of witnessing white southerners demean and stereotype black foodways while they identified the best of southern fare as a white privilege, in soul food African Americans have an avenue through which the community can express blackness as a positive and essential part of the southern experience. Soul food also affords the African American community the opportunity to negotiate various meanings of blackness as they debate the best ways to feed and sustain contemporary black bodies. At the same time, however, the designation of black fare as "soul food" has offered white southerners the opportunity to continue to interpret regional foodways as necessarily white—even if they do it in the same kind of coded language essential to the southern strategy. Words like "southern" and "country" are tied to the white community, and whiteness remains normative for the region and its fare.

By defining its fare as country, this coded language has enabled Cracker Barrel to perpetuate dining in public spaces across the South as a white activity without aggressively transgressing the plain language of the Civil Rights Act or the notion of civil rights progress more generally. Cracker Barrel's white customers continue to understand the restaurant's country fare as their food. If you visit Cracker Barrel's website today, you will find a corporation taking great care to seem inclusive. It clearly articulates antidiscrimination policies toward customers, employees, and vendors in an effort to create a "diverse community." The website even lists "animal welfare principles" that include a preference for suppliers that meet or exceed industry standards.[5] This carefully constructed image masks a corporate history built largely on catering to white customers who long to recapture a predominately white, rural—but mythical—culinary past.[6]

When he founded the Cracker Barrel chain, Evins specifically tried to harness white southerners' sense of nostalgia for a rural past filled with vegetable-laden suppers and country stores.[7] For most white southerners in 1969, however, the country store theme also would have implied nostalgia for the racial etiquette that had permeated these spaces. Country stores were generally operated by white proprietors, and black trade at those stores depended on an intricate set of unwritten rules that required deference and restraint on the part of African Americans. The historian Melton A. McLaurin's grandfather owned and operated a store in the small town of Wade, North Carolina, near the town's black neighborhood. He recalls that his grandfather provided black customers with more than just the items displayed on the store's shelves. African Americans turned to "Mr. Lonnie" for store credit, cash loans, check cashing, and job recommendations. "For many he was their link to 'the system,'" McLaurin writes of the important role of the white store owner to the black community, "their contact with the modern world . . . that passed them by." The relationship between the white storekeeper and the black customer often resembled the paternalism practiced on southern plantations.[8]

This relationship could have positive consequences for some African American customers. In one case, McLaurin's grandfather helped Viny Love, a local black resident, by interceding with the welfare office on her behalf. When the office failed to enroll her for benefits, Lonnie took Love and her disabled son to the welfare office to complain in person. McLaurin acknowledges that his grandfather's frustration over the bureaucracy's failure to help Love related less to his empathy toward Love's poverty and more to anger over the welfare director's obvious refusal to take Lonnie's word that Love deserved assistance. McLaurin's grandfather interpreted the situation as an assault on his standing in the community. But the fact that Love eventually received the welfare check she needed to make ends meet reveals the significant place of the white storekeeper in the lives of black southerners.[9]

The power of the white storekeeper, however, could also disappoint black customers. McLaurin also recalls the anger that many African American customers tried to hide when Lonnie refused to extend them credit. "I have seen grown men, black men twice the size of Granddaddy, choke back their anger and frustration," McLaurin writes, "and in their helplessness turn abruptly and silently stalk out of his store, their hopes and plans dashed by his final and unequivocal no." Regardless of the outcome of their quest, African Americans always approached the white storekeeper in a way that reassured him of his superiority in the negotiations. McLaurin describes the "centuries-old script" that such negotiations followed—the black customer portraying "childlike naiveté and innocence" and entering the store "head bent slightly forward, eyes downcast . . . face a sorrowful study of helplessness." The country store revolved around this paternalistic system, which required African Americans to continually reaffirm their supposed inferiority.[10] Certainly, by designing the Cracker Barrel restaurants around a historical space in which African Americans had been expected to debase themselves to the white merchant and participate in their own subservience, Evins created a modern space that incorporated this same type of racial subordination in its culture.

Not only would the country store be unlikely to engender much nostalgia among black southerners, it would more likely prompt feelings of trepidation and outright fear. Grace Elizabeth Hale reminds us that early twentieth-century country stores often sold postcards depicting lynchings or even displayed the dismembered body parts of black lynching victims. Such "souvenirs" of racial violence no doubt served as reminders to black customers of the dangers that existed in transgressing segregation culture. "Even as they sold goods to African Americans," Hale writes, "storekeepers participated in the sale and display of racial otherness that was so central to the creation of mass products at the national level."[11] Country stores were also sites where fatal transgressions of segregation culture could take place. Only fourteen years before Evins opened the first Cracker Barrel, the Chicago teenager Emmett Till breached Mississippi's unwritten racial customs by allegedly flirting with a white woman in a country store. The store's white owner, along with a male relative, later murdered Till in a lynching that garnered national attention; the men were acquitted.[12] In these many ways, country stores functioned as spaces where whites constantly monitored and enforced the racial hierarchy.

Cracker Barrel has perpetuated the practice of representing black "otherness" in the stores connected to its restaurants. In his study on foodways and southern tourism, Anthony Stanonis points out that the company sold mammy dolls and souvenirs decorated with the Confederate battle flag in its stores during its first several decades of business. Writing about the culture of Cracker Barrel, Susie Penman attributes the "increasing public discomfort" over the company's public image to such racialized inventory.[13] Like the grotesque "souvenirs" detailed in Hale's study of segregation, the Confederate flags and mammy dolls served as reminders of the tenuous nature of black freedom in the rural South.

Finally, Cracker Barrel reveals the necessity of civil rights activism— through a combination of due process and public protest—to the successful remediation of the discrimination that has persisted in southern eating places. In 1999 the National Association for the Advancement of Colored People and several individual plaintiffs brought suit against Cracker Barrel for racial discrimination. The charges included discriminatory seating policies, pervasive racial slurs, and limiting the advancement of black employees. As late as 2002 one African American customer recalled waiting for a table while whites who arrived after him were seated. The Cracker Barrel host finally seated him in the smoking section, even though he had requested a nonsmoking table. In a separate investigation, the Justice Department determined that Cracker Barrel allowed white servers to refuse to serve black customers altogether. One black employee claimed she made extra money from white servers who paid her to serve other African Americans—with the management's full knowledge. In 2004 Cracker Barrel settled the NAACP case for $8.7 million. The restaurant chain settled the Justice Department suit by agreeing to implement diversity training and policies—which no doubt led to the company's current online inclusiveness.[14] The cases pursued by individuals, the federal government, and civil rights organizations reveal that white southern restaurants continue to cater to white southerners by creating a racially exclusive environment. Cracker Barrel has thrived on the desire of many white southerners to return to the days before the civil rights movement disrupted the carefully constructed racial codes by which all southerners learned to live, and before soul food laid claim to southern cuisine by reinterpreting "traditional" foods as black foods.

Although new southern quick-service restaurants like Cracker Barrel conduct business as the spiritual inheritors of anti–civil rights crusaders like Ollie McClung and Lester Maddox, national fast-food chains have taken an alternate route and attempted to embrace black customers. McDonald's early history involved a corporate culture that purposefully identified its typical customer as white and middle class. By the end of the twentieth century, however, this national chain was making efforts to cultivate its relationship with black communities, perhaps recognizing that the disproportionate poverty of minority populations made them appropriate targets for the marketing of cheap food. In the twenty-first century the chain's website features a section called "365 Black" to focus attention on and celebrate black history and culture. The public can browse articles about African Americans in music, the Essence Festival in New Orleans, and Ronald McDonald House charities in black communities while also studying the McDonald's menu and learning about the company's newest promotions.[15] In this way, the fast-food megalith now actively pursues African American consumers as a ready market for its inexpensive fare.[16]

The myth and reality of southern foodways have served to both unite and divide this fractious region at various times. Although white supremacists like Maddox and Bessinger no longer control the discourse surrounding food practices, the structural inequalities that their rhetoric helped to create and perpetuate continue to exist. Although the region is inextricably connected to national food systems, a diverse community of southerners continues to construct southern food as a distinctive entity through popular culture and, increasingly, academic scholarship. In short, despite the dominance of modern national food systems, the distinctions of the culinary South continue to exist because southerners continue to want them.

Notes

INTRODUCTION. THE OLLIE'S BARBECUE CASE AND THE FOODSCAPE
OF THE URBAN SOUTH

1. *Polk's Birmingham, Alabama, City Directory* (Birmingham, Ala.: R. L. Polk, 1927), 1507; Ancestry.com, *Alabama Deaths and Burials Index, 1881–1974* (Provo, Utah: Ancestry.com Operations, 2011); U.S. Census, 1900 (this and all subsequent references to federal Census records were accessed at http://search.ancestry.com); Jefferson County, Alabama, Registration Roll 1509396, Draft Board 3, U.S. World War I Draft Registration Cards, 1917–1918 (accessed at http://home.ancestry.com). The description of Ollie's Barbecue used in this paragraph is based on an entry in bhamwiki.com.

2. Transcript of record, *McClung v. Katzenbach*, 233 F. Supp. 815 (N.D. Ala.) (No. 64-448), 70–74, 80–81; "Barbecue and the Bar," *Newsweek*, September 28, 1964, 32; Ollie McClung Jr., interview by Joan Hoffman, November 5, 1975, tape and transcript, Oral History Collection, Mervyn H. Sterne Library, University of Alabama, Birmingham.

3. General Code of Birmingham, § 369 (repealed July 23, 1963); Civil Rights Act, Pub. L. No. 88-352, 78 Stat. 241 (1964); *Katzenbach v. McClung*, 379 U.S. 294 (1964).

4. Affidavit of Weaver Saterbak, *McClung v. Katzenbach*, 233 F. Supp. 815 (N.D. Ala.) (No. 64-448), 31–32; Transcript of Record, ibid., 75.

5. *Katzenbach v. McClung*, 379 U.S. 294 (1964). The Supreme Court had established this "aggregate theory" in *Wickard v. Filburn*, 317 U.S. 111 (1942) (upholding the Agricultural Adjustment Act of 1938).

6. *Civil Rights Cases*, 109 U.S. 3 (1883) (striking down the Civil Rights Act of 1875).

7. Grace Elizabeth Hale, *Making Whiteness: The Culture of Segregation in the South, 1890–1940* (New York: Pantheon, 1998).

8. Ibid., 21, 130–131.

9. Ibid., 187.

10. Katharine Du Pre Lumpkin, *The Making of a Southerner* (Athens: University of Georgia Press, 1992), 206. Other white southern memoirists who mention this prohibition include Lillian Smith, *Killers of the Dream* (New York: Norton, 1994), 97–98, and Virginia Foster Durr, *Outside the Magic Circle: The Autobiography of Virginia Foster Durr*, ed. Hollinger F. Barnard (Tuscaloosa: University of Alabama Press, 1985), 56–57. Gunnar Myrdal, *An American Dilemma: The Negro Problem and Modern Democracy* (New York: Harper and Row, 1944), discusses this taboo in the South as a racialized and gendered construct (609).

11. Smith, *Killers of the Dream*, 97–98.

12. Some of the leading works in interdisciplinary food studies include Jeffrey M. Pilcher, *Planet Taco: A Global History of Mexican Food* (Oxford: Oxford University Press, 2012); Harvey Levenstein, *Fear of Food: A History of Why We Worry about What We Eat* (Chicago: University of Chicago Press, 2012); Julie Guthman, *Weighing In: Obesity, Food Justice and the Limits of Capitalism* (Berkeley: University of California Press, 2011); Warren Belasco, *Appetite for Change: How the Counterculture Took on the Food Industry* (Ithaca, N.Y.: Cornell University Press, 2006); Donna Gabaccia, *We Are What We Eat: Ethnic Food and the Making of Americans* (Cambridge, Mass.: Harvard University Press, 1998); and Sidney Mintz, *Sweetness and Power: The Place of Sugar in Modern History* (New York: Viking-Penguin, 1985).

13. Psyche A. Williams-Forson, *Building Houses Out of Chicken Legs: Black Women, Food, and Power* (Chapel Hill: University of North Carolina Press, 2006). Doris Witt, *Black Hunger: Food and the Politics of U.S. Identity* (New York: Oxford University Press, 1999), also explores the dynamic between black women and food as a structuring narrative for the twentieth century.

14. Elizabeth S. D. Engelhardt, *A Mess of Greens: Southern Gender and Southern Food* (Athens: University of Georgia Press, 2011).

15. Among other important works on southern foodways, Marcie Cohen Ferris, *The Edible South: Food and History in an American Region* (Chapel Hill: University of North Carolina Press, 2014), addresses various cultural constructions of food across the American South; John T. Edge, Elizabeth Engelhardt, and Ted Ownby, eds., *The Larder: Food Studies Methods from the American South* (Athens: University of Georgia Press, 2013), reveals how scholars of various disciplines approach the topic; and Anthony J. Stanonis, ed., *Dixie Emporium: Tourism, Foodways, and Consumer Culture in the American South* (Athens: University of Georgia Press, 2008), connects southern food culture to memory, consumerism, and regional identity.

16. "Recipes That Generations of Cooks Have Sworn By," *Life*, January 3, 1955, 65; Mary R. Wheeler, letter to the editor, *Life*, January 24, 1955, 8.

17. This argument follows C. Vann Woodward, *The Strange Career of Jim Crow* (New York: Oxford University Press, 1957), and Hale, *Making Whiteness*. On the development of southern segregation and its lively historiography, see John W. Cell, *The Highest Stage of White Supremacy: The Origins of Segregation in South Africa and the American South* (Cambridge: Cambridge University Press, 1982), and C. Vann Woodward, "Strange Career Critics: Long May They Persevere," *Journal of American History* 75, no. 3 (December 1988): 857–868.

18. Andrew Haley, *Turning the Tables: Restaurants and the Rise of the American Middle Class, 1880–1920* (Chapel Hill: University of North Carolina Press, 2011), helps frame this discussion. He argues that the beginning of the twentieth century was when dining out transitioned from an elite to a middle-class activity.

19. Mary Douglas, *Purity and Danger: An Analysis of the Concepts of Pollution and Taboo* (London: Routledge and Kegan Paul, 1966), 1–6. Patricia Yaeger, *Dirt and Desire: Reconstructing Southern Women's Writing, 1930–1990* (Chicago: University of Chicago Press, 2000), applies Douglas's purity analogy to racial construction in the South.

20. Zillah Eisenstein, "N.C. Protests Highlight GOP's Turn to the Hard Right," on *Melissa Harris-Perry*, MSNBC, July 21, 2013, http://tv.msnbc.com/shows/melissa -harris-perry (accessed August 13, 2013).

21. Smith, *Killers of the Dream*, 87.

22. Ibid., 144–148.

23. Durr, *Outside the Magic Circle*, 56–57.

24. Of these two taboos, the first may have been more often transgressed. See, e.g., Joshua Rothman, *Notorious in the Neighborhood: Sex and Families across the Color Line in Virginia, 1786–1861* (Chapel Hill: University of North Carolina Press, 2003).

25. Kyla Wazana Tompkins, *Racial Indigestion: Eating Bodies in the Nineteenth Century* (New York: New York University Press, 2012), addresses some of these same ideas by connecting eating, bodies, and race construction. Among other things, she focuses on nineteenth-century reform and political imagery that often portrayed whites as "eaters" and nonwhite bodies as objects of consumption (8–10).

26. Don H. Doyle, *New Men, New Cities, New South: Atlanta, Nashville, Charleston, Mobile, 1860–1910* (Chapel Hill: University of North Carolina Press, 1990), xiii.

27. Martin Luther King Jr. famously called Birmingham "the most thoroughly segregated city in the United States" in "Letter from Birmingham City Jail" (May 1, 1963), King Center, http://www.thekingcenter.org/archive/document/letter -birmingham-city-jail-0. William B. Hartsfield referred to Atlanta as "the city too

busy to hate." See Alton Hornsby, "A City That Was Too Busy to Hate," in *Southern Businessmen and Desegregation*, ed. Elizabeth Jacoway and David R. Colburn (Baton Rouge: Louisiana State University Press, 1982), 120–136.

28. Although popular culture often limits the experiences of black women to trite stereotypes, a large academic literature critically examines these images. See, e.g., Kimberly Wallace-Sanders, *Mammy: A Century of Race, Gender, and Southern Memory* (Ann Arbor: University of Michigan Press, 2008); Micki McElya, *Clinging to Mammy: The Faithful Slave in Twentieth-Century America* (Cambridge, Mass.: Harvard University Press, 2007); and M. M. Manring, *Slave in a Box: The Strange Career of Aunt Jemima* (Charlottesville: University of Virginia Press, 1998).

29. Rebecca Sharpless, *Cooking in Other Women's Kitchens: Domestic Workers in the South, 1865–1960* (Chapel Hill: University of North Carolina Press, 2010), xi, 129–171.

30. This analysis aligns with scholarship finding that many white southerners believed that African Americans suffered a moral decline after emancipation. See, e.g., George M. Fredrickson, *The Black Image in the White Mind: The Debate on Afro-American Character and Destiny, 1817–1914* (New York: Harper and Row, 1971), 259–262. This perception caused fear among some whites over the effect of black servants on the welfare of white homes. See Tera W. Hunter, *To 'Joy My Freedom: Southern Black Women's Lives and Labors after the Civil War* (Cambridge, Mass.: Harvard University Press, 1997), 187–191.

31. Informative works on domestic service include Danielle T. Phillips, "Who Wants to Be an 'English' Mother? Irish and Southern African American Domestic Workers in New York, 1865–1935," *Journal of the Motherhood Initiative* 2, no. 1 (2011): 226–241; Andrew Urban, "Irish Domestic Servants, 'Biddy' and Rebellion in the American Home, 1850–1900," *Gender and History* 21, no. 2 (August 2009): 263–286; Amy Kaplan, "Manifest Domesticity," *American Literature* 70 (September 1998): 581–606; Elizabeth Clark-Lewis, *Living In, Living Out: African American Domestics in Washington, D.C., 1910–1940* (Washington, D.C.: Smithsonian Institution Press, 1994); Phyllis Palmer, *Domesticity and Dirt: Housewives and Domestic Servants in the United States, 1920–1945* (Philadelphia: Temple University Press, 1989); and Daniel E. Sutherland, *Americans and Their Servants: Domestic Service in the United States from 1800 to 1920* (Baton Rouge: Louisiana State University Press, 1981).

32. Lizbeth Cohen, *A Consumer's Republic: The Politics of Mass Consumption in Postwar America* (New York: Random House, 2004).

33. See, e.g., James M. McGoldrick, "*Katzenbach v. McClung*: The Abandonment of Federalism in the Name of Rational Basis," *BYU Journal of Public Law* 14, no. 1 (1999): 1–36; Richard C. Cortner, *Civil Rights and Public Accommodations: The Heart*

of Atlanta Motel and McClung Cases (Lawrence: University of Kansas Press, 2001); Jason Sokol, *There Goes My Everything: White Southerners in the Age of Civil Rights* (New York: Vintage, 2006); and Mark S. Weiner, "The Semiotics of Civil Rights in Consumer Society: Race, Law, and Food," *International Journal for the Semiotics of Law* 16, no. 4 (2003): 395–405.

34. Some scholarship explores the efforts among white southern businessmen to negotiate desegregation in downtown spaces, but this approach was an uneven, unreliable, and often disingenuous means by which to ensure civil rights. See, e.g., Glenn T. Eskew, *But for Birmingham: The Local and National Movements in the Civil Rights Struggle* (Chapel Hill: University of North Carolina Press, 1997), 274–280, and Elizabeth Jacoway and David R. Colburn, eds., *Southern Businessmen and Desegregation* (Baton Rouge: Louisiana State University Press, 1982), 5.

35. A literature of personal memoir and academic scholarship documents the efforts of college students in the 1960s-era sit-ins. See, e.g., M. J. O'Brien, *We Shall Not Be Moved: The Jackson Woolworth's Sit-In and the Movement It Inspired* (Jackson: University of Mississippi Press, 2013); Rodney L. Hurst Sr., *It Was Never about a Hot Dog and a Coke: A Personal Account of the 1960 Sit-In Demonstrations in Jacksonville, Florida* (Livermore, Calif.: Wingspan, 2008); John Lewis and Michael D'Orso, *Walking with the Wind: A Memoir of the Movement* (New York: Harcourt Brace, 1998); and Anne Moody, *Coming of Age in Mississippi: The Classic Autobiography of Growing Up Poor and Black in the Rural South* (1968; rpt., New York: Dell, 1976).

PART 1. SOUTHERN FOOD CULTURE IN TRANSITION, 1876–1935

1. *Atlanta City Directory* (Atlanta: Thomas J. Maloney, 1900), 1522, 1543; *Atlanta City Directory* (Atlanta: Thomas J. Maloney, 1901), 1579, 1598; *Atlanta City Directory* (Atlanta: Thomas J. Maloney, 1902), 1756, 1783–1784; *Atlanta City Directory* (Atlanta: Thomas J. Maloney, 1903), 1547–1548, 1572 (all accessed via microfilm at the Kenan Research Center, Atlanta History Center).

CHAPTER ONE. SCIENTIFIC COOKING AND SOUTHERN WHITENESS

1. Eugene Walter and Katherine Clark, *Milking the Moon: A Southerner's Story of Life on This Planet* (New York: Crown, 2001), 16–17.

2. Don H. Doyle, *New Men, New Cities, New South: Atlanta, Nashville, Charleston, Mobile, 1860–1910* (Chapel Hill: University of North Carolina Press, 1990), 19.

3. Harvey Levenstein, *Revolution at the Table: The Transformation of the American Diet* (Berkeley: University of California Press, 2003).

4. Helen Bullock, *The Williamsburg Art of Cookery; or, Accomplished Gentlewoman's Companion* (Williamsburg, Va.: Colonial Williamsburg Foundation, 1966); George P. Rawick, *The American Slave: A Composite Autobiography* (Westport, Conn.: Greenwood, 1972), 6:239–241, 256; Lily May Spaulding and John Spaulding, eds., *Civil War Recipes: Receipts from the Pages of Godey's Lady's Book* (Lexington: University Press of Kentucky, 1999), 17; Gerry Schremp, *Celebration of American Food: Four Centuries in the Melting Pot* (Golden, Colo.: Fulcrum, 1996), 18; Eleanor T. Fordyce, "Cookbooks of the 1800s," in *Dining in America 1850–1900*, ed. Kathryn Grover (Amherst: University of Massachusetts Press, 1987), 88–92; Mary Ann Bryan Mason, *The Young Housewife's Counsellor and Friend: Containing Directions in Every Department of Housekeeping including the Duties of Wife and Mother* (New York: E. J. Hale and Son, 1875), 186–188, http://docsouth.unc.edu/nc/mason/mason.html#p.

5. Atlanta Woman's Club, *Atlanta Woman's Club Cook Book* (Atlanta: Atlanta Woman's Club, 1921), 10–11; Megan J. Elias, *Food in the United States, 1890–1945* (Denver, Colo.: Greenwood, 2009), 48–52; Edward Ayers, *The Promise of the New South* (New York: Oxford University Press, 1992), 100.

6. Jane W. Fickling, ed., *Recipes from Old Charleston: Catherine Lee Banks Edwards* (Birmingham, Ala.: Banner, 1989), 11.

7. *The Dixie Cook-Book* (Atlanta: L. A. Clarkson, 1883), 9.

8. Atlanta Woman's Club, *Atlanta Woman's Club Cook Book*, 40–49; [Henrietta Stanley] Dull, *Southern Cooking* (1941; rpt., Athens: University of Georgia Press, 2006), 167–173; Ginter Park Woman's Club, *Famous Recipes from Old Virginia* (Richmond, Va.: Richmond Press, 1935), 121–136.

9. "Display Ad 7—No Title," *Atlanta Constitution*, September 1, 1906.

10. Isma Dooly, "Old-Time Darkies and Old-Time Plantations Passing Away but Few That Are Left Preserve Their Quaint Character," *Atlanta Constitution*, March 21, 1915; Ayers, *Promise of the New South*, 100.

11. "Local Servant Problem and Its Latest Incident," *Atlanta Constitution*, September 29, 1907.

12. Robert Preston Brooks, "Sanitary Conditions among the Negroes of Athens, Georgia," *Bulletin of the University of Georgia* 18, no. 7 (1918): 23. Tera W. Hunter describes how African American women exercised their freedom by choosing occupations that improved their families' circumstances and lessened the threat of sexual exploitation by white men in *To 'Joy My Freedom: Southern Black Women's Lives and Labors after the Civil War* (Cambridge, Mass.: Harvard University Press, 1997), 57–65, 106.

13. "Local Servant Problem and Its Latest Incident."

14. "Mrs. Stetson Discusses the Servant Problem," *Atlanta Constitution*, February 28, 1899; "National Household Economic Association," *Everyday Housekeeping* 12, no. 4 (January 1900): 155; Denise D. Knight, ed., *The Abridged Diaries of Charlotte Perkins Gilman* (Charlottesville: University Press of Virginia, 1998), 204. Gilman divorced Walter Stetson in 1894 and married George Houghton Gilman in 1900. She spent the years in between her marriages traveling the country to lecture on social reform. Cynthia J. Davis, *Charlotte Perkins Gilman: A Biography* (Stanford, Calif.: Stanford University Press, 2010), 160, 175–176, 236.

15. Katharine Du Pre Lumpkin, *The Making of a Southerner* (Athens: University of Georgia Press, 1992), 106; Timothy B. Tyson, *Blood Done Sign My Name: A True Story* (New York: Crown, 2004), 112.

16. Victoria Byerly, *Hard Times Cotton Mill Girls: Personal Histories of Womanhood and Poverty in the South* (Ithaca, N.Y.: Cornell University Press, 1986), 38–39. As an adult, Cannon was one of the first African American women to work in a North Carolina textile mill; she eventually became a scholar of Christian ethics. Katie Geneva Cannon, *Katie's Canon: Womanism and the Soul of the Black Community* (New York: Continuum, 1995).

17. Virginia Foster Durr, *Outside the Magic Circle: The Autobiography of Virginia Foster Durr*, ed. Hollinger F. Barnard (Tuscaloosa: University of Alabama Press, 1985), 13.

18. Many scholars assess the use of domestic labor as a marker of class and race. Phyllis Palmer discusses how the labor of a black woman in 1950s Texas enabled her white family to maintain a level of "respectability" even though it was headed by a working white woman. See *Domesticity and Dirt: Housewives and Domestic Servants in the United States, 1920–1945* (Philadelphia: Temple University Press, 1989), ix–x. Andrew Urban identifies domestic service as "a labor relationship that defined and maintained [the] class and racial identity" of the native-born white middle class and says that their enhanced standing presumed this population's fitness to engage in the nation's immigration debates. "An Intimate World: Race, Migration, and Chinese and Irish Domestic Servants in the United States, 1850–1920" (PhD diss., University of Minnesota, 2009).

19. Durr, *Outside the Magic Circle*, 90.

20. Hale, *Making Whiteness*, 122–197. M. M. Manring, *Slave in a Box: The Strange Career of Aunt Jemima* (Charlottesville: University of Virginia Press, 1998), describes how mass advertisers used white consumer attitudes toward black service to sell pancakes starting in the late nineteenth century.

21. Urban, "An Intimate World."

22. Annie Kendrick Walker, "Mrs. Kirk, President of Fenelon Club, Writes of Ser-

vant Problem," *Birmingham Age-Herald*, May 2, 1899. Danielle T. Phillips examines Irish and African American servants in New York and finds that white employers saw both "races" as disease-ridden, unintelligent, and unreliable workers. These employers nevertheless relied on both groups as a source of cheap, available labor. See "Who Wants to Be an 'English' Mother? Irish and Southern African American Domestic Workers in New York, 1865–1935," *Journal of the Motherhood Initiative* 2, no. 1 (2011): 226–240.

23. "The Domestic Servant Problem," *Atlanta Constitution*, July 31, 1901.

24. Mrs. W. H. Felton, letter to the editor, *Atlanta Constitution*, July 28, 1901. In addition to her distinction as the first woman to serve in the U.S. Senate, when the governor appointed her to temporarily fill the seat vacated by Tom Watson's death, Rebecca Latimer Felton is notorious for her racist views, which included active support for lynching to "protect" white womanhood. Leon Litwack, *Trouble in Mind: Black Southerners in the Age of Jim Crow* (New York: Knopf, 1998), 100, 213, 221, 282–283, 304–313.

25. "Much Interest Aroused in Mrs. Felton's Suggestion: Necessity of Providing Work for White Women Discussed," *Atlanta Constitution*, July 30, 1901.

26. George M. Fredrickson, *The Black Image in the White Mind: The Debate on Afro-American Character and Destiny, 1817–1914* (New York: Harper and Row, 1971), 259–262; Hunter, *To 'Joy My Freedom*, 187–191.

27. *Dixie Cook-Book*, 2; "Miss Clarkson's Death," *Atlanta Constitution*, February 12, 1896.

28. "Display Ad 41—No Title," *Atlanta Constitution*, September 3, 1899.

29. Catharine E. Beecher, *A Treatise on Domestic Economy for the Use of Young Ladies at Home and at School* (Boston: Thomas H. Webb, 1843); American Home Economics Association, "History and Outline of First Conference, 19–25 September 1899," in *Lake Placid Conference on Home Economics*, vols. 1–3: *Proceedings from the First, Second, and Third Conferences* (Washington, D.C.: American Home Economics Association, 1901), 3–9; American Home Economics Association, "Ten Years of the Lake Placid Conference on Home Economics: Its History and Aims," in *Lake Placid Conference on Home Economics*, vol. 10: *Proceedings from the Tenth Conference* (Washington, D.C.: American Home Economics Association, 1908), 19–25. These and all subsequent references to materials from the Lake Placid Conference were accessed at http://hearth.library.cornell.edu.

30. Christine Terhune Herrick and Marion Harland, *Modern Domestic Science* (Chicago: Debower-Chapline, 1909), 2:4–5.

31. Ellen H. Richards, "Nomenclature," *Lake Placid Conference on Home Economics*, vol. 6: *Proceedings of the Sixth Annual Conference* (Washington, D.C.: American

Home Economics Association, 1904), 63–64; Ellen H. Richards, *Euthenics: The Science of Controllable Environment* (Boston: Whitcomb and Barrows, 1912), vii–viii. The term "euthenics" never caught on, and the new discipline came to be known most commonly as home economics or domestic science. See Emma Seitfrit Weigley, "It Might Have Been Euthenics: The Lake Placid Conference and the Home Economics Movement," *American Quarterly* 26, no. 1 (March 1974): 79–96. Although the terms are not entirely synonymous, in this book I use the phrases "home economics," "domestic science," and "scientific cooking" interchangeably.

32. Edward J. Larson, *Sex, Race, and Science: Eugenics in the Deep South* (Baltimore, Md.: Johns Hopkins University Press, 1995), 2; Edward J. Larson, "'In the Finest, Most Womanly Way': Women in the Southern Eugenics Movement," *American Journal of Legal History* 39, no. 2 (April 1995): 119–147.

33. Mary E. Frayser, "House Plans for New Homes and for the Alteration of Homes," *Proceedings of the Second Annual Conference, Alabama Home Economics Association* 10, no. 11 (October 1916): 16–17; Atlanta Woman's Club, *Atlanta Woman's Club Cook Book*, 10–11. The Frayser document is found in the 1916 catalog of the Alabama Girls Technical Institute in the Anna Crawford Milner Archives and Special Collections, Carmichael Library, University of Montevallo, Montevallo, Alabama.

34. Atlanta Woman's Club, *Atlanta Woman's Club Cook Book*, 10–11.

35. William N. Henderson, "Outlines for a Brief Course in Chemistry of Food and Nutrition," *Bulletin, Alabama Girls Technical Institute* 21 (ca. 1912): 38–40.

36. Mary Randolph, *The Virginia Housewife with Historical Notes and Commentary* (Columbia: University of South Carolina Press, 1984), 141.

37. Fannie Merritt Farmer, *The 1896 Boston Cooking School Cook Book* (1896; rpt., New York: Gramercy, 1997), 27–29.

38. Henderson, "Outlines for a Brief Course," 38–40.

39. Mason, *Young Housewife's Counsellor*, 235–237.

40. Annie Mae Bryant, ed., *Athens Woman's Club Cook Book* (Athens, Ga.: McGregor, 1922), 89–100.

41. Atlanta Woman's Club, *Atlanta Woman's Club Cook Book*, 62.

42. Laura Shapiro, *Perfection Salad: Women and Cooking at the Turn of the Century* (New York: Modern Library, 2001).

43. Culinary scholars agree that cookbooks need to be assessed carefully. For one, these sources probably do not reflect the everyday practices of cooks or housekeepers during the period. I and many other scholars use these sources, supplemented by other types of texts, to examine the "collective value system" of the women who drafted and may have experienced these texts. See Anne Bower, ed., *Recipes for*

Reading: Community Cookbooks, Stories, Histories (Boston: University of Massachusetts Press, 1997), 4. See also Janet Theophano, *Eat My Words: Reading Women's Lives through the Cookbooks They Wrote* (New York: Palgrave Macmillan, 2002).

44. "Other 16—No Title," *Atlanta Constitution*, March 20, 1925.

45. "The Science of Cooking," *Milledgeville* (Ga.) *Union Recorder*, May 9, 1899. This and all subsequent references to the *Milledgeville Union Recorder* were accessed at http://milledgeville.galileo.usg.edu/milledgeville.

46. "The African Negro . . . Living near to Nature His Digestion Is Perfect," *Atlanta Constitution*, February 9, 1908. Compare this erroneous assessment of African foodways to actual West African cooking practices as described in James E. McWilliams, *A Revolution in Eating: How the Quest for Food Shaped America* (New York: Columbia University Press, 2005), 33–34.

47. "The Science of Cooking," *Milledgeville Union Recorder*, May 9, 1899.

48. Smith, *Killers of the Dream*, 87–89.

49. Ibid., 87.

50. Georgia Branch of the National Congress of Parents and Teachers, ed., *P.T.A. Interpretations of Food* (Atlanta: Walter W. Brown, 1928), 61.

51. "Scientific and Industrial," *Atlanta Constitution*, December 30, 1894.

52. "Article 4—No Title," *Atlanta Constitution*, September 21, 1885; "Habits of the Tennessee Mountaineers and Clay-Eaters," *Timely Topics*, September 10, 1897, 267.

53. "Earth Eaters Who Find a Remedy for Disease in Dirt as a Diet," *Montgomery Advertiser*, March 30, 1919. Other writings that discuss dirt eating as an international phenomenon include "Eating Clay," *Good Housekeeping*, March 19, 1887, 236; "Article 11—No Title," *Atlanta Constitution*, December 3, 1921; "Earth as Medicine and Food," *Literary Digest* 53, no. 17 (October 21, 1916): 1027; N. W. T., "Earth-Eaters in India," *Nature* 74, no. 1926 (September 27, 1906): 543–544; "They Eat Dirt as Butter," *Atlanta Constitution*, January 21, 1900; Frederick L. Hoffman, *Race Traits and Tendencies of the American Negro* (New York: Macmillan, 1896), 137; "Folks Who Eat Clay . . . This Custom Is Found in Mexico, Japan and Georgia," *Atlanta Constitution*, October 20, 1895; "Clay Eating," *Scientific American* 72, no. 12 (March 23, 1895): 186.

54. "What's New in Medicine," *Science Digest* 2, no. 4 (April 1942): 50–51; "Negroes Eat Clay," *Atlanta Constitution*, June 12, 1909; Hoffman, *Race Traits and Tendencies of the American Negro*, 135–137.

55. J. Montgomery M'Govern, "The Clay Eaters of Carolina," *Everybody's Magazine*, March 1900, 246–247; "The Clay Eaters," *Atlanta Constitution*, March 6, 1897; "Eat Yellow Clay," ibid., August 30, 1896; "Folks Who Eat Clay—Habit Is Hereditary and Stronger than Any Drug," ibid., October 20, 1895; Alfred C. Newell, "The

Clayeaters—A Strange Colony in Middle Georgia and How They Live," ibid., February 18, 1894; "Article 4—No Title," ibid., September 21, 1885.

56. Smith, *Killers of the Dream*, 89.

57. "Article 4—No Title," *Atlanta Constitution*, September 21, 1885.

58. "The Negro Problem: How It Appeals to a Southern White Woman," *Independent . . . Devoted to the Consideration of Politics, Social and Economic Tendencies, History, Literature, and the Arts* 54, no. 2807 (September 18, 1902): 2224.

59. Robert W. Twyman, "The Clay Eater: A New Look at an Old South Enigma," *Journal of Southern History* 37, no. 3 (August 1971): 439–448, finds that the practice goes back to colonial times. Although he suggests there may be medical reasons behind the practice, he concludes that it is largely a cultural ritual passed down through the generations of predominately lower-class families.

60. M'Govern, "Clay Eaters of Carolina," 246.

61. Sarge Plunkett, "With the State Press," *Atlanta Constitution*, July 1, 1904.

62. "Pure Food Show to Begin Tonight," *Atlanta Constitution*, March 6, 1900.

63. "Housekeepers' Exposition Offers Many Prizes Today," *Atlanta Constitution*, May 21, 1908; Athens Woman's Club Minutes, 1912–1920, June 4, 1914, 58, Athens Woman's Club Collection, Heritage Room, Athens–Clarke County Library, Athens, Georgia.

64. Mary S. Hoffschwelle, "The Science of Domesticity: Home Economics at George Peabody College for Teachers, 1914–1939," *Journal of Southern History* 57, no. 4 (November 1991): 659–680, finds that from the Progressive era through the Great Depression home economics education at this Nashville school changed "from a reform program that promised women professional and social importance to a training course in domestic skills."

65. The school is now Georgia College and State University (hereafter referred to as Georgia College).

66. "Normal and Industrial College," *Milledgeville Union Recorder*, November 19, 1889; "Our Girls—The Normal and Industrial College: The President's First Report to the Board of Directors . . . ," *Milledgeville Union Recorder*, June 16, 1891; "Announcement of the Opening of the Girls Normal and Industrial College," *Milledgeville Union Recorder*, September 29, 1891; Georgia Normal and Industrial College, *First Annual Announcement of Catalogue of the Georgia Normal and Industrial College, Milledgeville, Georgia, 1891–92* (Atlanta: Jas. P. Harrison, 1892), 20, 29, 32. The Georgia College catalogs were accessed at the Georgia College Archives, Georgia College and State University, Milledgeville.

67. Lucille B. Griffith, *Alabama College, 1896–1969* (Montevallo, Ala.: University of Montevallo, 1969), 3–4. The white women's school at Montevallo changed names

from the Alabama Girls Industrial School to the Alabama Girls Technical Institute to Alabama College to the University of Montevallo. In this book I refer to the school as the "Alabama Girls Industrial School" or "Montevallo."

68. Georgia Normal and Industrial College, *First Annual Announcement of Catalogue*, 28.

69. "Our Girls—The Normal and Industrial College: The President's First Report to the Board of Directors . . . ," *Milledgeville Union Recorder*, June 16, 1891; Georgia Normal and Industrial College, *First Annual Announcement of Catalogue*, 20; Alabama Girls Technical Institute, *Catalogue of the Alabama Girls Technical Institute for the Twentieth Annual Session 1915–1916 and Announcements 1916–1917* (Montevallo: Alabama Girls Technical Institute, 1917), 42.

70. These conclusions are based on a family history review of Montevallo students who graduated with a degree in scientific cooking, home economics, or domestic science during the school's first two decades. The names and fields of study of the graduates were obtained from the annual school catalogs for the years 1891–1918. Fathers' occupations and property ownership were obtained by reviewing federal Census records for the years 1880, 1900, 1910, 1920, and 1930. The marital and employment statuses of the graduates were obtained from alumnae lists in school catalogs, when available, and federal Census records. School catalogs were accessed at the Anna Crawford Milner Archives and Special Collections, Carmichael Library, University of Montevallo, Montevallo, Alabama.

71. Alabama Girls Technical Institute, *Catalogue of the Alabama Girls Technical Institute for the Fifteenth Annual Session 1910–11* (Birmingham, Ala.: Dispatch Printing, 1909–1910), 54, 68; Alabama Girls Technical Institute, *Catalogue of the Alabama Girls Technical Institute for the Eighteenth Annual Session 1913–1914 and Announcements 1914–1915* (Montevallo: Alabama Girls Technical Institute, 1915), 5; Alabama Girls Technical Institute, *Catalogue of the Alabama Girls Technical Institute for the Twenty-Third Annual Session 1918–1919 and Announcements 1919–1920* (Montevallo: Alabama Girls Technical Institute, 1920), 5; U.S. Census, 1900.

72. *Catalogue of the Alabama Girls Technical Institute for the Nineteenth Annual Session 1914–1915 and Announcements 1915–1916* (Montevallo: Alabama Girls Technical Institute, 1916), 59; U.S. Census, 1900, 1910, 1920, 1930.

73. Lynne Anderson Rieff, "'Rousing the People of the Land': Home Demonstration Work in the Deep South, 1914–1950" (PhD diss., Auburn University, 1995), 50, 68–72, 79, 81–82. In *A Mess of Greens*, Elizabeth S. D. Engelhardt shows how these efforts nevertheless helped to empower rural girls by providing them with economic opportunity through tomato clubs (83–117).

74. Lever Food and Fuel Control Act, Pub. L. No. 65-41, 40 Stat. 276 (1917); Wil-

liam Clinton Mullendore, *History of the United States Food Administration 1917–1919* (Stanford, Calif.: Stanford University Press, 1941), 51–53, 56; Witold S. Sworakowski, "Herbert Hoover, Launching the American Food Administration, 1917," in *Herbert Hoover: The Great War and Its Aftermath, 1914–23*, ed. Lawrence E. Gelfand (Iowa City: University of Iowa Press, 1979), 44.

75. Harvey Levenstein, *Revolution at the Table: The Transformation of the American Diet* (Berkeley: University of California Press, 2003), 137–146.

76. Tuskegee Normal and Industrial Institute, *Catalogue of the Tuskegee Normal and Industrial Institute 1895–96* (Tuskegee, Ala.: Tuskegee Normal and Industrial Institute, 1895), 57–59.

77. Courtney Sanabria Woodfaulk, "The Jeanes Teachers of South Carolina: The Emergence, Existence, and Significance of Their Work" (EdD diss., University of South Carolina, 1992); Bernadine S. Chapman, "Northern Philanthropy and African-American Adult Education in the Rural South: Hegemony and Resistance in the Jeanes Movement" (EdD diss., Northern Illinois University, 1990).

78. "Negro Fair Open in Central City," *Atlanta Constitution*, November 13, 1906.

79. "Display Ad 8—No Title," *Atlanta Constitution*, January 17, 1902.

CHAPTER TWO. SOUTHERN CAFÉS AS CONTESTED URBAN SPACE

Parts of this chapter were first published, in substantially different form, as "'The Customer Is Always White': Food, Race, and Contested Eating Space in the South," in *The Larder: Food Studies Methods from the American South*, edited by John T. Edge, Elizabeth Engelhardt, and Ted Ownby (Athens: University of Georgia Press, 2013).

1. William Faulkner, *Light in August* (1932; rpt., New York: Vintage, 1990), 172–200.

2. Ibid., 176.

3. "Vienna Restaurant, 133–135 S. Fourth Street, Louisville, Jefferson County, Kentucky," Photographs Historical and Descriptive Data, Historic American Buildings Survey, 1974 and 1981, American Memory, Library of Congress, http://memory.loc .gov (accessed March 2011).

4. "Thompson's Restaurant," *Atlanta Constitution*, November 3, 1869; "Thompson's Cafe," ibid., April 6, 1873; "Other 12—No Title," ibid., October 27, 1869; "Thompson's Restaurant," ibid., December 5, 1871; "Thompson's Restaurant," ibid., December 16, 1871.

5. "Thompson's Restaurant and Ladies' Dining Rooms," *Atlanta Constitution*, November 2, 1882; *Sholes' Atlanta Directory* (Atlanta: Sholes, 1880), 91.

6. "Pease and His Wife," *Atlanta Constitution*, December 9, 1868; untitled advertisement, *Richmond Times-Dispatch*, March 19, 1908.

7. "Classified Ad 5—No Title," *Atlanta Constitution*, September 23, 1868; "Classified Ad 2—No Title," ibid., June 10, 1869; "Alas and Alack Free Lunches Going," ibid., April 17, 1897; "Other 8—No Title," ibid., June 22, 1890; "Passing of the Pretzel," ibid., May 27, 1897; "Down with Free Lunch and Beer," ibid., June 12, 1897.

8. "Alas and Alack Free Lunches Going."

9. "Luncheons," Home Economics Lab Notebook, box 1, Cherry Waldrep Clements Papers, Special Collections Library, Georgia College and State University, Milledgeville.

10. Joseph R. Smith to Robert Jemison Jr., October 23, 1962, folder 17.2, Hill Ferguson Papers, Birmingham Archives, Birmingham Public Library, Birmingham, Alabama.

11. "Some Mistakes of Restaurant Living," *Galveston Daily News*, March 17, 1915.

12. "Lunch Counters May Be Banished," *Atlanta Constitution*, June 8, 1897; "Foes to Free Lunch, These Saloon Men," ibid., June 9, 1897; "Council Names Free Lunch Bill of Fare," ibid., August 19, 1898; "Lunch Ordinance Is in Effect," ibid., August 21, 1898.

13. "Wail from Patrons of Free Lunch Counters," *Macon Telegraph*, June 27, 1901.

14. Untitled advertisements in *Richmond Times-Dispatch*, September 12, 1902; *Birmingham News*, April 15, 1902; *Richmond Times-Dispatch*, July 14, 1907; *Birmingham News*, April 25, 1902; *Birmingham News*, April 15, 1902; *Richmond Times-Dispatch*, July 14, 1907; *Louisville Courier*, March 25, 1913, 7–8.

15. Switching from the American plan to the European plan was a national trend. See Richard Pillsbury, *From Boarding House to Bistro* (Boston: Unwin Hyman, 1990).

16. "Chinese Grocers," Southern Foodways Alliance Oral Histories, http://www.southernfoodways.org/oral-history/chinese-grocers-in-the-mississippi-and-arkansas-deltas; "Delta Lebanese," Southern Foodways Alliance Oral Histories, http://www. southernfoodways.org/oral-history/delta-lebanese; Yitzchak Kerem, "The Settlement of Rhodian and Other Sephardic Jews in Montgomery and Atlanta in the 20th Century," *American Jewish History* 85 (1997): 373–392.

17. Oral History of Nicholas Christu by Sofia Petrou, February 3, 1977, 1–10, transcript and recording, Mervyn H. Sterne Library, University of Alabama at Birmingham.

18. Marios Christou Stephanides, *History of the Greeks in Kentucky, 1900–1950* (Lewiston, N.Y.: Edwin Mellen Press, 2001), 4–7.

19. "Grocery and Luncheon Mr. and [. . .] Phil's" (ca. 1925), photograph, Vanish-

ing Georgia Collection, Georgia Department of Archives and History, Office of the Secretary of State, Morrow, http://dlg.galileo.usg.edu/vanga/id:ful0136.

20. "Some Mistakes of Restaurant Living," *Galveston Daily News*, March 17, 1915. This concern is particularly ironic because in the original eighteenth-century French incarnation, a "restaurant's" primary purpose was to sustain customers whose gastrointestinal tracts could not handle the rigors of modern city life. The French term originally referred to a thick meat broth served to invalids whose weak constitutions could not handle heavier foods and only later came to apply to the public spaces where such fare could be consumed. Rebecca L. Spang, *The Invention of the Restaurant: Paris and Modern Gastronomic Culture* (Cambridge, Mass.: Harvard University Press, 2000), 1.

21. "Classified Ad 1—No Title," *Atlanta Constitution*, August 5, 1903.

22. "Negro Thief Escapes," *Atlanta Constitution*, April 6, 1909.

23. "Three Blind Tigers Get Limit of the Law," *Atlanta Constitution*, February 7, 1912.

24. "Crap-Shooters Pay Penalty of the Law in Recorder's Court," *Atlanta Constitution*, May 5, 1914.

25. "Can't Sell Beer in Restaurant: Recorder Broyles Hands Down an Interesting Opinion," *Atlanta Constitution*, April 17, 1906; "No More Liquor in Restaurants: City Council Has Adopted a New Rule for Future," ibid., September 27, 1906; "Many Matters before Council . . . License of Restaurants," ibid., May 21, 1907.

26. Marni Davis, *Jews and Booze: Becoming American in the Age of Prohibition* (New York: New York University Press, 2012), describes how Atlanta authorities targeted Jewish saloonkeepers on Decatur Street for selling to African American customers (126–127).

27. "No More Liquor in Restaurants"; "Mayor Talks of Resolutions: All Restaurants Should Not Have Been Included, Says Woodward," *Atlanta Constitution*, September 28, 1906.

28. "Must Pay Debts Says the Mayor: Closing of Saloons Has Cut Down the Revenue," *Atlanta Constitution*, October 6, 1906.

29. J. Francis Keeley, "Keeley on the Correct Thing: General Comment on the Unique," *Atlanta Constitution*, May 24, 1908.

30. *Nicrosi v. the State*, 52 Ala. 336 (1875).

31. "Lays Blame on Council: Montgomery Chief Says He Needs More Laws," *Atlanta Constitution*, October 19, 1904.

32. "Orders College Inn Closed after Trial: Witnesses Declare Women Sat in Escorts' Laps, and That Couples Embraced," *Atlanta Constitution*, May 31, 1914.

33. "At the Police Matinee: Old Sarah Brown's Hashery," *Atlanta Constitution*, March 1, 1900; "All Worked for Old Woman: Nearly Every Female Negro Vagrant Arrested Said She Worked in 'Old Lady Brown's' Restaurant," ibid., September 3, 1903; Clifford M. Kuhn, Harlon E. Joye, and E. Bernard West, *Living Atlanta: An Oral History of the City, 1914–1948* (Athens: University of Georgia Press, 1990), 37; U.S. Census, 1900.

34. Albert P. Maurakis, *Never Saw Sunset* (Fredericksburg, Va.: Sheridan, 1998), 98, 131.

35. "Café Proprietors Receive Warning from Ku Klux," *Savannah Tribune*, February 5, 1921.

36. Glenn Feldman, *Politics, Society, and the Klan in Alabama, 1915–1949* (Tuscaloosa: University of Alabama Press, 1999); Wyn Craig Wade, *The Ku Klux Klan in America: The Fiery Cross* (New York: Oxford University Press, 1987).

37. John Katsos, *The Life of John Katsos* (Greenville, S.C.: A Press, 1985), 127.

38. "Dives Are Run as Restaurants: Chief of Police Will Abolish Them," *Atlanta Constitution*, August 30, 1906,.

39. "Saloons on Red Bridge Road Violate the Sunday Law: Citizens Appeal to Courts for Relief," *Montgomery Advertiser*, March 17, 1902.

40. Atlanta Woman's Club, *Atlanta Woman's Club Cook Book* (Atlanta: Atlanta Woman's Club, 1921), 13.

41. Dorothy Dickins, *Some Contrasts in the Levels of Living of Women Engaged in Farm, Textile Mill, and Garment Plant Work* (State College: Mississippi Agricultural Experiment Station, 1941), 27.

42. For some common attitudes toward dating among Alabama college co-eds, see Lisa Lindquist Dorr, "Fifty Percent Moonshine and Fifty Percent Moonshine: Social Life and College Youth Culture in Alabama, 1913–1933," in *Manners and Southern History*, ed. Ted Ownby (Oxford: University Press of Mississippi, 2007), 45–75.

43. *Birmingham News*, April 26, 1902.

44. Britt Craig, "Shuffling Out 'Cakes' to Mr. Hungry Business Man Has Cotton Factory Beat Forty Ways, Says Mamie," *Atlanta Constitution*, January 10, 1915.

45. See, e.g., Nancy MacLean, "The Leo Frank Case Reconsidered: Gender and Sexual Politics in the Making of Reactionary Populism," in *Jumpin' Jim Crow: Southern Politics from Civil War to Civil Rights*, ed. Jane Dailey, Glenda Gilmore, and Bryant Simon (Princeton, N.J.: Princeton University Press, 2000), 183–218. MacLean argues that white anxiety over the increasing tendency for young white farm women to take factory work contributed to the conviction and lynching of the Jewish factory manager Leo Frank in Atlanta.

46. Craig, "Shuffling Out 'Cakes.'"

47. Jonathan Daniels, *A Southerner Discovers the South* (New York: Macmillan, 1938), 129.

48. Coleman L. Blease, "Message from the Governor," in *Journal of the House of Representatives of the General Assembly of the State of South Carolina Being the Regular Session, Beginning Tuesday, January 13, 1914* (Columbia, S.C.: Gonzales and Bryan, 1914), 37–38.

49. Ibid.

50. Ibid.; "Blease Shoots at Everything and Everybody: Annual Message of South Carolina Governor Loaded to Guards with Denunciation," *Atlanta Constitution*, January 14, 1914.

51. James Jones, *Bad Blood: The Tuskegee Syphilis Experiment* (New York: Free Press, 1993), 16–29; Lisa Lindquist Dorr, *White Women, Rape, and the Power of Race in Virginia, 1900–1960* (Chapel Hill: University of North Carolina Press, 2004), 98; Tera W. Hunter, *To 'Joy My Freedom: Southern Black Women's Lives and Labors after the Civil War* (Cambridge: Harvard University Press, 1997), 189, 196.

52. *The Charter and Ordinances of the City of Atlanta, Code of 1924* (Atlanta: Byrd, 1924), 673–678.

53. Edward B. Klewer, *The Memphis Digest*, vol. 1 (Memphis: S. C. Toof, 1931), § 1261, rule 27.

54. Ibid., §§ 1082, 1083, 1261, rule 1.

55. Faulkner, *Light in August*, 193.

56. Ordinance No. 276-c, "An Ordinance to Prohibit the Condcuting [*sic*] of Resturants [*sic*] or Lunch Counters for White and Colored Persons in the Same Room," Regular Meeting of the Board of Commissioners of the City of Birmingham, sp-33, December 15, 1914, microfilm, Birmingham Archives, Birmingham Public Library, Birmingham, Alabama.

57. "To Stop Serving of Whites and Blacks in Same Restaurant: Judge Lane Will Introduce Ordinance Today Prohibiting Black and Tan Lunch Rooms," [Birmingham] *Age-Herald*, December 15, 1914.

58. Some racial segregation ordinances include *Code of the City of Montgomery, Alabama* (Charlottesville, Va.: Michie City Publications, 1952), § 191.10.14; *Code of Ordinances City of Fairfield, Alabama* (Tallahassee, Fla.: Municipal Code Corporation, 1957), §§ 14–29; *Code of the City of Eufaula, Alabama* (Eufaula, Ala.: City Council, 1952), § 346; *City Code of Gadsden, Alabama* (Charlottesville, Va.: Michie City Publications, 1946), §§ 12, 13; and *Code of the City of Bessemer, Alabama* (Charlottesville, Va.: Michie City Publications, 1944), § 3311.

59. *City Directory of Birmingham and Gazetteer of Surrounding Section for 1884–5*

(Atlanta: Interstate Directory, 1884), 290; *Birmingham Directory 1904* (Birmingham, Ala.: Wiggins Directories Publishing, 1904), 1097. See the restaurant and lunchroom listings in the *Birmingham City Directory* from 1884–1885 through 1904 to see this transition. Birmingham's first city directory, published in 1883, divided residences into a "white department" and a "colored department" but did not mark any black businesses—suggesting that it did not list black business operations or, less likely, it did not distinguish businesses by race. See *First City Directory of Birmingham and County Gazetteer for 1883–4* (Atlanta: C. M. Gardner, 1883). By 1904, the city directory intermixed black and white residences, noting African American residents with an asterisk, but separated black and white businesses.

60. See the *Atlanta City Directory* for the years 1884, 1885, and 1886, in which black and white proprietors are included alphabetically in the "Restaurant" listings, and the *Atlanta City Directory* for 1901, 1902, and 1903, in which all "Restaurants" are white and most "Lunch Rooms" are black. *Weatherbe's Atlanta, Ga. Duplex City Directory* (Atlanta: Ch. F. Weatherbe and Dunlop and Cohen, 1884), 92; *Weatherbe's Atlanta, Ga. Duplex City Directory* (Atlanta: Ch. F. Weatherbe and Dunlop and Cohen, 1885), 93; *Weatherbe's Atlanta, Ga. Duplex City Directory* (Atlanta: Ch. F. Weatherbe and Dunlop and Cohen, 1886), 91–92; *Atlanta City Directory* (Atlanta: Thomas J. Maloney, 1901), 1579, 1598; *Atlanta City Directory* (Atlanta: Thomas J. Maloney, 1902), 1756, 1783–1784; *Atlanta City Directory* (N.p.: n.p., 1903), 1547–1548, 1572.

61. Although formal segregation in public eating places did not occur until the 1910s and 1920s, southern white legislators segregated other public spaces, especially trains and streetcars, by the turn of the twentieth century. Despite significant resistance by black communities, the Supreme Court validated such laws in *Plessy v. Ferguson*, 163 U.S. 537 (1896). See Blair L. M. Kelly, *Right to Ride: Streetcar Protests and African American Citizenship in the Era of Plessy v. Ferguson* (Chapel Hill: University of North Carolina Press, 2010).

62. "Mitchell's Cafe Open," *Birmingham Wide Awake*, January 13, 1906; U.S. Census, 1880; *Birmingham, Suburban and Bessemer Directory* (N.p.: R. L. Polk, 1888), 226; *Birmingham City Directory 1889* (N.p.: R. L. Polk, 1889), 165; *Wilda's Birmingham and Suburban Directory 1893* (N.p.: R. W. A. Wilda, 1893), 229; *Roberts and Son Directory of the City of Birmingham and Suburbs 1896* (Birmingham, Ala.: Roberts and Son, 1896), 172; "P. M. Edwards," *Birmingham Wide Awake*, November 23, 1905.

63. *Maloney's Birmingham 1900 City Directory* (Atlanta: Maloney Directory, 1900), 839, 1087; *City Directory of Birmingham, Alabama, 1898* (N.p.: Maloney Di-

rectory, 1897), 388, 791; *City Directory of Birmingham, Alabama, 1899* (N.p.: Maloney Directory, 1898), 473, 643. There is no known family relationship between Mitchell Edwards and Dora Edwards.

64. *Birmingham City Directory 1902* (Atlanta: Mutual, 1902), 689.

CHAPTER THREE. SOUTHERN NORMS AND NATIONAL CULTURE

1. *Virginia Cookery—Past and Present* (Franconia, Va.: Woman's Auxiliary of Olivet Episcopal Church, 1957), 5–20; Karen Hess, "Bibliography," in Mary Randolph, *The Virginia Housewife with Historical Notes and Commentary* (Columbia: University of South Carolina Press, 1984), 319–320.

2. "Historical Census Browser," Geospatial and Statistical Data Center, University of Virginia, 2004, http://mapserver.lib.virginia.edu (accessed August 9, 2013).

3. Ross Netherton and Nan Netherton, *The Preservation of History in Fairfax County, Virginia: A Report Prepared for the Fairfax County History Commission, Fairfax County, Virginia, 2001* (New York: University Press of America, 2002), 5–6.

4. Ibid.; Franconia Museum website, http://www.fairy-lamp.com/Franconia /Franconia_Main.html (accessed August 9, 2013); Historical Society of Fairfax County, Virginia, website, http://www.fairfaxhistoricalsociety.org/index.html (accessed March 17, 2014); Fairfax County History Commission website, http://www .fairfaxcounty.gov/histcomm (accessed March 17, 2014).

5. In the 1930s a group of southern intellectuals, collectively referred to as the Southern Agrarians or the Fugitives, lamented the loss of supposedly traditional rural ways to a growing industrial culture. See Roger Biles, *The South and the New Deal* (Lexington: University of Kentucky Press, 1994), 15.

6. Numan V. Bartley, "The Era of the New Deal as a Turning Point in Southern History," in *The New Deal and the South*, ed. James C. Cobb and Michael V. Namorato (Jackson: University Press of Mississippi, 1984), 135–146, describes the New Deal era as a period of significant change in the South for many reasons, including the breakdown of plantation agriculture and the migration from rural areas to cities. He concludes by discussing the relative affluence of whites and the prevalence of social mobility for whites in the post–World War II South.

7. "Housing Projects Here Start in 60 Days: Atlanta Sponsors of Developments Ready for Work," *Atlanta Constitution*, October 15, 1933; "University Homes Will Open Today: 31 Negro Families to Move In, with More Following Tomorrow, Saturday," ibid., April 15, 1937. In 1937 the architect Simon Breines claimed that these housing projects were too expensive to accommodate the poorest residents and they

mostly housed the middle class or lower middle class—"store clerks, servicemen, salesmen, and small business operators." Robert D. Leighninger Jr., "Public Housing under the New Deal," *Journal of Progressive Human Services* 16, no. 2 (2005): 76. Even so, evidence reveals that such apartments may have been an improvement for this group as well because prior to the New Deal even some middle-class accommodations did not have a stove or refrigerator.

8. Eleanor Arnold, ed., *Voices of American Homemakers* (Bloomington: Indiana University Press, 1998), 177.

9. Mary S. Hoffschwelle, "The Science of Domesticity: Home Economics at George Peabody College for Teachers, 1914–1939," *Journal of Southern History* 57, no. 4 (November 1991): 659.

10. Ibid., 680.

11. Sheila Hibben, "Cookbooks Aren't Sacred!" *Atlanta Constitution*, June 26, 1938.

12. Kay Burdette, *Cookery of the Old South (Translated from Southern Lore)* (Glendale, Calif.: n.p., 1938).

13. Ibid., 99.

14. Ibid., 153.

15. "Ginter Park Historic District," National Park Service, U.S. Department of the Interior, http://www.nps.gov (accessed April 10, 2011); "History," Ginter Park Residents Association website, http://www.ginterpark.org/ginter-park-history.php (accessed August 10, 2013).

16. Ginter Park Woman's Club, *Famous Recipes from Old Virginia* (Richmond, Va.: Richmond Press, 1935), 9–12.

17. Ibid., 24–58.

18. Ibid., 54.

19. This is an example of the cultural appropriation of black women's recipes by and for the benefit of white women. Rebecca Sharpless is one of many scholars who explore this theme. See her *Cooking in Other Women's Kitchens: Domestic Workers in the South, 1865–1960* (Chapel Hill: University of North Carolina Press, 2010), xx–xxiv.

20. Ginter Park Woman's Club, *Famous Recipes from Old Virginia*, 55. Maria Howard Weeden was a white poet and artist from Huntsville, Alabama. She is best known for drawings that depict African American servants and for poems featuring a stereotypical black dialect. The verse cited by Tunstall comes from the poem "Beaten Biscuit" in Howard Weeden, *Bandanna Ballads* (New York: Doubleday and McClure, 1899), 70. The version quoted in *Famous Recipes from Old Virginia* does not exactly match Weeden's original.

21. Ginter Park Woman's Club, *Famous Recipes from Old Virginia*, 2nd ed. (Richmond, Va.: Clyde W. Saunders and Sons, 1941), 21–26.

22. Ibid., 277.

CHAPTER FOUR. RESTAURANT CHAINS AND FAST FOOD

1. All quotations in this and subsequent paragraphs are from Wilber Hardee, *The Life and Times of Wilber Hardee* (New York: Writers Press Club, 2000), 55–60.

2. John A. Jakle and Keith A. Sculle, *Fast Food: Roadside Restaurants in the Automobile Age* (Baltimore, Md.: Johns Hopkins University Press, 1999), 42–45.

3. Ibid.

4. John Vachon, "Harlingen, Texas, Barbecue Stand" (May 1943), Farm Security Administration, Office of War Information, Black and White Negatives, Library of Congress, http://www.loc.gov/pictures/item/owi2001029944/PP.

5. Russell Lee, "Negro Sitting on Bench at Side of Barbecue Stand Made of Galvanized Metal, Corpus Christi, Texas" (February 1939), Farm Security Administration, Office of War Information, Black and White Negatives, Library of Congress, http://www.loc.gov/pictures/item/fsa1997025366/PP.

6. Marion Post Wolcott, "Barbecue Stand near Fort Benning, Columbus, Georgia" (December 1940), Farm Security Administration, Office of War Information, Black and White Negatives, Library of Congress, http://www.loc.gov/pictures/item/fsa2000037017/PP.

7. Jakle and Sculle, *Fast Food*, 46.

8. Daly, "Gas Station and Lunch Room near Yulee, Florida" (July 1941), Farm Security Administration, Office of War Information, Black and White Negatives, Library of Congress, http://www.loc.gov/pictures/item/fsa1998024203/PP.

9. Dorothea Lange, "Roadside Stand and Filling Station near Ennis, Texas" (June 1937), Farm Security Administration, Office of War Information, Black and White Negatives, Library of Congress, http://www.loc.gov/pictures/item/fsa2000001390/PP.

10. "Tired, Hungry and Angry" (ca. 1954), reel 8, Congress of Racial Equality Papers (microfilm), Library of Congress, Washington, D.C. (hereafter referred to as CORE Papers).

11. *The Negro Motorist Green Book* (New York: Victor H. Green, 1949), http://www.autolife.umd.umich.edu/Race/R_Casestudy/87_135_1736_GreenBk.pdf.

12. E. W. Ingram Sr., *"All This from a 5-Cent Hamburger": The Story of the White Castle System* (New York: Newcomen Society in North America, 1964), 10–11, 14–15; Upton Sinclair, *The Jungle* (1906), http://www.gutenberg.org/files/140/140-h/140-h.htm.

13. Ingram, *All This from a 5-Cent Hamburger,* 10.

14. Karen Plunkett-Powell, *Remembering Woolworth's: A Nostalgic History of the World's Most Famous Five-and-Dime* (New York: St. Martin's, 1999), 44–50, 151–155; "Woolworth to Occupy the Eiseman Building," *Atlanta Constitution,* August 25, 1915.

15. "12 by 16 Foot Restaurant Space Sells One Million Hamburgers and 160 Tons of French Fries a Year," *American Restaurant Magazine,* July 1952, 44–45; Ray Kroc and Robert Anderson, *Grinding It Out: The Making of McDonald's* (Chicago: Henry Regnery, 1977), 5–11, 65–68; James W. McLamore, *The Burger King: Jim McLamore and the Building of an Empire* (New York: McGraw-Hill, 1998), 15–18.

16. "12 by 16 Foot Restaurant Space," 44–45; Kroc and Anderson, *Grinding It Out,* 5–11, 65–68; McLamore, *The Burger King,* 15–18.

17. Kroc and Anderson, *Grinding It Out,* 5–11, 65–68; McLamore, *The Burger King,* 15–18.

18. Kroc and Anderson, *Grinding It Out,* 116.

19. McDonald's Corporation, *McDonald's First Annual Report* (Chicago: McDonald's Corporation, 1963). Annual reports for the McDonald's Corporation for the years 1963–1973 (excluding 1964) were located at Purdue University.

20. Kroc and Anderson, *Grinding It Out,* 89.

21. McDonald's Corporation, *1965 Annual Report* (Chicago: McDonald's Corporation, 1965), 7.

22. Kroc and Anderson, *Grinding It Out,* 6, 108.

23. McLamore, *The Burger King,* 18–21.

24. Ibid.

25. Ibid., 15, 21–22, 28–29.

26. Ibid., 23.

27. Ibid., 33.

28. Ibid., 33–35.

29. Ibid., 43–47.

30. "Meat, Potatoes, and Money," *Time,* November 3, 1961.

31. McDonald's Corporation, *McDonald's First Annual Report,* 4.

32. McDonald's advertisement, *Reader's Digest,* October 1963, 297; McDonald's Corporation, *McDonald's First Annual Report,* 5–6.

33. McDonald's Corporation, *1965 Annual Report,* 7–8.

34. Kroc and Anderson, *Grinding It Out,* 81–82.

35. Eric Schlosser, *Fast Food Nation: The Dark Side of the All-American Meal* (Boston: Houghton Mifflin, 2001).

36. Growing up in small-town Arkansas, Maya Angelou recalls that the butcher put the orders of black customers aside if a white person entered the shop. *Hallelu-*

jah! The Welcome Table: A Lifetime of Memories with Recipes (New York: Random House, 2004), 46.

37. Hardee, *Life and Times of Wilber Hardee*, 58.

38. Kroc and Anderson, *Grinding It Out*, 81.

39. Hulda Beth Taylor, "Account of My Participation in the Sit-Ins" (May 1963), *Civil Rights Movement Veterans*, http://www.crmvet.org.

40. "In Arkansas: McDonald's Boycott Called," *Student Voice*, December 9, 1963, in *The Student Voice, 1960–1965: Periodical of the Student Nonviolent Coordinating Committee*, ed. Clayborne Carson (Westport, Conn.: Meckler, 1990), 90.

41. Plunkett-Powell, *Remembering Woolworth's*, 159.

42. Herb Kelman to George Houser, December 7, 1953, reel 8, CORE Papers.

43. Kroc and Anderson, *Grinding It Out*, 80.

44. McDonald's Corporation, *McDonald's First Annual Report*.

45. McDonald's Corporation, *1966 Annual Report* (Chicago: McDonald's Corporation, 1966).

PART 3. THE CIVIL RIGHTS REVOLUTION, 1960–1975

1. John Lewis and Michael D'Orso, *Walking with the Wind: A Memoir of the Movement* (New York: Harcourt Brace, 1998), 43–47.

CHAPTER FIVE. THE POLITICS OF THE LUNCH COUNTER

1. Ibid., 74–97.

2. Ibid., 86–92.

3. "Lunch Bar Protests Bring Store Closing," *Nashville Tennessean*, February 7, 1960; "Lunch-Counter Ban Brings New Protests: White Students Join Demonstrators in Durham, Stores Close Doors," ibid., February 9, 1960; "Lunch Counter Dispute Spreads," ibid., February 10, 1960.

4. Lewis and D'Orso, *Walking with the Wind*, 92.

5. Ella Baker, "Bigger than a Hamburger," *Southern Patriot*, May 1960.

6. Lizabeth Cohen, *A Consumer's Republic: The Politics of Mass Consumption in Postwar America* (New York: Knopf, 2003).

7. For examinations of these important civil rights events, see Tony Freyer, *Little Rock on Trial: Cooper v. Aaron and School Desegregation* (Lawrence: University of Kansas Press, 2007), and Kenneth M. Hare, *They Walked to Freedom, 1955–1956: The Story of the Montgomery Bus Boycott* (Montgomery, Ala.: Advertiser Company, 2005).

8. Peter Madsen, Lunch Counter Stool, U.S. Patent 1,862,755, filed October 4, 1926, and issued June 14, 1932; John S. Reid, Food-Display Case for Lunch Counters, U.S. Patent 1,744,081, filed January 25, 1928, and issued January 21, 1930.

9. Luther L. Knox, Lunch-Counter Structure, U.S. Patent 1,584,035, filed April 19, 1924, and issued May 11, 1926; Clinton O. Larmore, Lunch-Counter Partition, U.S. Patent 1,563,381, filed April 4, 1925, and issued December 1, 1925.

10. *Browder v. Gayle*, 352 U.S. 903 (1956).

11. "Civil Rights Leader Diane Nash" (April 12, 2013), Anna Julia Cooper Project on Gender, Race, and Politics in the South, Newcomb College Institute, Tulane University, New Orleans, Louisiana, http://www.c-spanvideo.org/program/DianeN.

12. W. Ralph Eubanks, *Ever Is a Long Time: A Journey into Mississippi's Dark Past* (New York: Basic, 2003), 18–19, 36–37.

13. Karen Plunkett-Powell, *Remembering Woolworth's: A Nostalgic History of the World's Most Famous Five-and-Dime* (New York: St. Martin's, 1999), 145–152.

14. Ibid., 142.

15. Columbia Broadcasting System, *Anatomy of a Demonstration*, Civil Rights Collection, Nashville Public Library, Nashville, Tennessee.

16. Henry Kraus, interview by U-M Flint Labor History Project (May 5, 1982), edited by Michael Van Dyke, and "Strike Organization," *Flint Sit-Down Strike Audio Gallery*, http://flint.matrix.msu.edu.

17. Larry Jones, interview by U-M Flint Labor History Project (June 9, 1978), edited by Michael Van Dyke, "Strike," and "Aftermath," ibid.

18. Floyd Root, interview by U-M Flint Labor History Project (June 4, 1978), edited by Michael Van Dyke, and "Strike," ibid.

19. Dana Frank, "Girl Strikers Occupy Chain Store, Win Big: The Detroit Woolworth's Strike of 1937," in *Three Strikes: Miners, Musicians, Sales Girls, and the Fighting Spirit of Labor's Last Century*, ed. Howard Zinn, Dana Frank, and Robin D. G. Kelley (Boston: Beacon, 2001), 61–79.

20. Ibid., 76–113.

21. Phyllis Haeger to Catherine Raymond, June 10, 1949, reel 8, CORE Papers.

22. Colorado Committee of Racial Equality, [affiliation blank], ca. 1953, reel 8, CORE Papers; Philadelphia CORE, [affiliation blank], ca. 1953, ibid.

23. Warren Baumann and Lawrence Gorham to George M. Houser, November 12, 1949, reel 8, CORE Papers.

24. Helen W. Brown to Friend, April 25, 1958, reel 8, CORE Papers.

25. "The Tea Cup Project: Berkeley Committee of Racial Equality," reel 8, CORE Papers.

26. Ruth W. Brown to George Houser, February 1, February 2, March 11, and August 11, 1950, reel 9, CORE Papers. Louise S. Robbins connects Brown's story to civil rights activism, censorship, and McCarthyism in *The Dismissal of Miss Ruth Brown: Civil Rights, Censorship, and the American Library* (Norman: University of Oklahoma Press, 2000).

27. Lewis and D'Orso, *Walking with the Wind*, 92.

28. Ibid. (emphasis in original).

29. Ibid., 94.

30. Ibid., 93–96.

31. National Broadcasting Company, *NBC White Paper*, Civil Rights Collection, Nashville Public Library, Nashville, Tennessee.

32. "State Reports," *Student Voice* 1, no. 2 (August 1960), in *The Student Voice 1960–1965: Periodical of the Student Nonviolent Coordinating Committee*, ed. Clayborne Carson (Westport, Conn.: Meckler, 1990), 9.

33. Hulda Beth Taylor, "Account of My Participation in the Sit-Ins" (May 1963), *Civil Rights Movement Veterans*, http://www.crmvet.org.

34. "The Atlanta Story," *Student Voice* 1, no. 3 (October 1960), in Carson, *Student Voice 1960–1965*, 13–14; Glenn T. Eskew, *But for Birmingham: The Local and National Movements in the Civil Rights Struggle* (Chapel Hill: University of North Carolina Press, 1997), 274; "Civil Rights Leader Diane Nash"; "The Nashville Story: Whites Meet Challenge," *Southern Patriot*, September 1960, 1–3.

35. "Negro Students Issue Warning: Threaten to Enroll at Auburn if Alabama Reprisals Continue," *Nashville Tennessean*, February 27, 1960; "Students Plan Mass Walkout: Object to Alabama Governor's Expel 'Advice' on Demonstrators," ibid., March 1, 1960.

36. "Alabama College Ousts 9 Negroes," *Nashville Tennessean*, March 3, 1960; *Dixon v. Alabama State Board of Education*, 186 F. Supp. 945 (M.D. Ala. 1960), rev'd, 294 F.2D 150 (5th Cir. 1961).

37. "Alabama Negro Students Strike: Retaliation Move Made for Expulsion of Campus Leaders," *Nashville Tennessean*, March 5, 1960.

38. Ibid.

39. *Dixon v. Alabama State Board of Education*; Adam M. Peck, "Due Process and Fairness in Student Affairs: How to Do All That Is Due," *Bulletin* 73, no. 2 (March 2005), http://www.acui.org/publications/bulletin/article.aspx?issue=410&id=1952.

40. James Farmer to Friends of CORE, March 22, 1962, reel 26, CORE Papers.

41. Anne Moody, *Coming of Age in Mississippi: The Classic Autobiography of Growing Up Poor and Black in the Rural South* (1968; rpt., New York: Dell, 1976), 286–290.

42. Rodney L. Hurst Sr., *It Was Never about a Hot Dog and a Coke: A Personal Account of the 1960 Sit-In Demonstrations in Jacksonville, Florida, and Ax Handle Saturday* (Livermore, Calif.: Wingspan, 2008), 54–77.

43. "White Students Join in Lunch Counter Protests," *Atlanta Daily World*, March 3, 1960; "46 Arrested in Greensboro, N.C., Sit-Down Protest," ibid., April 22, 1960; "Supreme Court Asked to Review Va. Sit-In Cases," ibid., August 4, 1961; Dan Day, "Capital Spotlight: Court's Ruling Skirts More Serious Constitutional Questions," ibid., December 27, 1961.

44. Transcript of Record, *Peterson v. City of Greenville*, 373 U.S. 244 (1963).

45. *Civil Rights Cases*, 109 U.S. 3 (1883).

46. *Burton v. Wilmington Parking Authority*, 365 U.S. 715 (1961).

47. *Peterson v. City of Greenville*, 244.

48. J. M. Breckenridge to Albert Boutwell, May 23, 1963, Collection 987.1.30, Birmingham, Alabama, Law Department, Civil Rights Files and Related Materials, Department of Archives and Manuscripts, Birmingham Public Library, Birmingham, Alabama.

49. Eskew, *But for Birmingham*, 294n37.

50. Ibid., 317.

51. *Gober v. City of Birmingham*, 373 U.S. 374 (1963) (per curiam) (holding, pursuant to *Peterson*, that Birmingham City Code § 369 represented an unconstitutional violation of the Fourteenth Amendment).

52. Columbia Broadcasting System, *Report to the American People on Civil Rights, 11 June 1963*, 16 mm film, 13:41, John F. Kennedy Presidential Museum and Library, Boston, Massachusetts, http://www.jfklibrary.org/Asset-Viewer/LH8F_0Mzv oe6Ro1yEm74Ng.aspx (accessed August 14, 2013); Eskew, *But for Birmingham*, 310–311.

53. Civil Rights Act, Pub. L. No. 88-352, 78 Stat. 241 (1964).

54. Lyndon B. Johnson, "Annual Message to the Congress on the State of the Union, January 8, 1964," in *Public Papers of the Presidents of the United States: Lyndon B. Johnson, 1963–64*, vol. 1 (Washington, D.C.: Government Printing Office, 1965), entry 91, 112–118.

55. Nicholas D. Katzenbach Oral History Interview I, interview by Paige E. Mulhollan, November 12, 1968, online transcript, 14–18, Lyndon Baines Johnson Library, University of Texas, Austin, http://www.lbjlib.utexas.edu/johnson/archives .hom/oralhistory.hom/Katzenbach/KATZENB1.PDF (accessed January 25, 2005).

56. Lewis and D'Orso, *Walking with the Wind*, 273–274.

57. "Score Victory in Integration," *Chicago Defender*, August 26, 1958; "Okla.

Youngsters Fight Color Line," ibid.; "Youths Sit Down for Integration," ibid., August 30, 1958.

CHAPTER SIX. WHITE RESISTANCE IN SEGREGATED RESTAURANTS

1. "A Bill to Eliminate Discrimination in Public Accommodations Affecting Interstate Commerce: Hearings before the Committee on Commerce, United States Senate," S. 1732, 88th Cong., 1963 (statement of John G. Vonetes), 1059–1062.

2. Ibid., 1062–1063.

3. Ibid., 1061–1064.

4. Ibid., 1059–1060.

5. In Maurice Bessinger's obituary, his son Lloyd Bessinger, who took over the family business, noted that he is no longer interested in furthering any particular political philosophy. "We want to serve great barbecue," the younger Bessinger stated. John Monk, "Barbecue Eatery Owner, Segregationist Maurice Bessinger Dies at 83," *State*, February 24, 2014, http://www.thestate.com/2014/02/24/3288326 /barbecue-eatery-owner-segregationist.html.

6. The U.S. attorney general regularly brought charges against restaurants that defied the Civil Rights Act, and intervened in lawsuits brought by activists. The McClungs reportedly filed suit to request a declaratory judgment that the Civil Rights Act did not apply to their business after the attorney general brought suit against several restaurants and lunch counters in nearby Tuscaloosa, Alabama. Transcript of record, *McClung v. Katzenbach*, 233 F. Supp. 815 (N.D. Ala.) (No. 64-448), 89; "15 Tuscaloosans Ask Racial Suit Dismissal," *Birmingham Post Herald*, August 18, 1964. When the federal district court issued a permanent injunction against these Tuscaloosa restaurants, it used the decision in *Katzenbach v. McClung* as the controlling precedent. "Restaurants, Hospital Cited in Rights Case," *Birmingham News*, April 15, 1965.

7. Transcript of Record, *McClung v. Katzenbach*, 233 F. Supp. 815 (N.D. Ala.) (No. 64-448), 79.

8. Lester Maddox, *Speaking Out: The Autobiography of Lester Garfield Maddox* (Garden City, N.Y.: Doubleday, 1975), 1–25, 27–29.

9. Ibid., 31–32; "Lester G. Maddox Guest Book," http://www.legacy.com (accessed March 27, 2008).

10. Maddox, *Speaking Out*, 30–32, 54–57.

11. Ibid., 30–32, 54–57, 62; "Maddox Holds Gun, Bars 3 Negroes," *Atlanta Constitution*, July 4, 1964; Horace Cort, "Lester Maddox, Lester Maddox Jr." (July 3, 1964), Associated Press photograph, http://www.apimages.com/metadata/Index

/Watchf-Associated-Press-Domestic-News-Georgia-U-/a264ffe1f1d94480887d4cf0
a50fc1d2/5/0.

12. Maurice Bessinger, *Defending My Heritage: The Maurice Bessinger Story* (West
Columbia, S.C.: Lmbone-Lehone, 2001), 1–15.

13. Ibid., 15.

14. Ibid., 15, 28.

15. Ibid., 26.

16. Ibid., 69.

17. Rebecca Sharpless, *Cooking in Other Women's Kitchens: Domestic Workers
in the South, 1865–1960* (Chapel Hill: University of North Carolina Press, 2010),
74–77, 154.

18. Bessinger, *Defending My Heritage*, 58–59; "50s Piggie Park," Maurice's Piggie
Park bbq, http://www.mauricesbbq.com (accessed March 21, 2011).

19. Bessinger, *Defending My Heritage*, 75–78; "60s Piggie Park," Maurice's Piggie
Park bbq, http://www.mauricesbbq.com (accessed March 21, 2011); *Newman v. Piggie Park Enterprises*, 390 U.S. 400 (1968).

20. Psyche A. Williams-Forson, *Building Houses Out of Chicken Legs: Black
Women, Food, and Power* (Chapel Hill: University of North Carolina Press, 2006),
53–57, 136.

21. Bessinger, *Defending My Heritage*, 27–28.

22. "A Bill to Eliminate Discrimination in Public Accommodations Affecting Interstate Commerce: Hearings Before the Committee on Commerce, United States
Senate," S. 1732, 88th Cong., 1963 (statement of U.S. attorney general Robert F. Kennedy), 19–20.

23. Maddox, *Speaking Out*, 34.

24. Transcript of record, *McClung v. Katzenbach*, 233 F. Supp. 815 (N.D. Ala.) (No.
64-448), 77, 86.

25. "Say Sit-In Law Can Be Used to Evict Anyone," *Atlanta Daily World*, November 13, 1960.

26. Lallage Longshore to Lister Hill, June 24, 1963, folder 121, box 495, Lister Hill
Papers 1921–1968, W. S. Hoole Special Collections Library, University of Alabama,
Tuscaloosa.

27. Transcript of record, *McClung v. Katzenbach*, 233 F. Supp. 815 (N.D. Ala.) (No.
64-448), 70, 79.

28. "2 Lester Maddox Waitresses Say Man Tried Dates," *Atlanta Daily World*,
April 12, 1962.

29. Bruce Galphin, *The Riddle of Lester Maddox* (Atlanta: Camelot, 1968), 22.

30. Bessinger, *Defending My Heritage*, 73.

31. The white southern assumption that white women faced imminent threats of rape from black men developed after Reconstruction as a method to limit black political power and peaked during the first part of the twentieth century. In actuality, white female accusations of rape were complicated by competing racial, class, and gender considerations. Nevertheless, the image of the black rapist continued to influence white supremacist rhetoric. Lisa Lindquist Dorr, *White Women, Rape, and the Power of Race in Virginia, 1900–1960* (Chapel Hill: University of North Carolina Press, 2004), 7–10.

32. "Who Needs Protection?" *Citizen*, December 1964, 2, 23.

33. Durr, *Outside the Magic Circle*, 276.

34. "Recently Desegregated—Negro Is Killed in Fight in Cafe," *Birmingham Post-Herald*, October 30, 1964.

35. "McClungs Agree to Serve Negroes," *Birmingham News*, December 16, 1964; "Ollie's Complies, Negroes Served," *Birmingham Post-Herald*, December 17, 1964; "Ala. Restaurant Owner to Bow to Rights Bill," *Birmingham World*, December 23, 1964; Ollie McClung Jr., interview by Joan Hoffman, November 5, 1975, tape and transcript, Oral History Collection, Mervyn H. Sterne Library, University of Alabama, Birmingham.

36. Regina A. Thurston, "Evaluation Report: Social Services, Parent Participation, Volunteer Services, Southwest Mississippi Child Development Council," April 29, 1968–May 2, 1968, p. 4, folder "MISS CG-3155 Southwest Mississippi Opportunity, Inc. Woodville, Mississippi," box 12, RG381, National Archives at Atlanta, Morrow, Georgia.

37. *U.S. v. Boyd*, 327 F. Supp. 998 (S.D.Ga. 1970).

38. Philip P. Ardery, "Federal Suit Bolsters Picketers in Bogalusa," *Southern Courier*, July 23, 1965; "Bogalusa, Louisiana, Incident Summary: January 25–February 21 [1965]," *Civil Rights Movement Veterans*, http://www.crmvet.org/docs/65_core_bogalusa_incidents.pdf; *Katzenbach v. Jordan*, 302 F. Supp. 370 (E.D.La. 1969).

39. Scholarly works on the Bogalusa movement include Rickey Hill, "The Bogalusa Movement: Self-Defense and Black Power in the Civil Rights Struggle," *Black Scholar* 41, no. 3 (Fall 2011): 43–54, and Lance Hill, *The Deacons for Defense: Armed Resistance and the Civil Rights Movement* (Chapel Hill: University of North Carolina Press, 2004).

40. "Pickrick Restaurant and Employees" (ca. 1964), Lester Maddox Photographs, VIS105.06, Kenan Research Center, Atlanta History Center (emphasis in original); Don McKee, "Maddox's Actions Called Political, Not Racial," *Birmingham Post-Herald*, February 2, 1965, and "Maddox's Confusion Stressed," *Birmingham News*, February 3, 1965, both in *Civil Rights Scrapbook*, p. 15, Birmingham Archives, Bir-

mingham Public Library, Birmingham, Alabama; "Maddox Says He'll Comply, Wife Weeps," *Birmingham News*, February 7, 1965, and "Maddox Blames Reds for Cafe Troubles," *Birmingham Post-Herald*, February 24, 1965, both ibid., p. 19.

41. WSB-TV, "Newsfilm Clip of Lester Maddox Pushing African Americans Away from His Cafeteria with an Ax Handle, Atlanta, Georgia" (January 29, 1965), Digital Library of Georgia and Walter J. Brown Media Archives and Peabody Awards Collection, University of Georgia Libraries, Athens, http://dlg.galileo.usg.edu/crdl /id:ugabma_wsbn_47697.

42. *Willis v. Pickrick Cafeteria*, 231 F. Supp. 396 (N.D.Ga. 1964); "In Front of the Pickrick after the Closing," in Maddox, *Speaking Out*, picture 6; Justin Nystrom, "Lester Maddox (1915–2003)," in *New Georgia Encyclopedia*, http://www.georgia encyclopedia.org/articles/government-politics/lester-maddox-1915-2003.

43. John Monk, "God, Barbecue, Slavery Meet at Maurice's," *State*, August 27, 2000; Bessinger, *Defending My Heritage*, 155–163.

44. R. Kevin Dietrich, "Stores Stand Firm on Sauce's Ban," *State*, December 26, 2000; Bessinger, *Defending My Heritage*, 165–170; Jack Hitt, "A Confederacy of Sauces," *New York Times*, August 26, 2001.

CONCLUSION. CRACKER BARREL AND THE SOUTHERN STRATEGY

1. "Heritage and History," Cracker Barrel website, http://crackerbarrel.com /about-us/heritage-and-history (accessed August 15, 2013).

2. Susie Penman, "Cracker Barrel's Culture: Exporting the South on America's Interstate Exits" (master's thesis, University of Mississippi, 2012).

3. Rick Perlstein, "Exclusive: Lee Atwater's Infamous 1981 Interview on the Southern Strategy," *Nation*, November 13, 2012; Joseph A. Aistrup, *The Southern Strategy Revisited: Republican Top-Down Advancement in the South* (Lexington: University of Kentucky Press, 1996), 6–11.

4. Frederick Douglass Opie, *Hog and Hominy: Soul Food from Africa to America* (New York: Columbia University Press, 2008), 121–138; William C. Whit, "Soul Food as Cultural Creation," in *African American Foodways: Explorations of History and Culture*, ed. Anne Bower (Urbana: University of Illinois Press, 2007), 45–58.

5. "Our Social Responsibility," Cracker Barrel website, http://www.crackerbarrel .com/about-us/social-responsibility (accessed August 15, 2013).

6. In her master's thesis, Penman explores the company's strategy to target white nostalgia for the racially segregated space of the country store and analyzes the company's name with reference to the term "cracker," which among other things is derogatory slang used to describe poor rural whites. "Cracker Barrel's Culture," 82–107.

7. "Heritage and History," Cracker Barrel website.

8. Melton A. McLaurin, *Separate Pasts: Growing Up White in the Segregated South* (Athens: University of Georgia Press, 1998), 112.

9. Ibid., 121–132.

10. Ibid., 28–29, 111–113.

11. Grace Elizabeth Hale, *Making Whiteness: The Culture of Segregation in the South, 1890–1940* (New York: Pantheon, 1998), 174.

12. Stephen J. Whitfield, *A Death in the Delta: The Story of Emmett Till* (Baltimore, Md.: Johns Hopkins University Press, 1988), 15–21.

13. Anthony Stanonis, "Just Like Mammy Used to Make," in *Dixie Emporium: Tourism, Foodways, and Consumer Culture in the American South*, ed. Anthony Stanonis (Athens: University of Georgia Press, 2008), 226; Penman, "Cracker Barrel's Culture," 93.

14. Julie Schmit and Larry Copeland, "Cracker Barrel Customer Claims Bias was 'Flagrant,'" *USA Today*, May 7, 2004.

15. "365 Black," http://www.mcdonalds.com/365black/en/home.html (accessed August 16, 2013).

16. Most food scholars and activists see this as a negative development because of health concerns associated with fast food. See, for example, Naa Oyo A. Kwate, Chun-Yip Yau, Ji-Meng Loh, and Donya Williams, "Inequality in Obesigenic Environments: Fast Food Density in New York City," in *Taking Food Public: Redefining Foodways in a Changing World*, ed. Psyche Williams-Forson and Carole Counihan (New York: Routledge, 2011), 115–126.

Selected Bibliography

MANUSCRIPT, ORAL HISTORY, AND PHOTOGRAPH COLLECTIONS

Associated Press Photographs, http://www.apimages.com
Athens–Clarke County Library, Athens, Georgia, http://dlg.galileo.usg.edu
    Athens Woman's Club Collection
Birmingham Archives, Birmingham Public Library, Birmingham, Alabama, http://
    bplonline.cdmhost.com
    Civil Rights Files and Related Materials
    Civil Rights Scrapbook
    Hill Ferguson Papers
    Meeting Minutes, Board of Commissioners, City of Birmingham
Congress of Racial Equality (CORE) Papers, 1959–1976, Wisconsin Historical Society
Georgia Department of Archives and History, Office of the Secretary of State, Morrow
    Vanishing Georgia Collection, http://dlg.galileo.usg.edu
Kenan Research Center, Atlanta History Center, Atlanta, Georgia
    Lester Maddox Photographs
Library of Congress, Washington, D.C., http://www.loc.gov
    Farm Security Administration, Office of War Information, Black and White
        Negatives
    Photographs Historical and Descriptive Data
Lyndon Baines Johnson Library, University of Texas, Austin, http://www
    .lbjlibrary.org
    Nicholas D. Katzenbach Oral History Interview I
Martin Luther King Jr. Center for Nonviolent Social Change, Atlanta, Georgia,
    http://www.thekingcenter.org
    Digital Archive

National Archives at Atlanta, Morrow, Georgia
    RG381, Records of the Community Services Administration
Oral History Collection, Mervyn H. Sterne Library, University of Alabama at Birmingham
Oral History Collection, Southern Foodways Alliance, www.southernfoodways.org
Special Collections Library, Georgia College and State University, Milledgeville
    Cherry Waldrep Clements Papers
W. S. Hoole Special Collections Library, University of Alabama, Tuscaloosa
    Lister Hill Papers, 1921–1968

NEWSPAPERS

Atlanta Constitution
Atlanta Daily World
Birmingham Age-Herald
Birmingham News
Birmingham Post-Herald
Birmingham Wide Awake
Birmingham World
Chicago Defender
Galveston Daily News
Louisville Courier

Macon Telegraph
Milledgeville (Ga.) *Union Recorder*
Montgomery Advertiser
Nashville Tennessean
New York Times
Richmond Times-Dispatch
Savannah Tribune
State (Columbia, S.C.)
USA Today

PUBLISHED WORKS

"12 by 16 Foot Restaurant Space Sells One Million Hamburgers and 160 Tons of French Fries a Year." *American Restaurant Magazine*, July 1952, 44–45.

Aistrup, Joseph A. *The Southern Strategy Revisited: Republican Top-Down Advancement in the South*. Lexington: University of Kentucky Press, 1996.

Alabama Girls Technical Institute. *Catalogue of the Alabama Girls Technical Institute for the Eighteenth Annual Session 1913–1914 and Announcements 1914–1915*. Montevallo: Alabama Girls Technical Institute, 1915.

———. *Catalogue of the Alabama Girls Technical Institute for the Fifteenth Annual Session 1910–11*. Birmingham, Ala.: Dispatch Printing, 1909–10.

———. *Catalogue of the Alabama Girls Technical Institute for the Nineteenth Annual Session 1914–1915 and Announcements 1915–1916*. Montevallo: Alabama Girls Technical Institute, 1916.

———. *Catalogue of the Alabama Girls Technical Institute for the Twentieth Annual Session 1915–1916 and Announcements 1916–1917*. Montevallo: Alabama Girls Technical Institute, 1917.

———. *Catalogue of the Alabama Girls Technical Institute for the Twenty-Third Annual Session 1918–1919 and Announcements 1919–1920*. Montevallo: Alabama Girls Technical Institute, 1920.

American Home Economics Association. *Lake Placid Conference Proceedings*. 10 vols. Washington, D.C.: American Home Economics Association, 1901–1908. http://hearth.library.cornell.edu.

Angelou, Maya. *Hallelujah! The Welcome Table: A Lifetime of Memories with Recipes*. New York: Random House, 2004.

Ardery, Philip P. "Federal Suit Bolsters Picketers in Bogalusa." *Southern Courier*, July 23, 1965. http://www.southerncourier.org/hi-res/Vol1_N002_1965_07_23.pdf.

Arnold, Eleanor, ed. *Voices of American Homemakers*. Bloomington: Indiana University Press, 1998.

Atlanta City Directory. Atlanta: Thomas J. Maloney, 1900, 1901, 1902, 1903.

Atlanta Woman's Club. *Atlanta Woman's Club Cook Book*. Atlanta: Atlanta Woman's Club, 1921.

Ayers, Edward. *The Promise of the New South*. New York: Oxford University Press, 1992.

Baker, Ella. "Bigger than a Hamburger." *Southern Patriot*, May 1960.

"Barbecue and the Bar," *Newsweek*, September 28, 1964.

Beecher, Catharine E. *A Treatise on Domestic Economy for the Use of Young Ladies at Home and at School*. Boston: Thomas H. Webb, 1843.

Belasco, Warren. *Appetite for Change: How the Counterculture Took on the Food Industry*. Ithaca, N.Y.: Cornell University Press, 2006.

Bessinger, Maurice. *Defending My Heritage: The Maurice Bessinger Story*. West Columbia, S.C.: Lmbone-Lehone, 2001.

Biles, Roger. *The South and the New Deal*. Lexington: University of Kentucky Press, 1994.

Birmingham City Directory 1889. N.p.: R. L. Polk, 1889.

Birmingham City Directory 1902. Atlanta: Mutual, 1902.

Birmingham Directory 1904. Birmingham, Ala.: Wiggins Directories Publishing, 1904.

Birmingham, Suburban and Bessemer Directory. N.p.: R. L. Polk, 1888.

Bower, Anne ed. *Recipes for Reading: Community Cookbooks, Stories, Histories*. Boston: University of Massachusetts Press, 1997.

Brooks, Robert Preston. "Sanitary Conditions among the Negroes of Athens, Georgia." *Bulletin of the University of Georgia* 18, no. 7 (1918): 23.

Bryant, Annie Mae, ed. *Athens Woman's Club Cook Book*. Athens, Ga.: McGregor, 1922.

Bullock, Helen. *The Williamsburg Art of Cookery; or, Accomplished Gentlewoman's Companion*. Williamsburg, Va.: Colonial Williamsburg Foundation, 1966.

Burdette, Kay. *Cookery of the Old South (Translated from Southern Lore)*. Glendale, Calif.: n.p., 1938.

Byerly, Victoria. *Hard Times Cotton Mill Girls: Personal Histories of Womanhood and Poverty in the South*. Ithaca, N.Y.: Cornell University Press, 1986.

Cannon, Katie Geneva. *Katie's Canon: Womanism and the Soul of the Black Community*. New York: Continuum, 1995.

Carson, Clayborne, ed. *The Student Voice, 1960–1965: Periodical of the Student Nonviolent Coordinating Committee*. Westport, Conn.: Meckler, 1990.

Cell, John W. *The Highest Stage of White Supremacy: The Origins of Segregation in South Africa and the American South*. Cambridge: Cambridge University Press, 1982.

Chapman, Bernadine Sharpe. "Northern Philanthropy and African-American Adult Education in the Rural South: Hegemony and Resistance in the Jeanes Movement." EdD diss., Northern Illinois University, 1990.

City Directory of Birmingham, Alabama, 1898. N.p.: Maloney Directory, 1897.

City Directory of Birmingham, Alabama, 1899. N.p.: Maloney Directory, 1898.

City Directory of Birmingham and Gazetteer of Surrounding Section for 1884–5. Atlanta: Interstate Directory, 1884.

Clark-Lewis, Elizabeth. *Living In, Living Out: African American Domestics in Washington, D.C., 1910–1940*. Washington, D.C.: Smithsonian Institution Press, 1994.

"Clay Eating." *Scientific American* 72, no. 12 (March 23, 1895): 186.

Cobb, James C., and Michael V. Namorato, eds. *The New Deal and the South*. Jackson: University Press of Mississippi, 1984.

Cohen, Lizabeth. *A Consumer's Republic: The Politics of Mass Consumption in Postwar America*. New York: Knopf, 2003.

Cortner, Richard C. *Civil Rights and Public Accommodations: The Heart of Atlanta Motel and McClung Cases*. Lawrence: University of Kansas Press, 2001.

Daniels, Jonathan. *A Southerner Discovers the South*. New York: Macmillan, 1938.

Davis, Cynthia J. *Charlotte Perkins Gilman: A Biography*. Stanford, Calif.: Stanford University Press, 2010.

Davis, Marni. *Jews and Booze: Becoming American in the Age of Prohibition.* New York: New York University Press, 2012.

Dickins, Dorothy. *Some Contrasts in the Levels of Living of Women Engaged in Farm, Textile Mill, and Garment Plant Work.* State College: Mississippi Agricultural Experiment Station, 1941.

The Dixie Cook-Book. Atlanta: L. A. Clarkson, 1883.

Douglas, Mary. *Purity and Danger: An Analysis of the Concepts of Pollution and Taboo.* London: Routledge and Kegan Paul, 1966.

Doyle, Don H. *New Men, New Cities, New South: Atlanta, Nashville, Charleston, Mobile, 1860–1910.* Chapel Hill: University of North Carolina Press, 1990.

Dull, [Henrietta Stanley]. *Southern Cooking.* 1941. Rpt., Athens: University of Georgia Press, 2006.

Durr, Virginia Foster. *Outside the Magic Circle: The Autobiography of Virginia Foster Durr,* edited by Hollinger F. Barnard. Tuscaloosa: University of Alabama Press, 1985.

"Earth as Medicine and Food." *Literary Digest* 53, no. 17 (October 21, 1916): 1027.

"Eating Clay." *Good Housekeeping,* March 19, 1887, 236.

Edge, John T., Elizabeth Engelhardt, and Ted Ownby, eds. *The Larder: Food Studies Methods from the American South.* Athens: University of Georgia Press, 2013.

Elias, Megan J. *Food in the United States, 1890–1945.* Denver, Colo.: Greenwood, 2009.

Engelhardt, Elizabeth S. D. *A Mess of Greens: Southern Gender and Southern Food.* Athens: University of Georgia Press, 2011.

Eskew, Glenn T. *But for Birmingham: The Local and National Movements in the Civil Rights Struggle.* Chapel Hill: University of North Carolina Press, 1997.

Eubanks, W. Ralph. *Ever Is a Long Time: A Journey into Mississippi's Dark Past.* New York: Basic, 2003.

Farmer, Fannie Merritt. *The 1896 Boston Cooking School Cook Book.* 1896. Rpt., New York: Gramercy, 1997.

Faulkner, William. *Light in August.* 1932. Rpt., New York: Vintage, 1990.

Feldman, Glenn. *Politics, Society, and the Klan in Alabama, 1915–1949.* Tuscaloosa: University of Alabama Press, 1999.

Ferris, Marcie Cohen. *The Edible South: Food and History in an American Region.* Chapel Hill: University of North Carolina Press, 2014.

Fickling, Jane W., ed. *Recipes from Old Charleston: Catherine Lee Banks Edwards.* Birmingham, Ala.: Banner, 1989.

First City Directory of Birmingham and County Gazetteer for 1883–4. Atlanta: C. M. Gardner, 1883.

Frank, Dana. "Girl Strikers Occupy Chain Store, Win Big: The Detroit Woolworth's Strike of 1937." In *Three Strikes: Miners, Musicians, Sales Girls, and the Fighting Spirit of Labor's Last Century*, edited by Howard Zinn, Dana Frank, and Robin D. G. Kelley, 61–79. Boston: Beacon, 2001.

Frayser, Mary E. "House Plans for New Homes and for the Alteration of Homes." *Proceedings of the Second Annual Conference, Alabama Home Economics Association* 10, no. 11 (October 1916): 16–17.

Fredrickson, George M. *The Black Image in the White Mind: The Debate on Afro-American Character and Destiny, 1817–1914*. New York: Harper and Row, 1971.

Freyer, Tony. *Little Rock on Trial: Cooper v. Aaron and School Desegregation*. Lawrence: University of Kansas Press, 2007.

Gabaccia, Donna. *We Are What We Eat: Ethnic Food and the Making of Americans*. Cambridge, Mass.: Harvard University Press, 1998.

Galphin, Bruce. *The Riddle of Lester Maddox*. Atlanta: Camelot, 1968.

Georgia Branch of the National Congress of Parents and Teachers, ed. *P.T.A. Interpretations of Food*. Atlanta: Walter W. Brown, 1928.

Georgia Normal and Industrial College. *First Annual Announcement of Catalogue of the Georgia Normal and Industrial College, Milledgeville, Georgia, 1891–92*. Atlanta: Jas. P. Harrison, 1892.

Guthman, Julie. *Weighing In: Obesity, Food Justice and the Limits of Capitalism*. Berkeley: University of California Press, 2011.

Ginter Park Woman's Club. *Famous Recipes from Old Virginia*. Richmond, Va.: Richmond Press, 1935.

———. *Famous Recipes from Old Virginia*. 2nd ed. Richmond, Va.: Clyde W. Saunders and Sons, 1941.

Griffith, Lucille B. *Alabama College, 1896–1969*. Montevallo, Ala.: University of Montevallo, 1969.

Grover, Kathryn, ed. *Dining in America 1850–1900*. Amherst: University of Massachusetts Press, 1987.

"Habits of the Tennessee Mountaineers and Clay-Eaters." *Timely Topics*, September 10, 1897.

Hale, Grace Elizabeth. *Making Whiteness: The Culture of Segregation in the South, 1890–1940*. New York: Pantheon, 1998.

Haley, Andrew. *Turning the Tables: Restaurants and the Rise of the American Middle Class, 1880–1920*. Chapel Hill: University of North Carolina Press, 2011.

Hardee, Wilber. *The Life and Times of Wilber Hardee*. New York: Writers Press Club, 2000.

Hare, Kenneth M. *They Walked to Freedom, 1955–1956: The Story of the Montgomery Bus Boycott*. Montgomery, Ala.: Advertiser Company, 2005.

Henderson, William N. "Outlines for a Brief Course in Chemistry of Food and Nutrition." *Bulletin, Alabama Girls Technical Institute* 21 (ca. 1912): 38–40.

Herrick, Christine Terhune, and Marion Harland. *Modern Domestic Science*. Chicago: Debower-Chapline, 1909.

Hill, Lance. *The Deacons for Defense: Armed Resistance and the Civil Rights Movement*. Chapel Hill: University of North Carolina Press, 2004.

Hill, Rickey. "The Bogalusa Movement: Self-Defense and Black Power in the Civil Rights Struggle." *Black Scholar* 41, no. 3 (Fall 2011): 43–54.

Hoffman, Frederick L. *Race Traits and Tendencies of the American Negro*. New York: Macmillan, 1896.

Hoffschwelle, Mary S. "The Science of Domesticity: Home Economics at George Peabody College for Teachers, 1914–1939." *Journal of Southern History* 57, no. 4 (November 1991): 659–680.

Hornsby, Alton. "A City That Was Too Busy to Hate." In *Southern Businessmen and Desegregation*, edited by Elizabeth Jacoway and David R. Colburn, 120–136. Baton Rouge: Louisiana State University Press, 1982.

Hunter, Tera W. *To 'Joy My Freedom: Southern Black Women's Lives and Labors after the Civil War*. Cambridge, Mass.: Harvard University Press, 1997.

Hurst, Rodney L., Sr. *It Was Never about a Hot Dog and a Coke: A Personal Account of the 1960 Sit-In Demonstrations in Jacksonville, Florida, and Ax Handle Saturday*. Livermore, Calif.: Wingspan, 2008.

Ingram, E. W., Sr. *"All This from a 5-Cent Hamburger": The Story of the White Castle System*. New York: Newcomen Society in North America, 1964.

Jacoway, Elizabeth, and David R. Colburn, eds. *Southern Businessmen and Desegregation*. Baton Rouge: Louisiana State University Press, 1982.

Jakle, John A., and Keith A. Sculle. *Fast Food: Roadside Restaurants in the Automobile Age*. Baltimore, Md.: Johns Hopkins University Press, 1999.

Jones, James. *Bad Blood: The Tuskegee Syphilis Experiment*. New York: Free Press, 1993.

Kaplan, Amy. "Manifest Domesticity." *American Literature* 70 (September 1998): 581–606.

Katsos, John. *The Life of John Katsos*. Greenville, S.C.: A Press, 1985.

Kelly, Blair L. M. *Right to Ride: Streetcar Protests and African American Citizenship in the Era of Plessy v. Ferguson*. Chapel Hill: University of North Carolina Press, 2010.

Kerem, Yitzchak. "The Settlement of Rhodian and Other Sephardic Jews in Montgomery and Atlanta in the 20th Century." *American Jewish History* 85 (1997): 373–392.

Klewer, Edward B., ed. *The Memphis Digest.* Vol. 1. Memphis: S. C. Toof, 1931.

Knight, Denise D., ed. *The Abridged Diaries of Charlotte Perkins Gilman.* Charlottesville: University Press of Virginia, 1998.

Kroc, Ray, and Robert Anderson, *Grinding It Out: The Making of McDonald's.* Chicago: Henry Regnery, 1977.

Kuhn, Clifford M., Harlon E. Joye, and E. Bernard West. *Living Atlanta: An Oral History of the City, 1914–1948.* Athens: University of Georgia Press, 1990.

Kwate, Naa Oyo A., Chun-Yip Yau, Ji-Meng Loh, and Donya Williams. "Inequality in Obesigenic Environments: Fast Food Density in New York City." In *Taking Food Public: Redefining Foodways in a Changing World*, edited by Psyche Williams-Forson and Carole Counihan, 115–126. New York: Routledge, 2011.

Larson, Edward J. "'In the Finest, Most Womanly Way': Women in the Southern Eugenics Movement." *American Journal of Legal History* 39, no. 2 (April 1995): 119–147.

———. *Sex, Race, and Science: Eugenics in the Deep South.* Baltimore, Md.: Johns Hopkins University Press, 1995.

Leighninger, Robert D., Jr. "Public Housing under the New Deal." *Journal of Progressive Human Services* 16, no. 2 (2005): 71–76.

Levenstein, Harvey. *Fear of Food: A History of Why We Worry about What We Eat.* Chicago: University of Chicago Press, 2012.

———. *Revolution at the Table: The Transformation of the American Diet.* Berkeley: University of California Press, 2003.

Lewis, John, and Michael D'Orso. *Walking with the Wind: A Memoir of the Movement.* New York: Harcourt Brace, 1998.

Lindquist Dorr, Lisa. "Fifty Percent Moonshine and Fifty Percent Moonshine: Social Life and College Youth Culture in Alabama, 1913–1933." In *Manners and Southern History*, edited by Ted Ownby, 45–75. Oxford: University Press of Mississippi, 2007.

———. *White Women, Rape, and the Power of Race in Virginia, 1900–1960.* Chapel Hill: University of North Carolina Press, 2004.

Litwack, Leon. *Trouble in Mind: Black Southerners in the Age of Jim Crow.* New York: Knopf, 1998.

Lumpkin, Katharine Du Pre. *The Making of a Southerner.* 1971. Rpt., Athens: University of Georgia Press, 1992.

MacLean, Nancy. "The Leo Frank Case Reconsidered: Gender and Sexual Politics in the Making of Reactionary Populism." In *Jumpin' Jim Crow: Southern Politics from Civil War to Civil Rights*, edited by Jane Dailey, Glenda Gilmore, and Bryant Simon, 183–218. Princeton, N.J.: Princeton University Press, 2000.

Maddox, Lester. *Speaking Out: The Autobiography of Lester Garfield Maddox*. Garden City, N.Y.: Doubleday, 1975.

Maloney's Birmingham 1900 City Directory. Atlanta: Maloney Directory, 1900.

Manring, M. M. *Slave in a Box: The Strange Career of Aunt Jemima*. Charlottesville: University of Virginia Press, 1998.

Mason, Mary Ann Bryan. *The Young Housewife's Counsellor and Friend: Containing Directions in Every Department of Housekeeping including the Duties of Wife and Mother*. New York: E. J. Hale and Son, 1875. http://docsouth.unc.edu/nc/mason/mason.html#p.

Maurakis, Albert P. *Never Saw Sunset*. Fredericksburg, Va.: Sheridan, 1998.

McDonald's Corporation. *1965 Annual Report*. Chicago: McDonald's Corporation, 1965.

———. *1966 Annual Report*. Chicago: McDonald's Corporation, 1966.

———. *McDonald's First Annual Report*. Chicago: McDonald's Corporation, 1963.

McElya, Micki. *Clinging to Mammy: The Faithful Slave in Twentieth-Century America*. Cambridge, Mass.: Harvard University Press, 2007.

McGoldrick, James M. "*Katzenbach v. McClung*: The Abandonment of Federalism in the Name of Rational Basis." *BYU Journal of Public Law* 14, no. 1 (1999): 1–36.

McLamore, James W. *The Burger King: Jim McLamore and the Building of an Empire*. New York: McGraw-Hill, 1998.

McLaurin, Melton A. *Separate Pasts: Growing Up White in the Segregated South*. Athens: University of Georgia Press, 1998.

McWilliams, James E. *A Revolution in Eating: How the Quest for Food Shaped America*. New York: Columbia University Press, 2005.

"Meat, Potatoes, and Money," *Time*, November 3, 1961.

M'Govern, J. Montgomery. "The Clay Eaters of Carolina." *Everybody's Magazine*, March 1900, 246–249.

Mintz, Sidney. *Sweetness and Power: The Place of Sugar in Modern History*. New York: Viking-Penguin, 1985.

Moody, Anne. *Coming of Age in Mississippi: The Classic Autobiography of Growing Up Poor and Black in the Rural South*. 1968. Rpt., New York: Dell, 1976.

Moskos, Charles C. *Greek Americans: Struggle and Success*. New Brunswick, N.J.: Transaction, 2009.

Mullendore, William Clinton. *History of the United States Food Administration 1917–1919*. Stanford, Calif.: Stanford University Press, 1941.

Myrdal, Gunnar. *An American Dilemma: The Negro Problem and Modern Democracy.* New York: Harper and Row, 1944.

"The Nashville Story: Whites Meet Challenge," *Southern Patriot,* September 1960, 1–3.

"National Household Economic Association." *Everyday Housekeeping* 12, no. 4 (January 1900): 153–156.

The Negro Motorist Green Book. New York: Victor H. Green, 1949.

"The Negro Problem: How It Appeals to a Southern White Woman." *Independent . . . Devoted to the Consideration of Politics, Social and Economic Tendencies, History, Literature, and the Arts* 54, no. 2807 (September 18, 1902): 2224.

Netherton, Ross, and Nan Netherton. *The Preservation of History in Fairfax County, Virginia: A Report Prepared for the Fairfax County History Commission, Fairfax County, Virginia, 2001.* New York: University Press of America, 2002.

N. W. T. "Earth-Eaters in India." *Nature* 74, no. 1926 (September 27, 1906): 543–544.

O'Brien, M. J. *We Shall Not Be Moved: The Jackson Woolworth's Sit-In and the Movement It Inspired.* Jackson: University of Mississippi Press, 2013.

Opie, Frederick Douglass. *Hog and Hominy: Soul Food from Africa to America.* New York: Columbia University Press, 2008.

Palmer, Phyllis. *Domesticity and Dirt: Housewives and Domestic Servants in the United States, 1920–1945.* Philadelphia: Temple University Press, 1989.

Peck, Adam M. "Due Process and Fairness in Student Affairs: How to Do All That Is Due." *Bulletin* 73, no. 2 (March 2005). http://www.acui.org/publications/bulletin/article.aspx?issue=410&id=1952.

Penman, Susie. "Cracker Barrel's Culture: Exporting the South on America's Interstate Exits." Master's thesis, University of Mississippi, 2012.

Perlstein, Rick. "Exclusive: Lee Atwater's Infamous 1981 Interview on the Southern Strategy." *Nation,* November 13, 2012.

Phillips, Danielle T. "Who Wants to Be an 'English' Mother? Irish and Southern African American Domestic Workers in New York, 1865–1935." *Journal of the Motherhood Initiative* 2, no. 1 (2011): 226–241.

Pilcher, Jeffrey M. *Planet Taco: A Global History of Mexican Food.* Oxford: Oxford University Press, 2012.

Pillsbury, Richard. *From Boarding House to Bistro.* Boston: Unwin Hyman, 1990.

Plunkett-Powell, Karen. *Remembering Woolworth's: A Nostalgic History of the World's Most Famous Five-and-Dime.* New York: St. Martin's, 1999.

Polk's Birmingham, Alabama, City Directory. Birmingham, Ala.: R. L. Polk, 1927.

Public Papers of the Presidents of the United States: Lyndon B. Johnson, 1963–64. Vol. 1. Washington, D.C.: Government Printing Office, 1965.

Randolph, Mary. *The Virginia Housewife with Historical Notes and Commentary*. Columbia: University of South Carolina Press, 1984.

Rawick, George P. *The American Slave: A Composite Autobiography*. Vol. 6. Westport, Conn.: Greenwood, 1972.

"Recipes That Generations of Cooks Have Sworn By." *Life*, January 3, 1955, 65.

Richards, Ellen H. *Euthenics: The Science of Controllable Environment*. Boston: Whitcomb and Barrows, 1912.

Rieff, Lynne Anderson. "'Rousing the People of the Land': Home Demonstration Work in the Deep South, 1914–1950." PhD diss., Auburn University, 1995.

Robbins, Louise S. *The Dismissal of Miss Ruth Brown: Civil Rights, Censorship, and the American Library*. Norman: University of Oklahoma Press, 2000.

Roberts and Son Directory of the City of Birmingham and Suburbs 1896. Birmingham, Ala.: Roberts and Son, 1896.

Rothman, Joshua. *Notorious in the Neighborhood: Sex and Families across the Color Line in Virginia, 1786–1861*. Chapel Hill: University of North Carolina Press, 2003.

Schlosser, Eric. *Fast Food Nation: The Dark Side of the All-American Meal*. Boston: Houghton Mifflin, 2001.

Schremp, Gerry. *Celebration of American Food: Four Centuries in the Melting Pot*. Golden, Colo.: Fulcrum, 1996.

Shapiro, Laura. *Perfection Salad: Women and Cooking at the Turn of the Century*. New York: Modern Library, 2001.

Sharpless, Rebecca. *Cooking in Other Women's Kitchens: Domestic Workers in the South, 1865–1960*. Chapel Hill: University of North Carolina Press, 2010.

Sholes' Atlanta Directory. Atlanta: Sholes, 1880.

Sinclair, Upton. *The Jungle*. New York: Doubleday, Jabber, 1906. http://www.gutenberg.org/files/140/140-h/140-h.htm.

Smith, Lillian. *Killers of the Dream*. New York: Norton, 1994.

Sokol, Jason. *There Goes My Everything: White Southerners in the Age of Civil Rights*. New York: Vintage, 2006.

Spang, Rebecca L. *The Invention of the Restaurant: Paris and Modern Gastronomic Culture*. Cambridge, Mass.: Harvard University Press, 2000.

Spaulding, Lily May, and John Spaulding, eds. *Civil War Recipes: Receipts from the Pages of Godey's Lady's Book*. Lexington: University Press of Kentucky, 1999.

Stanonis, Anthony, ed. *Dixie Emporium: Tourism, Foodways, and Consumer Culture in the American South*. Athens: University of Georgia Press, 2008.

Stephanides, Marios Christou. *History of the Greeks in Kentucky, 1900–1950*. Lewiston, N.Y.: Edwin Mellen Press, 2001.

Sutherland, Daniel E. *Americans and Their Servants: Domestic Service in the United States from 1800 to 1920*. Baton Rouge: Louisiana State University Press, 1981.

Sworakowski, Witold S. "Herbert Hoover, Launching the American Food Administration, 1917." In *Herbert Hoover: The Great War and Its Aftermath, 1914–23*, edited by Lawrence E. Gelfand, 40–60. Iowa City: University of Iowa Press, 1979.

Theophano, Janet. *Eat My Words: Reading Women's Lives through the Cookbooks They Wrote*. New York: Palgrave Macmillan, 2002.

Tompkins, Kyla Wazana. *Racial Indigestion: Eating Bodies in the Nineteenth Century*. New York: New York University Press, 2012.

Tuskegee Normal and Industrial Institute. *Catalogue of the Tuskegee Normal and Industrial Institute 1895–96*. Tuskegee, Ala.: Tuskegee Normal and Industrial Institute, 1895.

Twyman, Robert W. "The Clay Eater: A New Look at an Old South Enigma." *Journal of Southern History* 37, no. 3 (August 1971): 439–448.

Tyson, Timothy B. *Blood Done Sign My Name: A True Story*. New York: Crown, 2004.

Urban, Andrew Theodore. "An Intimate World: Race, Migration, and Chinese and Irish Domestic Servants in the United States, 1850–1920." PhD diss., University of Minnesota, 2009.

———. "Irish Domestic Servants, 'Biddy' and Rebellion in the American Home, 1850–1900." *Gender and History* 21, no. 2 (August 2009): 263–286.

Virginia Cookery—Past and Present. Franconia, Va.: Woman's Auxiliary of Olivet Episcopal Church, 1957.

Wade, Wyn Craig. *The Ku Klux Klan in America: The Fiery Cross*. New York: Oxford University Press, 1987.

Wallace-Sanders, Kimberly. *Mammy: A Century of Race, Gender, and Southern Memory*. Ann Arbor: University of Michigan Press, 2008.

Walter, Eugene, and Katherine Clark. *Milking the Moon: A Southerner's Story of Life on This Planet*. New York: Crown, 2001.

Weatherbe's Atlanta, Ga. Duplex City Directory. Atlanta: Ch. F. Weatherbe and Dunlop and Cohen, 1884, 1885, 1886.

Weeden, [Maria] Howard. *Bandanna Ballads*. New York: Doubleday and McClure, 1899.

Weigley, Emma Seitfrit. "It Might Have Been Euthenics: The Lake Placid Conference and the Home Economics Movement." *American Quarterly* 26, no. 1 (March 1974): 79–96.

Weiner, Mark S. "The Semiotics of Civil Rights in Consumer Society: Race, Law, and Food." *International Journal for the Semiotics of Law* 16, no. 4 (2003): 395–405.

"What's New in Medicine," *Science Digest* 2, no. 4 (April 1942): 50–51.

Whit, William C. "Soul Food as Cultural Creation." In *African American Foodways: Explorations of History and Culture*, edited by Anne Bower, 45–58. Urbana: University of Illinois Press, 2007.

Whitfield, Stephen J. *A Death in the Delta: The Story of Emmett Till*. Baltimore, Md.: Johns Hopkins University Press, 1988.

"Who Needs Protection?" *Citizen*, December 1964, 2, 23.

Wilda's Birmingham and Suburban Directory 1893. N.p.: R. W. A. Wilda, 1893.

Williams-Forson, Psyche A. *Building Houses Out of Chicken Legs: Black Women, Food, and Power*. Chapel Hill: University of North Carolina Press, 2006.

Witt, Doris. *Black Hunger: Food and the Politics of U.S. Identity*. New York: Oxford University Press, 1999.

Woodfaulk, Courtney Sanabria. "The Jeanes Teachers of South Carolina: The Emergence, Existence, and Significance of Their Work." EdD diss., University of South Carolina, 1992.

Woodward, C. Vann. "Strange Career Critics: Long May They Persevere." *Journal of American History* 75, no. 3 (December 1988): 857–868.

———. *The Strange Career of Jim Crow*. New York: Oxford University Press, 1957.

Yaeger, Patricia. *Dirt and Desire: Reconstructing Southern Women's Writing, 1930–1990*. Chicago: University of Chicago Press, 2000.

Index

cooking and, 30–31, 33, 38; urban
clubs, 13, 20–21, 24, 25–27, 29, 30, 33,
37, 38, 60, 80–86, 93
women, black, 36, 149–50; civil rights
activism and, 14, 103, 107, 118; dining
out, 57–60; discrimination against,
13, 106–7, 109, 111–12, 116; education
and, 40–41; as entrepreneurs, 6, 51,
56–57, 69–70; as servants, 12–13,
23–27, 35, 40–41, 56–57, 75–76,
81–86, 108, 137; sexuality of, 37;
transgressing race lines, 10. *See also*
domestic servants
women, white: dining out, 45, 46–48,
52, 56, 60, 61–63, 109, 119; historical
memory and, 71, 79–86; Irish
immigrant, 25; middle class, 12–13,
15, 17–18, 24–28, 73–76, 93; in
the nineteenth century, 22–23,
32; protections of, 9–10, 11, 60,
62–63, 138–41; rural, 7, 39, 48, 77–78;
scientific cooking and, 19–21, 23,
29–33, 34–35, 38–40, 41–42, 74, 78,
148; as servants, 38; as servers, 43,
60–61, 64, 108, 139, 141; sexuality of,
11, 43, 64; transgressing race lines,
10; working class, 12–13, 18, 25–27,
43, 48, 61, 76, 77–78, 113. *See also*
domestic servants; woman's clubs
Woolworth's: civil rights activism in,
106, 111, 117, 122, 123; food service,
94, 110–11; founding of, 94; labor
activism in, 113; segregation in,
100–101, 111
World War I, 21, 40, 51
World War II, 128, 129, 131; civil rights
activity during, 76, 113–14; food
culture during, 71, 75, 83–86